A COLLECTION OF MEMORIALS

CONCERNING

DIVERS DECEASED MINISTERS AND OTHERS
OF THE PEOPLE CALLED QUAKERS

IN

PENNSYLVANIA, NEW JERSEY, AND PARTS ADJACENT,
FROM NEARLY THE FIRST SETTLEMENT
THEREOF TO THE YEAR 1787

WITH

SOME OF THE LAST EXPRESSIONS AND
EXHORTATIONS OF MANY OF THEM

Philadelphia Yearly Meeting Staff

Not by works of righteousness which we have done, but according to his mercy, he saved us, by the washing of regeneration, and renewing of the Holy Ghost. Titus iii–5.

HERITAGE BOOKS
2012

HERITAGE BOOKS
AN IMPRINT OF HERITAGE BOOKS, INC.

Books, CDs, and more—Worldwide

For our listing of thousands of titles see our website
at
www.HeritageBooks.com

A Facsimile Reprint
Published 2012 by
HERITAGE BOOKS, INC.
Publishing Division
100 Railroad Ave. #104
Westminster, Maryland 21157

Originally published
Philadelphia:
Printed by Joseph Crukshank, in
Market-Street, Between Second
and Third Streets.
1787

— Publisher's Notice —

In reprints such as this, it is often not possible to remove blemishes from the original. We feel the contents of this book warrant its reissue despite these blemishes and hope you will agree and read it with pleasure.

International Standard Book Numbers
Paperbound: 978-1-55613-327-5
Clothbound: 978-0-7884-9266-2

PREFACE.

ALTHOUGH they who are departed hence in the Lord, can receive no addition to their happiness by any testimonial of their surviving friends, however just; yet to the wise in heart, precious is the memory of the truly pious and upright, whose humble walking in the fear of God has livingly witnessed against the appearance of evil in its various transformations; their conformity in spirit and practice to the holy law of the Lord, evincing the delight and benefit to be found therein; for "Verily there
" is a reward for the righteous, verily he is
" a God that judgeth in the earth." Psalm lviii, verse 11.

" What scene in this life more dignifies
" humanity? what school is more profita-
" bly instructive than the death-bed of the
" righteous, impressing the understanding
" with a convincing evidence, that they
" have not followed cunningly devised fa-
" bles, but solid substantial truth; that
" there is a measure of divine light and
" grace in man, which if duly minded and
" obeyed, is sufficient to preserve thro' all the
" vicissitudes in life, to give him the vic-
" tory

"tory over his spiritual enemies, and in the end over death, hell, and the grave?"*

It is right therefore, that the remembrance of those should be preserved, whose lights have so shone before men as to excite the beholders of their good works to glorify God, the original, and source from whom all good is derived, that tho' being dead, the lustre of their pious example through life, and on the approach of death, may continue to speak the inviting language, "*Follow us as we have followed Christ.*"

With this view, our yearly-meeting considering that many memorials of our departed friends lay dormant on the records, directed a Collection to be made of such of them as were most likely to be of general benefit by publication, which the committee appointed for the service having performed to the best of their judgment, it is now presented to the readers, some of whom will be reminded of the sincere piety and virtue of their ancestors, who through the dangers and difficulties to which they were subjected, in their removal from their native land, and forming a new settlement in a wilderness, were happily preserved in a steady attention to their religious duty, and many of them faithfully engaged in promoting the cause of truth and righteousness among mankind, to whom others succeeded, who through obedience to the powerful influence of Divine grace, became alike eminent in their day, and serviceable in the church.

* Life of James Gough, page 53.

PREFACE.

The following Collection is affectionately recommended to the descendants of those worthies, to the readers in general, and particularly to the youth, who may derive profitable instruction by a serious observation of the happy effects of an early devotion of heart, and the inexpressible advantages of embracing the merciful visitation of the Most-High, to secure their true comfort in this life, and enduring felicity in that which is to come.

Though the language and style of these memorials may not be calculated to please such curious readers who in their estimate of the value of a Book, are too much amused by the display of wit and literary accomplishments in the composition, to give due attention to the instructive import of an artless account of the christian experiences of those, who have not been so solicitous for the approbation of men, as to be found humble followers of Christ, their meek and lowly pattern and redeemer; but it is hoped, that there are many to whom the contents of this Collection will afford information, edification, and encouragement in the pursuit of their most substantial interest, a life of true wisdom, piety, and virtue; and that the number of such may increase is the design of the following publication.

Philadelphia, 12th Month, 1787.

AN ALPHABETICAL INDEX.

A

	Page
Thomas Atkinson	10
Peter Andrews	168

B

	Page
John Bevan	75
Joseph Booth	94
Thomas Brown	179
Obadiah Borton	209
Rachel Brown	396
Anthony Benezet	411

C

	Page
Vincent Caldwell	58
Aaron Coppock	64
Hannah Carpenter	84
Thomas Chalkley	103
Esther Clare	109
John Cadwalader	118
Hannah Cooper	158
Joseph Cooper	159
Betty Caldwell	184
Hannah Carleton	194
Isaac Child	268
Grace Croasdale	278
John Churchman	323

D

	Page
John Delaval	17
James Daniel, senior	65
Lydia Dean	153
Nicholas Davis	165
Elizabeth Daniel	205
James Daniel (2d)	353

E

	Page
John Eckley	12
Rowland Ellis	91
Joseph Elgar	98
John Estaugh	119
Cadwallader Evans	130
Evan Evans	137
John Evans	175
Elizabeth Estaugh	210
Ellen Evans	234
Margaret Ellis	243
Mary Evans	276
Mary Emlen	370
Thomas Evans	409

F

	Page
Abraham Farrington	186
Peter Fearon	217

INDEX.

F

	Page
Josiah Foster	280
William Foulke	332
Hannah Foster	356
Rachel Farquhar	368
William Farquhar	384
David Ferris	390

G

	Page
Joseph Glaister	56
Alice Griffith	141
Thomas Goodwin	321
Joseph Gibson	367

H

	Page
Cuthbert Hayhurst	1
James Harrison	8
William Haig	52
Mary Haig	54
Hannah Hill	70
Jacob Holcombe	140
William Hammans	162
Isaac Hollingsworth	202
Isaac Hornor	208
Elizabeth Haydock	222
Ellis Hugh	223
William Hunt	296
William Horne	317
Zebulon Heston	349
Mary Hornor	351
John Hallowell	380
Joseph Husband	431

I

	Page
Thomas Janney	27
Benjamin Jordan	44
Robert Jordan	89
Joseph Jordan	99
Robert Jordan (2d)	109
Jane Jones	196
Cadwallader Jones	199
Dinah James	246

I

	Page
Samuel John	251
Joseph Jones	376
Griffith John	379
William and Katharine Jackson	426

K

	Page
Edmund Kinsey	204
Mary Knight	264

L

	Page
Roger Longworth	4
Thomas Langhorne	6
Thomas Lloyd	21
Thomas Lightfoot	63
John Lee	68
James Lord	74
William Levis	133
Thomas Lancaster	154
William Ladd	155
Michael Lightfoot	160
Joshua Lord	207
Samuel Large	238
Mary Lippincott	295
Rachel Lippincott	389
Susanna Lightfoot	400

M

	Page
Anthony Morris	60
Moses Mendenhall	93
Susanna Morris	163
Sarah Murfin	215
William Mott	240
Mary Moore	248
Abraham Marshall	257
Sarah Milhouse	331
Sarah Morris	334

O

	Page
Robert Owen	30
Robert and Jane Owen	32

INDEX

P

	Page
Ellis Pugh	48
Caleb Pusey	68
Ann Parson	95
Samuel Preston	126
Margaret Preston	127
Thomas Pleasants	128
Sarah Pleasants	144
Israel Pemberton	156
Agnes Penquite	198
Mary Pennel	229
Rachel Pemberton	231
Mary Pemberton	386

R

	Page
James Radcliff	13
Hugh Roberts	34
Ann Roberts	149
Thomas Redman	250
Edward Roberts	263
John Ridgway	318
John Reynell	423

S

	Page
John Simcock	36
Eleanor Smith	39
John Smith	42
Elizabeth Small	46
Sarah Shotwell	200
Eleanor Shotwell	216
John Smith (2d)	253
John Scarborough	274
Daniel Stanton	282
Elizabeth Shipley	371
Edith Sharples	434

T

	Page
Christopher Taylor	3
Richard Townsend	102
William Trotter	146
Evan Thomas	161
Joseph Tomlinson	197
Thomas Tilton	221
Benjamin Trotter	259
John Thomas	292
Ephraim Tomlinson	398
Phebe Trimble	420

U

	Page
Alexander Underwood	256

V

	Page
John Vail	319

W

	Page
William Walker	20
Henry White	41
Christopher Wilson	102
Elizabeth Wyatt	148
Anna Webster	212
Thomas Wood	266
John Woolman	301
Joseph White	359
Esther White	374

Y

	Page
William Yardley	14
Nathan Yarnall	393

A COLLECTION

A COLLECTION

OF

MEMORIALS OR TESTIMONIES

CONCERNING

Divers MINISTERS and ELDERS deceased.

An abstract of Nicholas Waln's *Testimony, concerning that faithful servant of the Lord,* CUTHBERT HAYHURST, *who departed this life, at his own house in the county of Bucks, in* Pennsylvania, *about the 5th of the first month,* 1682-3, *near the fiftieth year of his age.*

HE was born at Easington, in Bolland in the county of York, in Old England, and was one of the worthies in Israel. My spirit is comforted in a sense of that power, which did attend him in our meetings, for many years in the land of our nativity, and also after he came into these parts; having been a valiant soldier for the truth, and bore a faithful testimony to the same, in word,

word, life and conversation. He went through many great exercises and imprisonments, and was a comfort unto the faithful and true believers, who *follow the Lamb through many tribulations.* He was a worthy instrument in the Lord's hand, against the false teachers and hirelings, going several times to their steeple-houses, and testifying against their deceiving the people. He also went to several market towns, and at their crosses, declared and published the truth as it is in Jesus: I accompanied him and his dear wife at one of them, where he faithfully warned the people and exhorted them to repentance; the divine power and presence eminently attending him, which my soul was made sensible of to my comfort and satisfaction. I can say he was of great service to me and many others, being instrumental in bringing us near unto the Lord, whose name over all we have cause to bless on his behalf; and although his body is gone to the earth, his memorial liveth among the righteous, and I am persuaded his soul is in the enjoyment of peace with the Lord. I was often with him in the time of his sickness, and beheld his meek, innocent and lamb-like deportment; being also by his bed-side when he departed, which was in a quiet and truly resigned frame, like one falling into a sweet sleep; so that I have great cause to believe he is one of those *that died in the Lord, and is at rest with him forever.*

NICHOLAS WALN.

William Yardley's *Testimony concerning* CHRISTOPHER TAYLOR, *who died about the year* 1686.

HE was one of the Lord's worthies, strong and steadfast in the faith, very zealous for the truth and careful for the church; his life being hid with God in Christ. His ministry stood not in the wisdom of the flesh, but in the power of God. It was the birth born from above, that could receive him and was refreshed by him. In a word, he was a Jew inward whose praise is not of men but of God. And forasmuch as he was a man thus qualified, I could not well be satisfied that so worthy a man as dear Christopher Taylor, should be buried in oblivion. His chiefest joy was to feel friends in the invisible life; and although many exercises did attend him for the truth's sake, he was *faithful unto the death, and so has received a crown of life*; and though his departure from us is our loss, yet it is his gain; for *blessed are the dead which die in the Lord, they rest from their labours and their works do follow them.*

WILLIAM YARDLEY.

It appears our said friend came from Old England, his native country, on a religious visit to New England, in the year 1675; afterwards into Pennsylvania, among the first English, and settled at Philadelphia. He was of confiderable fervice in public affairs, and very active in fettling meetings for difcipline in thofe early times; the firft of that fort for the women, being held at his houfe in 1683.

William Yardley and Phineas Pemberton's Teftimony concerning ROGER LONGWORTH.

HE was born at Longworth, near Bolton in Lancafhire. We were well acquainted with him almoft from the time of his convincement, being a man of a peaceable difpofition, gentle and mild, ready and willing to ferve his friend to the utmoft of his ability, and a very diligent labourer in the work of the Lord, willing to fpend and be fpent, not counting any thing in this world too dear to part with, for the fame. The Lord did eminently blefs his miniftry, whereunto he was called about the year 1672, and travelled fometimes in that work, in his own country until 1675; after which time he was wholly given up and devoted to the fervice of the Lord, travelling much in England, where he fuffered imprifonment in feveral places; fix times he paffed through Holland, and fome others of thofe provinces; alfo part of Germany and thereabout, feveral times as far as Dantzick, where he laboured much for the releafe of friends,

friends, who then were prisoners there, writing to the king, magistrates and officers on their behalf. At Embden, where friends were sufferers, he laboured for their freedom, and it being a time of hot persecution, went through the streets, warning the people to repent of their wickedness, where they kept him two nights a prisoner: At another time in the said place, he delivered a paper to the council, relating to the liberty of friends; after the reading whereof, he was called in to the council room and received in a friendly manner, with promises of freedom to the people called Quakers, in matters of faith and worship; he also had good service with magistrates, lawyers, priests and collegians, and was several times a prisoner in those parts. Five times he passed through Ireland, visiting friends, where he had good service, sometimes among the Irish when at mass. Once he passed through part of Scotland, twice at Barbados, once through New England and Virginia, twice in Maryland and the Jerseys, and twice at Pennsylvania; having travelled by land above 20,000 miles, his travels by water, not being much less: And though he was often in storms and tempests at sea, perils by land, and met with bad spirits and exercises of divers kinds, yet the Lord stood by him and made him a successful instrument in his hand: Cheerfully passing through them all, by the power of him that called him thereto, not being slack to labour in word and doctrine,

trine, wherever he came, to the edifying of the brethren, and reconciling things where he found them amiss: Settling and establishing meetings in many parts where he came, to the great comfort and refreshment of the upright in heart, by which he got a name amongst the ancients, and is recorded among the worthies of the Lord. Not long after his arrival in Pennsylvania, he was taken ill with a fever; his distemper was violent upon him, yet he bore it patiently and passed away like a lamb, leaving a good favour. And though *the name of the wicked shall rot, yet the righteous shall be had in everlasting remembrance.*

WILLIAM YARDLEY.
PHINEAS PEMBERTON.

He died the 7th of the sixth month 1687, about the fifty-seventh year of his age.

John Hayton's *Testimony concerning* THOMAS LANGHORNE, *who died at his own habitation in* Bucks *county,* Pennsylvania, *the 6th of the eighth month* 1687.

I KNEW him 14 years, he having been made instrumental in the hand of the Lord, to turn me from the evil of my ways, and from darkness to his marvellous light; and I am a witness that he held his integrity until the finishing of his course, according

ing to the saying of David, "Mark the perfect man and behold the upright, for the end of that man is peace", And therein he laid down his head. Having experienced the work of regeneration in himself, he became qualified to strengthen the brethren, and went forth in the ministry and word of life, preaching the everlasting gospel of Christ Jesus; having freely received he freely gave, not fearing man but obeying God, who had committed a large measure, and clear manifestation of his spirit unto him, not only for his own profit and benefit, but many others received comfort thereby; for his doctrine dropped as the rain, and his speech distilled as the dew, to the renewing and refreshing the seed and plant of God.

Thus he went forth in the name of the Lord, and was valiant for truth upon earth; and though many weapons were formed, and many tongues rose up against him, yet the divine power which stopped the mouths of lions, and quenched the violence of fire, girded him with strength and valour, whereby he was enabled to encounter all his enemies, and such as endeavoured to stop the work which God has begun in the earth. After some time, he with his wife and two children came into this country, and whilst here, he bore a living, sound and faithful testimony for the Lord God, to the great satisfaction and comfort of the faithful in this wilderness, where his lot did fall. For having had the opportunity of being with him

him here in this solitary country, as well as in our native land, both in private and public places; I am a witness according to my measure, that the power and presence of the Lord did greatly attend him in preaching the everlasting truth. After he was taken sick, he grew weaker until his departure, saying "The will of the Lord be done." His short continuance here caused many to mourn when he was taken from them, yet not as those that mourn without hope, for tho' he be dead, yet he lives, and tho' his removal is our loss, it is his gain.

JOHN HAYTON.

William Yardley *and* Phineas Pemberton's *Testimony concerning* JAMES HARRISON.

THAT the righteous may not be buried in oblivion, we give forth this short testimony concerning our well beloved friend James Harrison, who was born near Kendal, in Westmoreland, and in the breaking forth of the truth in those parts he was early convinced thereof, and in a short time after, came forth in a public testimony for the same. His ministry was not "*In the wisdom of this world, but in the demonstration of the spirit and power of God*", By which many were convinced, the serpent's head was broken, the wisdom of the flesh confounded, and

and several came forth in a living testimony for God, who were begotten to the Lord by by him, and still remain seals of his ministry. As he was instrumental in *turninging many to God*, so he was helpful in the establishing of such as were converted, being a good pattern, as well in conversation as doctrine, *walking uprightly as in the daytime*, being bold and valiant for the truth, in opposing its enemies, whether professors or profane, tho' they often raged sore against him, so that his sufferings were very great, both by imprisonment and spoil of goods; yet he always with great courage steadily kept his ground against all those that rose up against him for the truth's sake, which was of more worth to him than all outward enjoyments. In the year 1682, he removed with his family into Pennsylvania, and as his testimony was in the power of God, when in the land of his nativity, so it was when here; he being likewise serviceable many ways. And tho' he had great concerns in this world, yet he earnestly laboured to keep a conscience void of offence, being a man of a peaceable spirit, and the Lord's power kept him a sweet favour to the end. He bore his sickness with much patience, tho' often greatly bowed down therewith to the time of his departure, laying down his head in peace, and passing away in much stillness, the sixth of the eighth month, 1687, in the fifty-ninth year of his age: His removal

removal being our loss but his gain, for, *blessed are the dead which die in the Lord, they rest from their labours and their works do follow them.*

 WILLIAM YARDLEY.
 PHINEAS PEMBERTON.

Jane Atkinson's *Testimony concerning her late husband* Thomas Atkinson.

HE was born at Newby in the County of York, being the son of John Atkinson, of Thrush-Cross, was convinced of the truth and had received a gift of the ministry before I knew him. We were joined in marriage in the year 1678, and lived together in love and unity. He was a zealous man for the truth, and according to the gift which he had received, bore a faithful testimony unto it, of which many were witnesses in that country from whence we came. In 1682 we came into this country, with one consent, and in the unity of our dear friends and brethren, who gave a good testimony for us, by a certificate from their monthly meeting; and my soul hath good cause to bless the Lord, and to prize his mercies, whose presence was with us by sea and land. Since we came into this part of the world, he retained his love and zeal for God and his truth, his treasure not being in this world, and as it often opened in his heart,

heart, did exhort others to stand loose from things which are here below, and diligently seek after those things that are above. He was a tender husband, ready to encourage and strengthen me in that which is good. About the latter end of the fifth month 1687, he was taken with the ague and fever, which much weakned his body, in which he continued a considerable time; being well content with the dealings of the Lord: His heart was often opened in prayer and supplication unto his God, to preserve him in patience unto the end of his days, and that none of us might think hard of any of those exercises that he is pleased to try us withal. At times he would look upon me and say, *my dear wife, the Lord preserve thee and take care of thee, for I must leave thee and go to my rest*; with many more sweet and heavenly expressions and exhortations, in the time of his great weakness, which continued until the 31*st* of the eighth month, when he once more exhorted me to be content, and that I would desire his brother (who was then absent) to be content also: After which he passed away as one falling into a quiet sleep. And as the Lord hath hitherto been my strength and my stay in the time of my great distress, so the desire of my heart is, that I, with my brethren and sisters, who yet remain behind, may also finish our course in faithfulness, that in the end we may receive the same reward with the righteous that are gone before.

JANE ATKINSON.

Samuel Jennings's *Testimony concerning* JOHN ECKLEY, *of* Philadelphia *in* Pennsylvania, *who died about the year* 1690.

I AM persuaded it is a justice due to the righteous, and a duty upon us, to contribute something to perpetuate the names of such who have left a fragrancy behind them, and *through faith have obtained a good report.* Tho' their bodies sleep in the grave, and by divine appointment, they die like other men, yet this signal difference hath the Lord declared, *the memory of the just is blessed, but the name of the wicked shall rot,* Pro. 10, 7. And to give testimony to those that die in the Lord, is not only just to them, but is very useful to the living; as many under great conflicts of spirit have experienced, that it hath been to their comfort and strength, to hear or read of the faithfulness and constancy of God to his own in all ages, and how he hath in due time, made them more than conquerors, and crowned their end with peace and dominion. These considerations, together with the sincere affection I had for this our dear friend, hath prevailed with me, in truth and soberness, to give the following testimony concerning him. As a man he was pleasant, courteous, discreet and grave, and in public services accompanied the foremost. *The word of wisdom was in his mouth, and he had received the tongue of the learned, to speak in due season.*
I might

I might truly say much of his innocency, love and zeal for truth, which hath left a lively impression upon the hearts of many. His last sickness was the small pox, a distemper often known to be very afflicting; notwithstanding which, he cheerfully and contentedly submitted to the providence of God in it, upon all occasions expressing a free and hearty resignation to his will; and was frequently filled with praises to God, and instructions to his people.

SAMUEL JENNINGS.

Mary Radcliff's *Testimony concerning her late husband* JAMES RADCLIFF, *who died in or about the year* 1690.

HE was an innocent man, and one that did truly fear the Lord, and wished the welfare of all. It was his chiefest care, faithfully to serve the Lord, and obey him in whatsoever he required; and it was often in his heart to exhort others to faithfulness, and to improve the gift which the Lord had committed to them. I knew him when he was young, we both belonging to the same meeting. He was a prisoner upon truth's account, when about fifteen years of age; after which his mouth was opened to bear a public testimony for the Lord and his blessed truth, travelling many miles, and undergoing many hardships, imprisonments and

and other exercises: And after we were married, he also passed thro' many deep sufferings and imprisonments, but the Lord preserved him through them all: And as he was of a mild lamb-like disposition, and lived an innocent harmless life, so he ended his days in innocency, and being redeemed from the earth, laid down his head in peace. And tho' his body be gone to the dust, from whence it came yet his spirit is ascended to God who gave it, and his living testimony and good favour that he hath left, are comfortable memorials upon my mind, desiring I may so live and so finish my course as he hath done.

MARY RADCLIFF.

Thomas Janney's *Testimony concerning* WILLIAM YARDLEY.

HE was born near Leek, in the north part of Staffordshire, of honest parents, who brought him up in the employment of a farmer. In his youth he sought more after the knowledge of God and the things of his kingdom, than the fading vanities or momentary pleasures of this world, and therefore joined himself in society with a people that were then the highest in profession in those parts, who called themselves, the family of love, among whom he walked for some time; but when it pleased the Lord

to

to send two of his faithful messengers, called in scorn Quakers, out of the north of England into the parts where William lived, he received their testimony, as did also several others of the aforesaid society. But this my friend received the truth with a ready mind and gladness of heart, and thought nothing too dear to part with for it, yea it was precious to him as *the pearl of great price*, and it wrought effectually in him, not only in opening his understanding, but also in its various operations, both to wound and to heal, to purge out the old leaven and to leaven anew into its holy nature and quality: And as the Lord had made him a living witness of the power and life of truth in himself, he called him to bear a testimony to the truth as he had received it, and also against the false ways and worships that were then extant in the world; for which he suffered several imprisonments, bearing the burden and heat of the day, being one of the first that received and bore witness to the truth in those parts. He was very serviceable in his public testimony, not only in convincing but also to the edification of many; yea he was a great stay and support to friends in the parts near where he lived: For he was an instrument of great service in the Lord's hand, being much esteemed for his works sake, not only at home but in other places where he travelled in truth's service.

In the year 1682, being in the fiftieth year of

of his age, he removed himself and family into America, and settled according to his intention in Pennsylvania, where he continued very serviceable amongst us, in his ministry, and sometimes visited places adjacent: He was also useful in some other services in our first settlement here. In short, as he was a sensible, so he was a serviceable member of the body, having a sense of and share in whatever tended to the strength and benefit thereof; as on the other hand, if any thing happened that caused grief or trouble, he bore his part of it.

He was a man of sound judgment and good understanding, not being drawn aside by any false spirit that hath risen in our day, nor joined with any that broke forth into separation, or sought to divide or make schisms in the body, either in England or America. He dearly loved the society of his brethren, and much prized unity, as one who knew the comfort and benefit thereof. He had a high esteem for all who were of a right spirit and of service in the church, although his younger brethren. His ministry was with a good understanding, not only of what he spoke from, but also what he spoke unto; and the things which he testified were *what he had learned of the Lord, and had himself seen, heard and tasted of in the good word of life, not boasting in other men's lines.* In the latter part of his days he grew weak in body by some infirmities which increased upon him, nevertheless,

less, he was often raised in meetings by the power of the Lord, and thereby carried on in his testimony, to our refreshment and comfort.

What I have here written concerning this my dear friend and brother, is from my own certain knowledge, we having been intimate friends, from our youth up, and since we came into America, we have had the advantage of frequent opportunities together, it being our lot to live near to each other, which now makes my loss in the want of him to be the greater, altho' I am satisfied *his removal is his gain*.

From my house in Makefield, in the county of Bucks, 26*th* of the sixth month 1693.

THOMAS JANNEY.

James Dickinson's *Testimony concerning* JOHN DELAVAL, *who died in* Philadelphia, *about the year* 1693, *supposed to have been written when on one of his visits to* America.

MY heart is opened by the power of truth, to give forth a testimony to the Lord's power, that hath wrought effectually in this latter age of the world, for the bringing many sons unto glory; of the number of whom I do believe was this my dear friend John Delaval, whose memory lives among the faithful that knew him, and needs not these characters, to set forth
that

that comelinefs which the Lord put upon him, but his name is recorded in Heaven, and fhall never be obliterated. Altho' he was one called in at the eleventh hour, yet he was faithful and zealous for the truth, a man of a tender broken fpirit, and loved the power of truth and the operation of it, which helped him through and over what was contrary to it. My foul loved him and was drawn near him the firft day I faw him, becaufe of the fincerity that I beheld in him; and as our familiarity increafed, fo I found the bent of his mind was to ferve the Lord in uprightnefs of heart. The Lord gave him a gift in the miniftry, and bleffed him in it, and enabled him to get his days work done in his day, whofe example I pray God, we that remain may follow; who was valiant for the truth upon earth, and turned not his back to the oppofers of it, nor would fpare the backfliders from it, but ftood faithful to the end. His bow abode in ftrength, and tho' many archers fhot at him, yet he kept the fhield of faith, by which the fiery darts of the wicked one were quenched, and his foul preferved in communion with the Lord, and in the faith of Chrift he finifhed his teftimony, with a heart full of love to God and his people: The Lord took him away from evil to come. And my defire is that we who remain, may keep to the fame power by which he was vifited; and love the operation of it, that thereby all may be
prepared

prepared for their latter end, which haftens upon us; fo obtain the crown that is laid up in ftore, for all them that fight the good fight and keep the faith, and keep their eyes fingle to Chrift Jefus the author of it, and keep the word of patience; thefe will be kept in the hour of temptation, and know an overcoming: And unto him that overcometh, faith Chrift, will I grant to fit with me in my throne, even as I alfo overcame, and am fat down with my father in his throne. Thefe fhall not be hurt of the fecond death, but know a part in Chrift, the firft refurrection, and know that they are the fons of God, as was anciently faid, " Now are we the fons of God, and it doth not yet appear what we fhall be." But " When Chrift, who is our life fhall appear, then fhall we alfo appear with him in glory." Let all keep to Chrift and know him to be their life, fo fhall they be made partakers of the better refurrection, even that unto life; when the fentence will be paffed upon all, either come ye bleffed, or go ye curfed, by the juft Judge of the whole earth, who will do rightly to every man, and give to every one according as their works fhall be: To whom all muft give an account, and happy will they be who keep to God's power, they will be kept by it to his glory, and their eternal falvation.

JAMES DICKINSON.

Elizabeth

Elizabeth Walker's *Testimony concerning her husband* WILLIAM WALKER.

THE love of God to him was great, in calling him out of the broad way to labour in his vineyard; and tho' it was late in the day, I believe he received his penny. Great was the care and awe that was on his mind, left he should do any thing to hinder his religious growth and service; for having no trade, and we possessing little but what my dear husband earned by hard labour, he was advised to learn a trade, to which he answered, " I dare not let out my mind to learn one, but can freely follow my present calling, if the Lord will enable me; because it is no incumbrance to my mind, and thro' God's goodness we do not want." However, in an unexpected time, way was made for our getting into a small business, which suited our capacities, and the Lord gave a blessing unto our endeavours. He often visited the sick, and his soul sympathized with the afflicted, being also willing to administer to the necessities of the poor as objects of charity presented. He was a tender husband unto me, and one whom my soul had true unity with in the life of Jesus; his delight and meditations being in the law of the Lord. Many were the seasons of divine love we enjoyed the little time we were together, which often tendered our hearts before the Lord, in our private retirements, so that

that praises have been returned to his pure name, in a sense of the aboundings of his love and life. And altho' his body is removed from me, I am well satisfied he hath obtained the recompence of reward with the redeemed of the Lord.

ELIZABETH WALKER.

The aforesaid William Walker, was born in Yorkshire, but removed to Pennsylvania, where he was convinced. In the latter end of the year 1693, he went to England on a religious visit, and died at London the 12*th* of the fourth month 1694. A further account of him and some of his last expressions, are inserted in the 2*d* part of the book, called piety promoted.

A Testimony from the Monthly-Meeting of Haverford in Pennsylvania, concerning THOMAS LLOYD.

THE love of God and the regard we have to the blessed truth, constrains us to give forth this testimony, concerning our dear friend Thomas Lloyd, many of us having had long acquaintance with him, both in Wales, where he formerly lived, and also in Pennsylvania, where he finished his course, and laid down his head in peace with the Lord, and is at rest and joy with him forevermore.

He

He was by birth of them who are called the gentry, his father being a man of a confiderable eftate and of great efteem in his time, of an ancient houfe and eftate called Dolobran, in Montgomeryfhire in Wales. He was brought up at the moft noted fchools, and from thence went to one of the univerfities; and becaufe of his fuperior, natural and acquired parts, many of account in the world had an eye of regard towards him: Being offered degrees and places of preferments, he refufed them all: The Lord beginning his work in him, and caufing a meafure of his light to fhine out of darknefs, in his heart, which gave him a fight of the vain forms, cuftoms and traditions of the fchools and colleges: And hearing of a poor defpifed people called Quakers, he went to hear them, and the Lord's power reached unto him and came over him, to the humbling and bowing his heart and fpirit; fo that he was convinced of God's everlafting truth, and received it in the love of it, and was made willing, like meek Mofes, to choofe rather to fuffer affliction with the people of the Lord, than the honours, preferments and riches of this world. The earthly wifdom came to be of no reputation with him, but he became a fool, both to it and his former affociates, and through felf denial, and taking up the daily crofs of Chrift Jefus, which crucified his natural will, affections and pleafures, he came to be a fcholar in Chrift's fchool, and

and to learn the true wifdom which is from above. Thus by departing from the vanities and iniquities of the world, and following the leadings, guidance and inftructions of the divine light, grace and fpirit of Chrift, he came more and more to have an underftanding in the myfteries of God's kingdom, and was made an able minifter of the everlafting gofpel of peace and falvation; his acquired parts being fanctified to the fervice of truth.

His found and effectual miniftry, his godly converfation, meek and lamb-like fpirit, great patience, temperance, humility, and flownefs to wrath; his love to the brethren, his godly care in the church of Chrift, that all things might be kept fweet, favoury and in good order; his helping hand to the weak, and gentle admonitions, we are fully fatisfied have a feal and witnefs in the hearts of all faithful friends who knew him, both in the land of his nativity and in thefe American parts. We may in truth fay, he fought not himfelf, nor the riches of this world, but his eye was to that which is everlafting, being given up to fpend and be fpent for the truth and the fake of friends.

He never turned his back on the truth, nor was weary in his travels Sion-wards, but remained a found pillar in the fpiritual building. He had many difputes with the clergy and fome called peers in England, and alfo fuffered imprifonments and much lofs of outward fubftance, to the honour of
truth,

truth, and stopping in measure, the mouths of gainsayers and persecutors. Yet these exercises and trials in the land of his nativity, which he sustained through the ability God gave him, were small and not to be compared to the many and great exercises, griefs and sorrows he met withal and went thro' in Pennsylvania, from that miserable apostate George Keith and his deluded company. Oh the revilings, the great provocations, the bitter and wicked language, and rude behaviour which the Lord gave him patience to bear and overcome. He reviled not again, nor took any advantage, but loved his enemies, and prayed for them that despitefully abused him. His love to the Lord, his truth and people was sincere to the last. He was taken with a malignant fever, the 5th of the seventh month 1694, and tho' his bodily pain was great, he bore it with much patience. Not long before his departure, some friends being with him, he said, " Friends, I love you all, I am go-
" ing from you, and I die in unity and
" love with all faithful friends: I have
" fought a good fight and kept the faith,
" which stands not in the wisdom of words,
" but in the power of God: I have fought,
" not for strife and contention, but for the
" grace of our Lord Jesus Christ, and the
" simplicity of the gospel. I lay down my
" head in peace and desire you may all do so;
" friends, farewell all." He further said to Griffith Owen, a friend then intending for England,

England, "I desire thee to mind my love to friends in England, if thou lives to go over to see them; I have lived in unity with them, and do end my days in unity with them; and desire the Lord to keep them all faithful to the end, in the simplicity of the gospel." On the 10th day of the seventh month aforesaid, being the 6th day of his sickness, it pleased the Lord to remove him from the many trials, temptations, sorrows and troubles of this world, to the kingdom of everlasting joy and peace; but the remembrance of his innocent life and meek spirit lives with us, and his memorial is, and will remain to be sweet and comfortable to the faithful.

He was buried in friends burial-ground in Philadelphia, aged about forty-five years, having been several years president and deputy governor of Pennsylvania.

The followng epistle, which appears to have been written soon after his arrival in Pennsylvania, is thought not improper to be here subjoined.

Philadelphia, 2d of sixth Month 1684.

My dear and well beloved friends, of and belonging to Dolobran *Quarterly-Meeting.*

THE warm and tender salutation of my love is unfeigned to you, with whom I have conversed and walked some years, in unity, zeal, concord, and endeavoured serviceableness:

viceablenefs: You are, becaufe of our nearnefs, familiar, yet honourable in my thoughts and efteem. The truth as it is in Jefus, profper and increafe daily in your minds, and reft bountifully on your habitations. My heart is affected with the remembrance of you, and efpecially of the virtue and operation of that living principle which traverfeth the deeps, and though it bounds the feas, yet cannot be bound thereby, but continues its being and intirenefs through and over all diftances, and makes us of many, one people to himfelf. The God of Ifrael and the excellency of Jacob is with us, and the prefent days are as the former, days of glad tidings, days of humility, days of holy fear, obedience and refrefhment, increafe and growth to the faithful. We and you are under refpective exercifes, the way of your trial may be in a more fevere manner at prefent. The Lord in his wonted tendernefs bear you up, and grant you a rejoicing in fimplicity and godly fincerity before him. That is no new thing to you, to fuffer joyfully in your perfons and goods; the Lord gave us ftrength, courage, fatisfaction and honours thereby. Whilft he is in our eyes, and his holy fear in our hearts, whether in bonds or free, in that or this part of the world, our prefervation we fhall witnefs.—Our meetings are very full: I guefs we had no lefs number than eight hundred laft firft day; we are glad to fee the faces of ferviceable friends here,

here, who come in God's freedom, who are persons of a good understanding and conversation, and will discharge their stations religiously; such will be a blessing to the province. The favourable revolution of Providence hath founded the government so here, that a man is at liberty to serve his Maker without contempt, discouragement, or restraint. Truth indeed makes men honourable, not only here, but in most places at last; but here truth receives a good entertainment at first. Our governor is embarking for England; our well wishes go with and attend him. He hopes to have an opportunity by testimony or writing, to express his love and remembrance to the several churches of Britain. Our friends from the neighbourhood are generally well, and tolerably settled. In love I lived with you, in love I took my leave of you, and in love I bid you a christain and brotherly farewel.

Your friend and brother
THOMAS LLOYD.

A Testimony from the Falls *Monthly-Meeting in* Bucks *county,* Pennsylvania, *concerning* THOMAS JANNEY.

HE settled with us at his first coming into these parts, labouring amongst us in word and doctrine divers years. We
loved

loved and highly efteemed him for his works fake, being an able minifter of the gofpel, found in doctrine, endowed with wifdom and a ready utterance; and favour'd with openings into the myfteries of the things of God's kingdom. He was not forward to offer his gift, having a true regard to the giver, who faid formerly, "Caft the net on the right fide of the fhip:" Therefore his "Bow abode in ftrength." And tho' the Lord had furnifhed him with fuch excellent qualifications, he had fo learned felf-denial as not to glory therein; but was ready to prefer his friends before himfelf, and give them the right hand of fellowfhip; being careful to keep the teftimony of truth clear on all accounts, faying, "Thofe that appear in public, are doubly bound fo to do." He was of a cheerful and peaceable temper, and innocent and blamelefs in life. As the Lord had beftowed on him a gift of the miniftry, beyond many of his fellows, fo he was careful to improve it to his honour and the comfort of his people, labouring therein, not only here in Pennfylvania and New-Jerfey, but he alfo feveral times vifited the churches in New-England, Rhode-Ifland, Long-Ifland and Maryland, and laftly he went on that fervice to Old-England, where he finifhed his courfe. And tho' our lofs of him is great, we are fatisfied he hath his portion, among *thofe that turn many to righteoufnefs, and fhine as the ftars forever and ever.*

There

There are other accounts concerning Thomas Janney, from which it appears, that he was born in Cheshire, and received the truth about the year 1654, and the twenty-first year of his age. In 1683 he came with his family into Pennsylvania: And in 1695 he went in company with Griffith Owen, to visit his brethren in England; where, in the course of his travels, he was taken ill at Hitchin; and two of his relations from Cheshire, going thither to visit him, he said to one of them, " It is some exercise to
" think of being taken away so far from
" my home and family, and also from my
" friends and relations in Cheshire. My
" care hath been for my sons, that they
" may be kept in the fear of God: I have
" been a good example to them. I have a
" care upon me, that they may be kept
" humble while they are young, that they
" may bend their necks under the yoke of
" Christ. If I am taken away, I am very clear
" in my spirit, I have answered the requir-
" ings of God. I have been faithful in my
" day, and I have nothing that troubles
" my spirit; my spirit is very clear." He also expressed his concern for his brethren of the ministry, especially the young, that they might observe the leadings of God's spirit in their ministry, and not lean upon their own natural parts. After this, he recovered

covered so as to be able to get down into Cheshire; but after some time his disorder returning, he said to his sister, "If it be "the will of God, that I be taken away "now, I am well content." He departed in much quietness of mind, the 12th of the twelfth month 1696, and was buried the 15th of the same month, in friends burying place in Cheshire. Aged sixty-three years. A public minister 41 years.

Hugh Roberts's *Testimony concerning his brother* ROBERT OWEN.

HE was one that feared the Lord from his youth, being convinced of the truth, when about seventeen years of age; he loved the company of such of his acquaintance as were most substantial in religion, and was also beloved by them and all sort of people that knew him, being greatly helpful to his brethren, and made a cause of gladness to those that were his fathers in the truth. The Lord not only opened his heart like Lydia's formerly, but he likewise opened his mouth to publish his name and truth amongst many, travelling several times through his native country Wales, where he was of good service. In 1690, he came into Pennsylvania, where he lived about seven years, visiting this and the adjacent provinces, and was also very useful in the meeting

meeting where he refided, both in doctrine and difcipline; he was indeed a ftrong pillar in the church: I never faw him take part with a wrong thing: Oh the want of him which I feel! his place is yet empty, I pray God, if it be his will, to fill it up. Oh my brother, my dear companion! how can they that knew thy faithfulnefs to truth, do lefs than leave a memorial to fucceeding generations? for thy name is worthy to be recorded in Ifrael. He was a man of peace and hated all appearance of contention, and indeed he was a fkilful peacemaker, being endued with wifdom and authority, yet full of mercy and compaffion unto every appearance of good. His removal is a great lofs unto us who are left. Well my dear brother, in the remembrance of thee, and the many good and precious opportunities we have had together, my foul is bowed and ready to fay, I fhall never have the like companion, fo fitted and knit together in every refpect; the more I confider my lofs of thee, the greater it appears; therefore conclude this my teftimony, and return to my own work and fervice, that I may be prepared to follow after thee.

HUGH ROBERTS.

He died the 8*th* of the fifth month, 1697, and was interr'd the 10*th* of the fame, in friends burying ground at Merion in Pennfylvania.

Rowland

Rowland Ellis's *Testimony concerning* ROBERT OWEN *before mention'd, and* JANE *his wife.*

WHEN I think of former times and days that are over and gone, wherein the Lord visited a remnant by the gathering hand of his power, in the land of our nativity, to wait for the renewing of his love from one meeting to another, to our great refreshment and daily encouragement, to run our race through many trials within and without: The Lord whom we waited for, hath been the strength of his people in this our age and generation, as in all by past ages. So the remembrance of those days and times, and that near fellowship which was between the little remnant in that part of the country, is at present brought to my view; tho' most of the ancients that bore the heat of the day are now removed, yet methinks their names and worthy acts should be had in remembrance, that generations to come might see and understand, by what instruments the Lord was pleased to carry on his work, by making a clear discovery of the good way once lost in the night of apostacy; amongst whom were my dear friends Robert Owen and Jane his wife. And altho' we are not to set up or praise that in man or woman which perisheth, but because they made choice of the better and most durable substance, therefore their names shall be had in remembrance.

He

He was defcended of a very ancient and (according to the worlds account) one of the greateſt families in thoſe parts, having by his father a competent inheritance, and in all his time had the right hand among his equals; brought up a ſcholar, quick in apprehenſion, and whatever he took in hand he did it with all his might. He was zealouſly devoted to religion, and a great ſearcher for the pearl of great price; being one of the firſt in our parts who ſought after it; and having found it, he ſold all to purchaſe the ſame.

After King Charles II came to the crown, he ſuffered five years cloſe impriſonment, for not taking the oath of allegiance and ſupremacy, being confined at the town of Dolgelly, in Merionethſhire, North Wales, within about a mile from his dwelling houſe, to which he was not permitted to go during the ſaid time: And it was obſerved, that the perſon who had the greateſt hand in proſecuting him, was viſited with ſickneſs, when remorſe of conſcience ſeized ſo hard upon him, that he could find neither reſt nor eaſe, until he ſent a ſpecial meſſenger to releaſe him.

And concerning his wife Jane Owen. She was daughter of a juſtice of peace, a man of great integrity and exceeding moſt of his rank at that time. She was a woman rarely endowed with many natural gifts, being an help-meet to her huſband in his exerciſes, ſolid in her deportment, and not given to many

many words. In all their exercises together for the truth's sake, they did not shrink nor give way for fear or flattery; not only their hearts, but their house was open to all upon truth's account; meetings being held therein for many years. They were serviceable in their places and much beloved in their native land, where having borne their share of the heat of the day, they embark'd therefrom in the fifth month 1690, and came into Pennsylvania, where they finished their course, and were buried within a few days of each other.

John Bevan's *Testimony concerning* HUGH ROBERTS.

TRUTH in the inward parts God loves, and those that love it and give way to the operation thereof, are made precious and lovely in the sight of God, and he makes them instrumental in his hand for the good of others; among whom was my dear friend and brother Hugh Roberts deceased, who was qualified by God's power, to be a serviceable instrument to the churches of Christ in our parts of America. He came to this country about 18 years since; we were near neighbours and entirely loved each other, not having had a cross word, nor I believe an hard thought one of another, at any time since our first acquaintance.

ance. Having paſſed through many trials and exerciſes, he could by experience ſpeak a word in ſeaſon for the encouragement of weary travellers; his doctrine often "dropping as the dew, and diſtilling as the ſmall rain upon the tender plants," for in the openings of life, "things new and old" came forth of the treaſury of wiſdom, which gladned our hearts and comforted our ſpirits in a ſenſe of God's love, who is the author of all good to his people. He was zealous for good order in the church, ſerviceable in the diſcipline, and ſkilful in accommodating differences. And it is my deſire, that we, eſpecially of that meeting he belonged to, and the adjacent meetings, which moſtly received the benefit and advantage of his labour of love, may lay to heart and conſider our loſs of him, and in the ſenſe thereof, may breathe and cry unto the Lord, who is the repairer of breaches, to raiſe up inſtruments in his room, for carrying on of his great work that he hath begun in the earth, to his own praiſe, who is alone worthy of the ſame forever.—I was twice with him over ſea, and in many places in our native land, alſo in Maryland, and in his laſt journey to viſit friends on Long-Iſland, Rhode-Iſland and New-England, where he had good ſervice. And though he was often very weakly, yet his heart was bent to accompliſh the work the Lord laid upon him, which he was enabled to perform to his great comfort and ſatisfaction.

On our return homeward, being sick and in much pain, at the house of our friend John Rodman, on Long-Island, he said *nothing lies in my way as an obstruction to hinder my peace and well being with God.* He afterwards came home, and a few days before his departure, a dear friend taking leave of him said, "I believe thy deep trials and exercises are near at an end, and that peace and joy everlasting will be thy portion from the Lord." In much brokenness of heart and sense of the sweet presence of God upon his spirit, he answered, *I am satisfied thereof, and can bless my God for it.*

He died the 18th of the sixth month 1702, and on the 20th was interred at Merion, after which a large meeting was held, wherein the Lord's presence was sweetly enjoyed, and several living testimonies borne concerning his faithfulness to God and friends satisfaction of his eternal well-being.

JOHN BEVAN.

Margaret Minshell's *Testimony concerning* JOHN SIMCOCK.

HE was a nursing father in Israel, tender over the seed of God, and wherever he saw it in the least appearance he was a cherisher of it without respect of persons; but he abhorred deceit and hypocrisy. I have known him

him near forty years, and may fay that his miniftry was found, edifying and helpful to myfelf and many others, he being endued with a fpirit of difcerning, and wifdom beyond many in fpiritual things. He was a great fufferer in Old England, for truth's fake, both by imprifonments and lofs of goods. He travelled pretty much in truth's fervice, and notwithftanding all his fufferings, he was no ways chargeable to any, but rather helpful to thofe that ftood in need.

MARGARET MINSHELL.

In Jofeph Beffe's hiftory of friends fufferings, are fome accounts of thofe fuftained by the aforefaid John Simcock, and of his pious, meek difpofition towards his oppreffors. Once he was imprifoned a year and three months, for accompanying his wife to a fteeple houfe, for a fign and teftimony againft their falfe ways and worfhips. His perfecutors at different times, diftrained from him to the amount of feveral hundred pounds fterling, for preaching; taking nineteen cattle at one time, and twelve at another, befides corn, cheefe, and other goods; all which he bore patiently. Once when they were driving away his cows, his fervant maid, who did not profefs amongft friends, faid to him, " Mafter, how can you ftand by and fee them drive away fo many cattle?" He replied, *it did not trouble him any more than if they had drove away fo many geefe.* He

He removed to Pennsylvania in early times, and settled in Chester county; and when the spirit of division began to appear in George Keith, he was active in visiting him, to endeavour to recover him; and when the labour of friends in that respect proved ineffectual, he joined steadily with faithful friends in testifying against the said George Keith and his party.

In the time of his last sickness, he appear'd to be in a heavenly frame of mind, and utter'd many lively expressions: At one time he said, " I have had many hard beset-
" ments with the enemy of my soul since
" I knew the truth, and have been in many
" straits, and great combats and buffetings
" for the trial of my faith; but the keeper
" of Israel is near to all them that wait up-
" on him, and truly put their trust in him,
" and their faith is made strong in him,
" whereby they are enabled to make war
" against the adversary of souls, and to
" fight the good fight of faith, for whom
" is laid up a crown of eternal and endless
" joy, peace and heavenly comfort and glo-
" ry. And now I may say in truth, that
" I have kept this living faith, in which
" my soul hath renewed cause to magnify
" the name of my holy Redeemer, and
" powerful Saviour Christ Jesus, in whom
" my faith hath been made strong at this
" time." The day before his departure, his wife and son, with some other friends being present, he bore a living testimony to the necessity

neceffity of dwelling in love, even that holy love which labours for the peace, welfare and everlafting good of all; concluding in thefe words, " And now I defire my love
" may be remembred to friends in general,
" and it is the defire and earneft prayer of
" my foul, that the heavenly fpring of true
" love and ftream of divine life, may ever
" be known to fpring and run amongft
" thofe who would be accounted children
" of God, and followers of Chrift Jefus
" our bleffed Lord and eternal Saviour, who
" laid down his life to be a ranfom for fall-
" en man, and to be an atonement for all
" them that would come to God by him,
" who is the living word and promifed feed
" of the covenant."
He died the 27*th* of the firft month, 1703.

A Teftimony from Derby *Monthly-Meeting, in* Pennfylvania, *concerning* ELEANOR SMITH, *wife of* John Smith.

SHE was born at Harborough, in Leicefterfhire, Old England, her maiden name was Eleanor Dolby. She received the truth about the age of thirteen years, and lived and died therein, being a religious exemplary woman, and fome years before her death was concern'd in a public teftimony. A little before her departure, defiring that her hufband and children fhould come and sit down by her, she spoke as follows, "I entreat you my children to walk soberly, plainly and keep to the truth, and the Lord will provide for you every way beyond your expectation. I am clear of you, having done the part of a tender mother to you: I leave and commit you to the Lord, who is able to keep you to the end of your days."—She desired them not to mourn if it shoud please God to remove her from amongst them, saying, "It will be my great gain." Often repeating her full assurance of future happiness, adding, "I can praise thy name O Lord in the midst of affliction, for surely thou art worthy of all praise, honour and glory, and that forever more; for thou neither leavest nor forsakest those that put their trust in thee." Then said, "Dear children be content, for I shall die in favour with God, and true love and unity with his people." She desired to be dissolved, saying, "I can freely give up husband and children and all this world, to be with the Lord, whose presence I feel flowing as a river into my soul."

She died the 10th day of the seventh month 1708, aged fifty-five years.

In the time of her last illness, she wrote the following epistle to the monthly-meeting of women friends at Derby, viz.

Dear Sisters,

Herewith I send you the last salutation of my love, with whom I have been many

times

times refreshed and truly comforted. I say I have travelled with you through various exercises and difficulties, when the Lord has been sometimes pleased to give us (as it were) the bread of adversity to eat, and the water of affliction to drink; yet blessed be his name, he has sweetened our cups many times as with honey, and sustained us as with the oil of the cruse; and by his sweet presence caused our cups to overflow, to the praise of his great name. Wherefore, dear sisters, I entreat you to dwell in the love of God, which love is the bond of peace. Let charity be found to dwell amongst you, and then I do believe, you will be neither barren nor unfruitful, but your branches laden with good and weighty fruit, which will find acceptance with God. So no more, but my tender love to you in the blessed truth. I take my leave and bid you farewell in the Lord. The last from your loving sister,

ELEANOR SMITH.

The following Testimony concerning HENRY WHITE, *is from the committee of the Yearly Meeting in* North Carolina.

HE was a minister of the gospel and a faithful friend, whose christian conduct and loving behaviour towards the Indians, who were numerous in these parts at that time, was such, as we have been credibly

bly informed, not only procured him great esteem and respect from them, but for his sake they shewed great love and tenderness towards others in the infant settlement of these parts.

He dwelt in Pasquotank county, and died the 3*d* of the eighth month 1712, aged about seventy-seven years.

A Testimony from Derby *Monthly-Meeting, in* Pennsylvania, *concerning* JOHN SMITH.

HE was born in Licestershire, in Old England in 1645, and was convinced of the truth at the age of fourteen years, and being faithful thereto, after some time he came forth in the ministry. He was an early settler in Pennsylvania, where he was well beloved. Being taking sick, he was visited by many friends; and about two days before his departure, being asked how he did, he answered, " I am very poorly and
" weak indeed, but much easier than I have
" been, for I was extreme ill, so sick and
" full of pain, such as I never had under-
" gone before; so that I could not retire in
" my mind to God, my extremity was so
" great; but now the Lord has been pleas-
" ed to give me ease, so that I can stay my
" mind on him, for which I am truly thank-
" ful: And now I feel the fresh remem-
" brance or renewings of the love of God,
" flowing

"flowing into my heart, which is of much more comfort to my foul than all tranfitory things that are here below. Now I feel his living divine prefence is with me, which bears up my fpirit over that which flefh and blood would or could not be able to bear." Shortly after, a friend taking leave of him, afked him if he thought he fhould recover, "That (faid he) I am not worthy to know, however I am content; and this I know, that if we abide faithful to God to the end, we fhall receive a godly portion, fo farewell, and the Lord go along with thee." At another time he faid, "He was full of pain, yet he could fing of the mercy and goodnefs of God to his foul in the midft of affliction." Afterwards adding, "Do not mourn for me, but be ftill and quiet, and let me pafs away quietly, that fo my foul may enter into God's everlafting reft; for my confcience is clear from guilt in the face of all men." Saying, "Come Lord Jefus, receive my foul, thy fervant is ready, come quickly." This he fpoke in great frefhnefs and cheerfulnefs of fpirit, faying, "Now I think I am near my end;" but reviving again, he fat up, and his children being prefent, he faid to them," " I was never covetous to get a great deal of this world's riches, but I have endeavoured to bring you up in the fear of the Lord, and educate you in the way of his truth to the beft of my underftanding;

"and

" and if you do but wait upon the Lord in
" the sincerity of your hearts, for the drop-
" ping down of the love of God upon your
" souls in the meetings and gatherings of
" the Lord's people, he will shed his bles-
" sings amongst you; for he hath been and
" is a father to the fatherless, and as a hus-
" band to the widow." This he spoke just
before his departure, being fresh in spirit,
and perfect in sense and memory to the last
hour.

He died the 11th day of the twelfth month
1714, aged sixty-nine years and four months.

A Testimony from the Yearly-Meeting of friends in Virginia, *concerning* BENJAMIN JORDAN.

HE was born the 18th of the seventh month 1674, in Nancemond county in Virginia, of believing parents, who were careful to educate their children in the blessed truth for which they suffered, whose examples, together with the influence of grace, were sanctified unto this our friend as well as several others of their numerous offspring. He was a man who gave up much of his time in waiting upon God and services for the church, being clerk both to the monthly and yearly meeting; was a good example of piety and charity, and kept his integrity to the last.

The day before he died, several neighbours coming to see him, one of them being in a flourishing state as to the world, to whom the way of truth seemed too low and despicable, he said, " Rejoice O young " man, in thy youth, and let thy heart " cheer thee in the days of thy youth, and " walk in the ways of thy heart, and in " the sight of thine eyes: But know thou, " that for all these things God will bring " thee into judgment." He looked upon another who seemed to be under some convincement of truth, but did not live in obedience, and said, " Blessed are they that " hear the word of God and do it." And to another that appeared to have sought after the honour of this world more than the Lord's honour, he said, " He looked too " big to enter in at the strait gate." He gave particular directions concerning the place and manner of his burial, desiring that no more provision might be made than was sufficient, having, whilst in health, borne a testimony against making such a time, a time of feasting instead of mourning. One of his brothers asking him how it was with him, he replied, " As to my " eternal state, nothing but well." Soon after, holding up his hands and looking upwards, he said, " Lord Jesus, into thy " hands I commit my spirit, Lord help me " at this time," And so departed in quietness, the 12th of the twelfth month 1716, aged about forty-two years.

A Testimony

A Testimony from friends in Virginia, *concerning* Elizabeth Small *wife of* Benjamin Small, *of* Nancemond county.

SHE was born the 31st of the sixth month 1666. Her parents Edmund and Elizabeth Betson, were pious friends and zealous for the truth, whose care in the education of their children, had the desired effect on this our much esteemed friend; for being obedient to the manifestation of divine light, it so improved a tender, affectionate and affable disposition, that she became qualified for and endowed with an excellent and acceptable gift in the ministry, so as suitably to dispense doctrine, edification and consolation to the churches. She was very diligent in attending meetings of friends in this colony, even beyond what could be reasonably expected from so weakly a constitution, and was earnest in and much devoted to the cause of truth, greatly desiring the growth and prosperity thereof, saying, " She " could lay down her natural life for it, if " required." She was a woman of a generous and kind disposition, as well in helping the poor as entertaining of friends, saying (to such as were ready to think she would do more than her circumstances would admit of) that she hoped the Lord would so provide for her, that she should never want what was convenient, having never desired long life or riches for herself or children, but that they might live in his fear.

She

She was taken ill the 21*st* of the seventh month 1717, being the first day of the yearly-meeting at Chuckatuk, which gave opportunity to divers friends from different parts of the country to visit her, to whom she signified her peace of mind and submission to the divine will, saying among other things, " If the Lord has any more work " for me to do, he can raise me up again; " otherwise I am easy and freely resigned " to his will." To a beloved relation she said, " Dear cousin, thou art bone of my " bone and flesh of my flesh; live in the " fear of the Lord, that every high thought " may be brought down." To two friends belonging to a distant meeting which she had often visited, she said, " I have not " ceased to admonish you heretofore, and " now again desire you would be valiant " for the truth and walk steadily therein, " and remember my dear love to friends of " the meeting to which you belong." She often spoke to friends, " To be steadfast in " the truth;" And once to a public friend belonging to the same meeting, earnestly desiring him " To be valiant for the good " cause." She told her son William, " She " hoped that that day would be a good one " to her," And said " She had prayed for " an easy passage;" And accordingly she quietly departed the 25*th* of the seventh month aforesaid, aged fifty-two, a minister about 11 years.

An account of Ellis Pugh, *extracted from a testimony from* Gwynedd *Monthly-Meeting concerning him, and also from a short summary of his life, both of which are prefixed to a book he wrote, called* A salutation to the Britains, *&c.*

ELLIS PUGH was born in the parish of Dolgelly, in the county of Merioneth, and dominion of Wales, in the sixth month 1656. His parents were religious people; but his father died before he was born, and his mother a few days after. In the days of his youth, when going with the multitude into folly, it pleased God by his judgment, to stand in his way, and caused him to consider the things that belonged to his soul's everlasting peace. And in the eighteenth year of his age, the Lord visited him more eminently, kindling a zeal in him to serve his Creator more diligently; having been also reached by the testimony of John-ap-John, one of the people called Quakers.

God who promised to be a father to the fatherless, took care of him; and about the year 1680, gave him a part in the ministry of the gospel of Christ, (notwithstanding he was not one of the wife of this world, nor had human learning) yet he was made a profitable instrument to turn divers from vanity, and to exhort and strengthen many in their spiritual journey, in his native land, and also in this country where he finished his course.

In the year 1686, he and his family, with divers of his acquaintance prepared to come over to Pennsylvania, and whilst they waited for the ship to be ready, there came great trouble and exercise upon him, so that he was sick for some days; in which strait the Lord shewed him, that they should meet with troubles and exercises in their way, and that he had a work for him in that country, and must return again to his native land. After they sailed, they met with storms, straits and troubles; and having been upon the tempestuous sea all winter, they arrived at Barbados, where they were joyfully and lovingly received by their friends, and the summer following, in the year 1687, they arrived in Pennsylvania; where this our friend was a serviceable instrument in the Lord's hand, to cherish and instruct us, in meekness and tenderness, to obey that which God made known unto us of his will, and to follow and understand the operation of his spirit, discovering to us the snares of the enemy of our souls. His pious labours (among others that were fitted for the same service) have been profitable in directing and edifying us in the way of truth; for by the tenderness and influence which came as dew upon our souls while we sat under his ministry, we believed his doctrine was of God.

In the year 1706 he was engaged to visit the inhabitants of his native country, according to what the Lord revealed unto him before he came from thence; which service he performed to the benefit and acceptance of many, and returned to his family in 1708. After he came home, three of his children, in the flower of their age, who from their youth walked orderly and were hopeful, died within one month; in the time of which trial the Lord was near unto him; he mourned not as one without hope. Strength was given him to bear his affliction. He said in a public meeting "If he could bear his affliction acceptably in the fight of God, it would be as marrow to his bones:" Which testimony, amongst several other things, was to the edification and comfort of the hearers. His residence was then nearer to us than before, which render'd his life and conversation more conspicuous, and his fellowship more known unto us. His ministry was living, profitable and to edification. He was of a meek and quiet spirit, considerate and solid in his judgment, of few words, honest and careful in his calling; and several were induced to speak of the benefit they received by his chaste conversation, and his loving and comfortable expressions while he was amongst them in their families. He was honourable among his friends and of good report among all people generally, therefore his memory will not soon wear out.

He was in a declining state of bodily health about a year and three months before his decease, so that he was not well able to follow his calling; but his candle shined brighter, as may be seen by perusing his treatise, called " A salutation to the Bri-" tains;" which he wrote in his own language, in the time of his long sickness, when his view was towards that which pertains to eternity, more especially to those, or for the sake of those to whom the salutation of his life reached over sea and land, for the encouragement and instruction of them that were seeking the way to Sion, the New Jerusalem, the city of the Great King, whose walls and bulwarks are salvation.

The last meeting he was at among us, he was weak in body, but fervent in spirit, as one taking his last leave in a great deal of love and tenderness, saying, that the Lord granted him his desire to come and visit us once more; putting us in mind to live in love and unity, and to keep out from amongst us as much as we could, all strife and discord; and when any thing appeared which had a tendency thereunto, that hands should be laid without delay to end it, and that none should depend upon his own hand, eye, or balance in judgment.—He was fitted to counsel others, because his life and conversation was answerable to his testimony; amongst his family tender and careful to counsel them to live in the fear of God.

We looked upon him as one who had finished his work, that the time of his diffolution drew nigh: And that he might fay in the words of Paul, according to his meafure, "I have fought a good fight, I have "finished my courfe, I have kept the faith. "Henceforth there is laid up for me a "crown of righteoufnefs, which the Lord "the righteous judge fhall give me at that "day; and not to me only, but unto all "them alfo that love his appearing."

Being patient in his tedious indifpofition, and contented to wait the Lord's time; he flept with his fathers on the 3d day of the tenth month 1718, in favour with God.

The following Teflimony concerning WILLIAM HAIG, *was furnifhed by a committee of the Yearly-Meeting of* North-Carolina.

WILLIAM HAIG fenior of Pafquotank county, who removed from Antigua with his family and fettled in this province, was of a loving and fweet fpirit. In his laft ficknefs, as fome friends were fitting by him, he was filled with heavenly joy, and faid, "Friends I am glad of your "company, I feel fo much of the bleffed "truth, as I hope will carry me into that "joy where I fhall praife the Lord amongft "the redeemed. I hear that truth profpers "mightily in England, bleffed be the Lord
"for

" for it." He exhorted all his children with many heavenly expreffions, took his folemn leave of them, and in a living fenfe of truth, prayed to God for his bleffing upon them; charging them " to love and obey their " mother, learn their books and keep to the " truth." He faid to his wife, " My dear, " thou haft been a true wife unto me; when " my mind was drawn to love thee, I did " not inquire what thou hadft, nor thou " what I had, but we came together in love " and we have lived in love." And when his fpeech was very low, he fpake to his wife thus, " The Lord blefs thee and my " children, God Almighty protect you." To a young woman who came to vifit him he faid, " Fear God, keep to the truth, " never turn thy back upon it, left the days " come in which thou fhalt fay, I have no " pleafure in them: As for me, I am going " to my place, and I hope it will be in ever- " lafting reft." To another who had been vifited with great ficknefs, he faid, " It had " been better for thee to have died in thy " ficknefs, than to live to forget God." He prayed that God would remember all his people, and that their dwelling might be with the Lord, adding, " But what fhall " I fay, there are too many that tread the " teftimony of truth under foot; O! gather " them into thy fold of reft, I pray thee " O Lord!" To a friend of the miniftry he faid, " Thou art of the miniftry and " haft been a great while, and I am but
" young,

"young, but I would advise thee to be careful in thy testimony, not to enlarge beyond thy gift or concern; and have a care, thou do not stand in the way of others, or speak any thing to hurt others that may be but small or tender; but wait until thou art filled and then be humble, and not puffed up with pride, for pride goeth before a fall." After praying unto the Lord to settle him upon the sure foundation and rock that can never be removed, he quietly departed this life, at his own house, on the 6th of the eleventh month 1718, and now rests in joy.

A Testimony from the same committee concerning MARY HAIG, *wife of the aforesaid* William Haig.

SHE was a woman of an exemplary life and conversation, of a sweet and loving behaviour, and was favoured with a gift in the ministry. In her last sickness, after imparting her mind to a friend about her outward concerns, she spoke as follows, "According to my small gift, I have discharged myself, so that nothing lieth at my door. O! that the people would remember the words that I have spoken among them, and that this young generation would come up in truth. As for me, I had never left the island of Antigua, if it were
"not

"not that I might have my poor children amongst faithful friends: I have seen the wonders of the Lord in the deep ocean, and witnessed his delivering arm in many exercises, and he hath kept me sweet and clean all along since I knew the truth. Oh! that my children may remember the advice they have received of their father and me; I am clear, having done my duty." And praised God; also uttered many sweet and comfortable expressions. At another time, she said to some friends, "When I was but nine years old, the Lord made himself known unto me, but I then lived where there were no friends; and after some time, I went to Pennsylvania, and there met with friends, but some were loose and light, others were solid and weighty, and with these I joined, and received much benefit from the family of the Lloyd's. After I was married, we went to Antigua, and there in the first meeting, the power of the Lord was greatly with me, insomuch that the peoples expectations were upon me for words; but soon after it pleased the Lord to send two of his servants, Josiah Langdale and Thomas Thomson, to visit the island, when the power of the Lord did break in upon me like thunder:" And signified she had been faithful ever since in her measure, in giving up to the work of the Lord. On the day of her decease, she said to some present, "Friends, be loving one to another

"ther, that the Lord may bless you. The love that I feel in my heart is inexpressible." After a while she desired a friend to remember her love to Lydia Lancaster, Elizabeth Rawlinson and friends generally, adding, "Tell them, I die in unity with all faithful friends." Afterwards she said, "My husband is gone, but I shall not be long a sorrowful widow; yet not my will but thine be done; my speech fails apace, sweet Lord Jesus, thou hast loved me from a child, and I have loved thee ever since I knew thee, and my case is no doubtful case, I come, I come, hasten thou my journey."

She died the 13*th* of the eleventh month 1718, aged about thirty-nine years.

A Testimony from the aforesaid committee, concerning JOSEPH GLAISTER.

JOSEPH GLAISTER of Pasquotank county, formerly of Cumberland in Great-Britain, who removed with his family and settled in North-Carolina, was a valuable minister, and very serviceable in discipline, being well qualified therefor; a constant attender of meetings with his family, and one who travelled much for the spreading of truth. In his last sickness, he said to some friends that visited him, "I am very ill, but am out of all doubt of "my

"my salvation, being well assured of it." Two other friends coming in, he added, "Now I think I have most of the chief "friends about me that I desired; dear "friends, give me up freely, that I may not "be kept longer in misery, for I can say "with one of old, Lord I have long wait- "ed for thy salvation, and now have an "assurance of it, and altho' the pains are "great, yet the comfort and pleasure I see "before me do outbalance them all."— Again he said, "He hoped that friends "might keep their places in being faithful, "and not to shrink one from another when "troubles or differences may arise in the "church, or amongst neighbours, by any "evil spirit that may get into any unfaith- "ful one, for want of a due, true and faith- "ful watch; and then if any such thing "do happen, pray friends, I hope that such "as now are, or may then be, do stand "firm together, and give judgment in or by "a living, fresh and divine spirit, and keep "constant in mind, and thereby the trans- "gressor or transgressors may be judged "down and not able to resist; but if you "see in them any thing tender, then dear "friends, turn to them with bowels of love "and perhaps in so doing, you may gain "such as in time past may have gone astray." He went on speaking of the great love and unity, and the many good times he had had with us; having his spirit borne up by the ancient arm that had been from time to time
his

his great support. Near his end, we were sensible of his being engaged in prayer, but being almost spent we could not hear every word so as to pen it down. Thus this good man ended his life, with a sense of the great love of God to his soul, on the 31*st* of the eleventh month 1718, aged about forty-five years, and a minister about 24 years.

A Testimony from Kennet *Monthly-Meeting in* Pennsylvania, *concerning* VINCENT CALDWELL.

HE was born in Derbyshire Great-Britain, and was convinced about the 17*th* or 18*th* year of his age, by the ministry of John Gratton; having received the truth in the love of it and continuing faithful, the Lord was pleased to commit to him a dispensation of the gospel, so that he had to declare to others of the goodness of God to his soul. He came over into Pennsylvania, and after his marriage settled in East Marlborough in Chester county. His ministry was sound and edifying, being attended with the power of truth and adorned with an exemplary conversation; in the exercise whereof he twice visited the meetings of friends in the southern provinces, and once in divers of the West-India islands, where he was made instrumental to the convincing of many; for tho' he had but little school-

school-learning, yet being as a good Scribe, well instructed unto the kingdom, did at times bring forth out of the treasury things new and old.

His last sickness continued about six days, wherein he was preserved in a sweet, sensible and tender frame of spirit, and at times spoke in substance as follows, viz. The doctor coming to visit him, he said with cheerfulness, " I would have thee speak thy " mind freely concerning me, for I am not " afraid to die." The doctor after some pause, signified the doubt he had of his recovery; which bringing an awful silence over his mind, he broke forth in earnest supplication to the Lord for the welfare of Sion, and exhorted friends present to love and unity, and to beware of that spirit which would lead into a separation. He spoke clearly to the states of some, warning them to fear the Lord and walk humbly before him, and then they would be made partakers of his divine and heavenly blessing. He prayed the Lord to prosper his work, and said, " The Lord will cause his glorious truth to break forth in the north country, and among the Ethiopians," In a sight and sense whereof he rejoiced. Another time, his wife sitting by him, he look'd earnestly at her and said, " My dear, don't be surprised, for in time thou wilt come into that rest that I am going into." She queried, " Dost thou think so?" He said " I have no doubt of it," Then taking
leave

leave of her, he said, "Thou hast been a loving wife, a tender mother and a good neighbour." Taking leave of his children one by one, he charg'd them to be loving and obedient to their mother, and not to go out in their marriages. He prayed the Lord to make his passage easy, and receive him graciously into his arms of rest and peace forever; and desired his love to friends in general at their monthly, quarterly and yearly meetings, and meeting of ministers. After which, being sensible his end drew near, he said, " Give me a little water, and " I think I shall not want any more, till I " drink at that fountain which springs up " into eternal life."—Thus in a resigned frame of mind, he finished his course, the 10th day of the first month 1719-20, in the forty-sixth year of his age, and was interr'd in friends burying-ground at Kennet. Concerning whom we believe, he is entered into the mansions of glory, where " The wicked cease from troubling and the weary are at rest."

A Testimony from the Monthly-Meeting of Philadelphia *concerning* ANTHONY MORRIS.

OUR ancient and well esteemed friend Anthony Morris, was a member of this meeting at the early institution thereof, and in the year 1701 appeared in the ministry,

ministry, and being obedient and faithful, he soon became acceptable and edifying, being found in word and doctrine. He was advanced to his forty-seventh year when he engaged in this service, and having a prospect of a great work before him, requiring his close application, he drew his worldly business into a narrow compass, and devoted his time principally to the service of truth; not only visiting neighbouring meetings, but also travelled through New-Jersey, Long-Island, Rhode-Island, New-England and Maryland; and about the year 1715 perform'd a visit to friends in South-Britain. He was early appointed clerk of our monthly-meeting which service he performed many years to satisfaction; being zealous and serviceable in the discipline, a diligent attender of all our religious meetings, careful in observing the time appointed and often concern'd to exhort such to amendment as were remiss herein.

In the eighth month 1721 his speech was much affected by frequent attacks of a paralytick disorder, but his understanding remaining clear, and being favour'd with the enjoyment of divine love, he was enabled to utter some sentences to those that visited him, saying, " That if consistent with the di-
" vine will the time of his dissolution was at
" hand, it would be more joyous to depart
" now, than continue longer in the body."
Yet express'd his free resignation to the will of God, and in an humble tender frame of
spirit

spirit mention'd the testimony Christ gave concerning the woman who poured on his head the precious ointment, saying " He was favoured with the evidence in himself, that he had done what he could, and felt peace," Expressing at the same time, " That his hope for eternal salvation was alone in the mercy of God through his son Christ Jesus, the only saviour and mediator." Some friends who were going to attend a neighbouring yearly-meeting coming to visit him, he took an affectionate leave of them, saying " Remember my dear love to friends in general; tell them I am going and all is well."

He departed this life the 23d of the eighth month 1721, aged sixty-seven years; and on the 25th his corpse was borne to our meeting house in High-street, accompanied by many friends and neighbours, as well as friends from the adjacent country meetings, and thence to our burial ground in this city where it was interr'd. Concerning whom we hope, he hath obtained an entrance into the mansions prepared by Christ Jesus our Lord, for those who continue faithful to the end of their time here, as did this our friend.

Two Extracts from Thomas Chalkley's *journal concerning* THOMAS LIGHTFOOT.

IN the eighth month 1725, I went to Derby to visit our worthy aged friend Thomas Lightfoot, who lay very weak in body, none expecting his recovery; I called as I went from home, and then he was very ill, and told me, " He thought that illness " would conclude his time in this world, " but said that all was well and likewise " that he had a great concern upon his " mind for the growth and prosperity of " truth in the earth, and desired with ten- " derness of spirit, that I would give his " dear love to all friends;" And he now said, " I never thought to see thee more, " but am glad to see thee." I stayed there all night and in the morning we had a comfortable heart-melting time together, in which was revived the remembrance of the many favourable seasons of God's love we had enjoy'd in our travels in the work of the ministry of the gospel of Christ, and we tenderly prayed if we never met more in this world, we might meet in that which is to come, where we might never part more, but might forever live to sing with all the saints and holy angels, hallelujah to God and the Lamb.

In the 9*th* month 1725, I was at the funeral of our worthy ancient friend Thomas Lightfoot. He was buried at Derby; the meeting was the largest that I have ever seen at that place. Our dear friend was greatly beloved for his piety and virtue, his sweet disposition and lively ministry: The Lord was with him in his life and death and with us at his burial.

This our friend removed from Ireland in an advanced age, and settled in Chester county Pennsylvania. In 1724 being then near fourscore years of age, he with Benjamin Kidd, a young minister from England, paid a general visit to friends in New-England.

A Testimony from Nottingham Monthly-Meeting in Pennsylvania, concerning AARON COPPOCK.

IT appears he was born in Cheshire in Old England, the 25*th* of the tenth month 1662, was convinced of the truth when a young man, came to America soon after and lived near Chester; about the year 1714 he, with his family, settled at Nottingham in said county; being a man of an exemplary conduct and much esteemed by friends, he was chosen an elder for the particular meeting of East-Nottingham, until he appeared in a public testimony, and therein was often concerned to exhort friends to a life of self denial, watchfulness and prayer, the which he did in great sincerity, zeal

zeal and innocency. In the forepart of his last illness he complained of much poverty, but before he died had a prospect of happiness, and a sure hope of obtaining the same. He departed this life on the 10th day of the tenth month 1725, and was buried in friends burying ground in East Nottingham. the 12th of the same month, aged sixty-three, and a minister 7 years.

A Testimony from Salem *Monthly-Meeting in* New-Jersey, *concerning* JAMES DANIEL senior.

THE memory of the righteous cannot soon be forgotten by those who follow their footsteps, but are as memorials, deeply engraven on their minds, and are worthy to be had in remembrance, of which number was that steady friend and exemplary elder James Daniel, whose pious life and savoury conversation is fresh in some of our memories.

He was born in Ireland about the year 1675; his father Neal Daniel brought him over sea when about five years of age, and settled in Alloway's-Creek township in the county of Salem West-Jersey; at which time the white people were but few, and the natives a multitude. He learned their language perfectly, and has frequently said, that at that time the natives were a sober, grave and temperate people, and used no manner of oath in their speech. About the 15th year of his age his father died, leaving him in the care of friends to be educated in the way of truth, which he embraced in the love of it; and as he grew in age, he grew in experience and divine favour, and had a share of the oversight of the flock and eldership conferred upon him, which he faithfully performed in the spirit of love and meekness, thereby rendering his service acceptable and obtaining a good report. He ruled his own house well, having his children in subjection: Diligent in attending meetings for worship and discipline, altho' for many years with difficulty, the country being new and roads not made; but afterwards he, with considerable cost and labour, got bridges erected over some creeks and a public road made near his own house. His house and heart were open to entertain friends according to his ability; was zealously concerned for the honour of God and promotion of truth. He often lamented that as the country grew older the people grew worse, and had corrupted the natives in their morals, teaching them bad words and the excessive use of strong drink, which he, during many years in the latter part of his time, for example's sake took none of, and frequently admonished such as were in the use thereof, to observe great temperance.

In the latter years of his life, he desired his eldest sons to take the care of his temporal

ral concerns upon them, for his mind seemed divested therefrom as much as tho' he possessed nothing, (a good example for all elders; for sorrowful experience shews us, that too many as they grow in years, grow more closely attached to the earth; which is a sorrowful prospect and poor example to the rising generation) but devoted his mind and time to truth's service, often accompanying friends in their religious engagements, to his great satisfaction.

Whilst in health, the Lord gave him a sense that his departure drew near; soon afterwards he was taken with the pleurisy and lay about eight days, during which time he gave much good advice to his family, friends and neighbours that came to see him, to whom he also gave evident proofs of a happy exit. The day before his departure, many friends and neighbours came and had a religious meeting, after which, several taking leave, he said, " I am glad of this " visit and of the meeting, but I have a " great concern on my mind for this gene- " ration," mentioning many growing evils then prevalent, and said, " Many of the " elders are called away and more must soon; " but I hope the Lord will raise up some " that shall be faithful and zealous." The evening of his decease, he took his solemn leave of all present, beginning with his wife, and afterwards his children in order, giving each something in charge; to one particularly he said, " Thou dost not know what ser- " vice

"vice the Lord hath for thee to do in thy
"generation." So remaining fenfible until
about the 10*th* hour, he departed like one
falling into a fweet fleep, at his own houfe
on the 26*th* of the tenth month 1726, in
the fifty-fecond year of his age.

Extract from Thomas Chalkley's journal *concerning* JOHN LEE.

THE 27*th* of the tenth month 1726, I heard the news of the death of my dear friend John Lee: It affected me with forrow, he being an old acquaintance and inward friend of mine, with whom I had travelled many miles. He was a living ferviceable minifter of the gofpel of Chrift, and inftrumental to convince divers of that principle of divine light and truth which we profefs: Our love and friendfhip was conftant and intire unto the end, having been acquainted about thirty-five years as near as I can remember.

A Teftimony from New-Garden *Monthly-Meeting in* Pennfylvania, *concerning* CALEB PUSEY.

HE was born in Berkfhire Old England, and educated in the Baptifts profeffion, but after he arrived to years of religious confideration;

consideration, he was convinced of the principles of truth as professed by the people called Quakers. In the year 1682, he removed to Pennsylvania and settled near Chester, where he resided a considerable time, then removed to Marlborough in the same county, where he dwelt the remainder of his days.

He was a worthy elder in the church, being endowed with a good natural capacity, sound in judgment, and zealous in maintaining the cause of truth against contrary and contending spirits. His constancy in attending meetings for worship and discipline was remarkable and worthy of imitation. Much might be said of his zeal and integrity for truth, which he retained to the last, but, for brevity's sake, let it suffice, *that he was a just man*, therefore let him be had in remembrance.

His last illness was heavy upon him for six days; during which he was preserved sensible; signifying *what a brave thing it was to be prepared for death*. The morning before he died, being asked by his son-in-law how he did, answered, " The time was near come that he must leave the world;" to which his son replied, " Father, I hope that is no surprize to thee;" he answered, " No, No;" after which he spoke little that could be understood, only desired " That friends might keep their meetings in uprightness."

He

He died the 25th of the twelfth month 1726-7, in the seventy-sixth year of his age, and was interr'd in friends burying ground at London Grove.

A Testimony from the Monthly-Meeting of Philadelphia, *concerning* HANNAH HILL.

OUR worthy and much esteemed friend Hannah Hill, wife of Richard Hill, and daughter of Thomas Lloyd (formerly governor of this province) by Mary the daughter of Gilbert Jones, of Welchpool, was born in Montgomeryshire North Wales, at the seat of her ancestors called Dolobran, the 21*st* of the seventh month 1666. She was a woman highly favoured of the Lord, possessed many excellent christian virtues, as well as natural accomplishments: Coming over into this country with her parents when young; soon after their arrival it pleased the Lord to remove her pious mother by death, when the care of the younger children devolved upon her: This close trial in the earlier part of her time, was abundantly sanctified to her; for her mind being engaged to seek the Lord for her portion, and her father's God for the lot of her inheritance, he was graciously pleased, not only to favour her with the knowledge of himself and the enjoyment of his living presence in the days of her youth, but also made

made her a singular instrument of good, and a blessing to her father's family. As she grew in years, her conspicuous virtues, joined with a courteous deportment, justly gained the esteem and favour of most if not all with whom she conversed. Being earnestly solicited in marriage by John Delaval, who (tho' a worthy man) was not at that time of the same religious communion, she, by her prudent conduct and pious resolution to maintain the principles she professed without deviating therefrom in a matter of such importance, did not agree thereto; until he after some time embraced the truth in sincerity of heart, and bore his cross like an humble follower of Christ; he received a gift in the ministry, and continued faithful therein to his death: Concerning whom she gave this testimony, viz. "That he never used to her an expression of anger, or the product of a disturbed mind." The decease of her said husband proved to her a time of deep probation, having been heard to say, that in eight weeks time she lost eight of her family by death, beginning with the decease of her beloved husband, and ending with that of her only child: Under which afflicting circumstances, as well as what attended her the remaining part of her life (of which she had a large share) she approved herself a shining example of patience in tribulation, and a meek, humble, self-denying follower of Christ.

In

In the affluent station wherein divine providence had placed her, her benevolent disposition was conspicuous in administring to the necessities of the indigent, her charity not being limited to those of her own profession. She was a true servant of the church, and in the sense of the apostle's expressions, "One that washed the saints feet," receiving with joy into her house, the ministers and messengers of the gospel, for whom her love was great: The low, the poor and the mean, were objects of her peculiar care.

In her younger years she received a gift in the ministry, which she retained with faithfulness to the end; and tho' not large in her appearance, yet with great modesty and soundness of expression, "Her doctrine dropped as the dew, and distilled as the small rain," and was therefore truly acceptable. She travelled in the service of the gospel, to New-England and divers other parts of this continent, and was also concern'd for the good order and discipline of the church, having for a number of years, served in the station of clerk of the women's monthly, quarterly and yearly meetings, wherein she gave satisfaction.

Although bodily weakness frequently attended her in the latter years of her life, it did not abate her love and zeal for the everlasting truth, which she experienced to be her support in every time of trial; and when her dissolution drew near, she made divers seasonable

seasonable remarks and observations, also signified her acquiescence with the divine will, in the dispensations of his providence towards her; at one time particularly mentioning the expressions of the apostle, "That no chastening for the present seemeth to be joyous, but grievous, nevertheless, afterward it yieldeth the peaceable fruit of righteousness unto them which are exercised thereby." This was her happy experience; and after a well-spent life, interspersed with a variety of exercising vicissitudes, she exchanged this state of existence (no doubt) for a blessed immortality in the regions of unmixed felicity; after about three weeks illness, on the 25*th* of the twelfth month 1726-7, in the sixty-first year of her age. Her corpse was respectfully attended by a large number of friends and others, to the High-street meeting-house in Philadelphia, where divers living testimonies were borne, after which it was interr'd in friends burial ground.

She was twenty-six years the wife of Richard Hill, who was a serviceable member both in church and state, and died in good esteem, the 4*th* of the seventh month 1729.

A Testimony

A Testimony from Haddonfield *Monthly-Meeting in* New-Jersey, *concerning* JAMES LORD.

HE received a lively gift of the gospel ministry whilst young in years, was frequently exercised therein to the edification and encouragement of friends; and was much concerned for the true Sioners, that they might hold on their way, and that the outcasts of Israel might be gathered home into the true fold of rest. An exemplary man, by which he greatly adorned the doctrine he preached; was called from works to rewards in the flower of his age, being in his thirty-fourth year and in the year 1727.

Extract from Thomas Chalkley's journal, *concerning the aforesaid* JAMES LORD.

ON second-day the 25th of the seventh month 1727, I had the sorrowful tidings of the death of my beloved friend James Lord; who, on his death-bed, desired that I might be sent for to his burial. In the consideration of that christian love which was between us, I think I may truly note, that we were always glad to meet each other; therefore the thoughts of this so sudden change and final parting, brought, for the present, a sadness and heaviness over my mind;

mind; confidering his ftation in that neighbourhood, and fervice in that congregation to which he did belong; for therein he was well-beloved and very ferviceable.

And Oh! the lofs that his dear wife and tender children will have of him, really affects me with forrow in penning thefe notes; but the forrow, in thefe things, is all on our fide; for he, without doubt, is at reft with his great mafter in Heaven. We had a larger meeting at his funeral than ever was known to be there before (as an ancient friend told me) which was folemn and ferviceable to many.

Some account of JOHN BEVAN, *copied from a manufcript, appearing to be a teftimony from a meeting in* Wales *concerning him, the conclufion of which is wanting. And tho' he was born and died in that country, yet having lived many years in* Pennfylvania, *the following memorial is thought not improper to be inferted in this Collection.*

OUR deceafed friend John Bevan, the worthy fubject of our teftimony, having deferved to have his name tranfmitted to pofterity, for his pious life and converfation, the following account of him, probably, will not only be fatisfactory to his relations, friends and acquaintance, but afford edification and comfort to thofe who knew him not. He

He was born about 1646, and well descended; his parents died when he was very young, leaving five children, of whom he was the eldest. In 1665 he married a religious woman. His father had left him a considerable estate, but the rest of the children were unprovided for; he therefore, when he came of age, (his sister being dead before) portioned all his brothers, and gave them a helpful subsistence in the world. Some years after, he was convinced of the blessed truth as it is in Jesus, the manner whereof, as he himself hath left it in writing, was thus,

‘ My wife was religiously inclined in her
‘ young years, and zealously concerned to
‘ observe the ceremonies of the church of
‘ England, and I believe (as she has often
‘ told me) she aimed sincerely therein at
‘ God's glory and the salvation of her im-
‘ mortal soul. After we were joined in mar-
‘ riage, she continued very zealous in that
‘ way; but when a weighty concern came
‘ upon my mind for the well-being of my
‘ immortal soul, I saw it very needful for
‘ me to make a narrow search after the best
‘ way, and those people who performed
‘ that worship and service that was accept-
‘ able before God; and being in a weighty
‘ frame of spirit, the people called Quakers
‘ came before the view of my mind; and
‘ hearing of a book of George Fox the
‘ younger's, to be at a relation's house, I
‘ was willing to go thither for it, and in the
‘ reading

'reading thereof, I was so well satisfied,
'that I can truly say, what I then read,
'answered the witness of God in my own
'bosom, as "Face answereth face in a glass:"
'But soon after I came home, my wife per-
'ceiving me to be more serious and weigh-
'ty in my spirit than formerly, was jealous
'I had an inclination towards that way
'which the people called Quakers made
'profession of; and finding I had the said
'book, came up to the chamber where I
'was, and cautioned me not to be beguil-
'ed: I spoke to her in simplicity and much
'brokenness of heart, of the sense and sa-
'tisfaction I had, that those who were faith-
'ful to that divine principle which the
'people called Quakers bore testimony to,
'were the people God owned, or to that
'import; and it reached to God's witness
'in her, that we parted in much tenderness
'at that time. However she continued some-
'what zealous in her way still, and would
'be often arguing with me in vindication
'thereof, much about twelve months; but
'at one time, when she was at their wor-
'ship, the Priest denounced his excommu-
'nication against me, and she being in a
'seat just under him, it came so near her
'that she was nigh to faint away; when
'their worship was over, she went to the
'Priest and spoke somewhat home to him,
'and that she thought she deserved more
'civility, at least so much as to know afore-
'hand of their excommunication, for he
'might

'might know that she sincerely loved her
'husband tho' he dissented from her in
'judgment. And after that time, she be-
'came more willing to search closely into
'the weighty work of the salvation of her
'immortal soul; and the Lord's love was
'manifested to her, that in a little while af-
'ter, her understanding came to be opened,
'and she came to be convinced of God's
'everlasting truth, that was promised "To
"lead into all truth." And having tasted of
'that living bread that gives life to the soul,
'she came withal to see there was no need of
'the outward bread, which formerly she was
'zealous and conscientious in the observa-
'tion of, to commemorate the death and
'passion of our Lord Jesus Christ; the true
'remembrancer being come and witnessed,
'even he "Who stands at the door of men's
"hearts for an entrance, that he may come
"to sup with them and they with him."

'Soon after our convincement, the ene-
'my of souls mustered his forces, and en-
'deavoured to stifle our convictions, and
'we were hard put to it both within and
'without, but as our eyes were to the Lord,
'and in poverty and humility of spirit we
'leaned upon him, he made the hard things
'easy, and in the sense of his divine love
'which was often shed abroad in our hearts,
'we were made willing to deny ourselves,
'to take up the cross, and to despise the
'shame. And tho' we were but a few, we
'thought it convenient to meet together to

'wait

'wait upon the Lord, being fully satisfied
'it was a duty incumbent upon his people
'in all ages; and in the performance of our
'duty herein in the year 1675, several
'friends were taken from our house at two
'several times, and brought before two
'justices of the peace, who tendered the
'oath of allegiance and supremacy to them,
'and because, for conscience sake, they
'could not break the command of Christ
'who said "Swear not at all," they were
'committed to prison, where they remain-
'ed about fourteen weeks, and then were
'set at liberty; ever since which, the meet-
'ing has been kept either at our house or
'at the meeting-house, quietly without any
'more disturbance.

'Sometime before the year 1683, we
'heard that our esteemed friend William
'Penn, had a patent from king Charles the
'second, for that province in America call-
'ed Pennsylvania; and my wife had a great
'inclination to go thither, and thought it
'might be a good place to train up children
'amongst sober people, and to prevent the
'corruption of them here, by the loose be-
'haviour of the youth and the bad example
'of too many of those of riper years; she ac-
'quainted me therewith, but I then thought
'it not likely to take effect for several reasons;
'but as I was sensible her aim was upright
'on account of our children, I was willing
'to weigh the matter in a true balance;
'and I can truly say, my way was made
'easy

'easy and clear to go thither, beyond my
'expectation; and it was the Lord's great
'mercy to preserve us over the great deep
'to our defired port: And what hardships
'we met at the beginning of our fettlement,
'the Lord was our helper and fupport to
'go through: And I can in a fweet re-
'membrance fay, many were the blessed fea-
'fons we had with God's people in that re-
'mote country, and I believe and am well
'fatisfied that the Lord has a remnant there,
'that fincerely aim at his glory and the
'profperity of his truth, blessed and praif-
'ed be his holy name forever.

'We ftaid there many years, and had
'four of our children married with our
'confent, and they had feveral children,
'and the aim intended by my wife, was in
'a good meafure anfwered.—When a weigh-
'ty concern came upon my mind to return
'to my native country, and that chiefly on
'truth's account. I laid it before my wife,
'and fhe could not be eafy to ftay behind
'me, and we came over in the year 1704;
'and through the Lord's great mercy we were
'preferved in that tedious voyage, north
'about Scotland through many difficulties,
'and from the cruelties alfo of the pri-
'vateers, of which there were many then
'on that coaft, as we were afterward in-
'formed.—This wonderful prefervation de-
'ferves to be remembered with thankfgiv-
'ing; having loft the fleet, we were only
'four fhips coming together from Virginia,
and

'and one of them belonging to Briftol, we
'thought to remove to that fhip, becaufe
'Briftol was nearer to our habitation in
'Wales than London, whither our veffel
'was bound; we agreed with the mafter
'for our paffage, and next morning we were
'to go on board, but that night I was un-
'der a weighty exercife about our removal,
'but in the morning it happened to be fo
'ftormy that he could not take us in, fo he
'parted from us, and bore his courfe to-
'wards Briftol; then the weight I was un-
'der was removed, and I was very eafy in
'my fpirit; and as I was afterward inform-
'ed, that fhip was taken near to Lundy Ifland:
'This deliverance therefore and prefervation
'of us, I afcribe to the Lord's great favour
'and mercy towards us, thanks, honour and
'praifes be rendered and afcribed to him for
'the fame and all other mercies forever.

'In this voyage, our youngeft daughter
'Barbara Bevan accompanied us, and fhe
'was of good fervice on truth's account,
'the fhort time fhe remained in the body;
'her innocency and fweet behaviour preach-
'ed truth wherever fhe came. It is my
'comfort and great fatisfaction, that fhe left
'a good favour, and has finifhed her courfe
'in peace with her maker, and is gone to
'her eternal reft in the manfions of blifs
'and joy, to laud and magnify him forever.†

'We

† A fhort teftimony concerning her, worthy of perufal, is printed in the 5th part of Piety Promoted.

'We landed at last at Shields in Northumberland, and staid over the meeting on first-day, where we were comforted with friends; next day we set forward toward our habitation in Wales, having near three hundred miles to travel. We had several good meetings in our way, and about the beginning of the eighth month 1704, we came to our home at Treveyricke; and from that time forward my dear wife was given up as before, to be serviceable on truth's account, and so continued during her pilgrimage here, being six years and upwards. Her house and heart since her convincement, were open to receive the Lord's messengers, both here and in America, and she was very careful and open hearted to help the poor and weak, both amongst us and others. In her last sickness, she was sensible she was not like to recover out of it, and she was satisfied and contented therein to submit to the Lord's will; speaking to me, she said, "I take it as a great mercy that I am to go before thee, we are upwards of forty-five years married, and our love is rather more now towards one another, than at the beginning, yet I am willing to part with all, for the Lord is better than all." 'She quietly departed this life the 26th of the eleventh month 1710; aged seventy-three years and about four months; and tho' my loss thereby is great, yet it is her eternal gain.'

Our

Our well esteemed friend having left us this just account of his convincement, and of the reasons of his removal to, and return from Pennsylvania to his native country again; it remains for us to add, that by their testimonials from Pennsylvania, we find they were all three of good service there, the old friends being examples of meekness, temperance and charity, and having lived in love and fellowship with the brethren and sisters there, were in good esteem amongst all. And the young friend being of an innocent and good life and conversation, was well beloved amongst them; and further, that the father and daughter had received a gift of the ministry, which had been to the comfort and edification of the churches thereaway.—We heard he visited New-England in particular with our friend Hugh Roberts, about the year 1701.—Soon after he returned from Pennsylvania, he and his daughter visited together several meetings of friends in South and North Wales, and were eminently favoured therein with the divine presence.—His sufferings, considering his faithfulness and the time he lived in, were not very many; his relations at times diverting the strokes from him; however after a long prosecution by the Vicar of the parish for his pretended dues, he was at last confined to Cardiff goal in 1721, upon an excommunicatio capiendo, but there being some error in it, he was discharged the following sessions, and ever after left unmolested.

He was endued with a good understanding in things spiritual and temporal, discreet and prudent in his ways, of an unspotted life and conversation, grave and solid in his deportment, and careful to keep concord and unity among friends, constant and unmoveable against that which would divide and rend, yet labouring to restore those that were beguiled thereby. In his last sickness, he had no small conflict, but he was favoured with much patience and possessed his soul therein, and bore his indisposition to admiration.—At one time he said, "Ever since I had the knowledge of the truth, I have endeavoured to be innocent." To a relation asking him how he did? he answered, "Weakly, but I find some strength to bear my weakness."

A Testimony from the Monthly-Meeting of Philadelphia, *concerning* HANNAH CARPENTER.

SHE was born at Haverford West in South Wales, where having the opportunity of seeing the patient, innocent and steady sufferings of friends who were imprisoned for their religious testimony, together with their good conversation in Christ, she was convinced of the blessed truth, and became very serviceable to those who were in bonds there for Christ's sake. She came over here in the early settling of this province, and after some time was married to our well esteemed friend Samuel Carpenter, of this city. She received a share of the gospel ministry, which was seasoned with a lively favour of divine sweetness; and though not frequent in her appearances, was very acceptable. Her heart and house stood open to receive and entertain the true gospel ministers, to whom she was a tender nursing mother both in sickness and in health; being full of warmth and love to faithful friends, a bright example of meekness in the church as well as in her own family; and her life and conversation being adorned with the christian virtues of benevolence and charity, render'd her beloved, respected and useful in her station.

She died the 24th of the fifth month 1728, in the eighty-third year of her age.

The following Epistle to parents concerning the education of children, manifesting her pious regard for the youth, and her anxiety for the increase and prosperity of the church of Christ, is thought proper to be here annexed, viz.

" UPON the 4th day of the fourth month, I was drawn forth to wait on the Lord, and as I was waiting, the consideration of my dear children whom the Lord had taken to himself in their innocency came before me, and my soul blessed his holy name for his
great

great love towards them and me, in that they are gone to their reſt, and ſhall never partake of thoſe exerciſes and ſorrows theſe do that remain in the world; and then my ſoul was poured forth before the Lord for them that remain, that as they grow up in years, they may grow in grace, and in the knowledge of our Lord and ſaviour Jeſus Chriſt; or elſe I would rather follow them to their graves whilſt they are young, than that they ſhould live to the diſhonour of his worthy name: And then a more general and weighty concern came upon me for friends children that are grown up and do not come under the yoke nor bear the croſs. Oh! the cry that ran through my ſoul, and in the anguiſh and bitterneſs of my ſpirit, I ſaid, *Lord what will thou do with friends children when we are gone off the ſtage of this world; will thou raiſe up children, and not thoſe of believing parents?* And this was the word that livingly ſprung up in my ſoul. *They reject my counſel and caſt my law behind their backs, and will have none of my reproofs, and tho' my hand be ſtretched forth all the day long, yet they will not hear, but go after their own hearts luſt.* Then I ſaid in my heart, *Lord are they all ſo?* The anſwer was, *there are ſome that are innocent, whom I will bleſs with a bleſſing from me, and they ſhall ſhine forth to my praiſe.* And now, Oh friends! that you may dwell and abide in the innocent life, that ſo the bleſſing of the Lord you may

may feel daily to descend upon you. But as for you that " Reject the counsel of the Lord and cast his law behind your backs, and will have none of his reproofs," which are sorrowful sayings concerning you who are the children of believing parents, you who are under the profession of the truth, which will do you no good, unless you return unto the Lord; therefore I desire you may all return unto him, whilst the day of a long-suffering merciful God lasteth: But if you still reject the counsel of the Lord, the many faithful warnings you have had, how will you answer it in the day when he cometh, " To render unto every one according to their deeds?" And now, something further is with me to parents of children. Dear friends, you that have been convinced of God's unchangeable truth, and have known the work and operation of it, working out and bringing down that which was of a contrary nature to it. And Oh! that we may all abide faithful in his work, and retain our integrity to the Lord, then let our breathing cries and prayers be offered up to the Lord for our children, that he would be pleased to look down in mercy upon them, and visit them as he did our souls. But as David said, " If I regard iniquity in my heart, the Lord will not hear me;" so I desire we may all be clear in our offerings before the Lord, that he may smell a sweet favour from them.

Dear

Dear friends, what is here written is with great caution, knowing that I have children of my own, and that many honest parents have bad children, which is no small exercise; but if we keep faithful to the Lord, and discharge our duty to them by precept and example, we shall be clear of them in the sight of God: And therefore friends, faithfulness is the word that runs through me, not only for our own souls, but for our children's also; that a generation may grow up to his praise in this part of the world, when our heads are laid in the dust. Great and manifold hath the love and mercy of God been towards us, the consideration of it, many times hath deeply affected my mind; and it was he by the same arm of power that reached unto us, and brought a concern upon us in our own native land; and I do believe that many had as clear a call to leave their native country, as some of old had, which caused many days and nights of sore travel and exercise before the Lord, and no ease could we have, but in giving up life and all unto him, saying, "Lord do what thou wilt with us, only let thy presence preserve us." And to his praise we can say, he hath been with us since we came to this country, and hath preserved us through many and various exercises, both inwardly and outwardly. And now that which lies on our parts I desire may be considered by us all, that so suitable returns may be made unto the Lord, by walking in in humility and godly fear before him; that so, good patterns we may be, by keeping our places "To the praise of him who hath called us," for he is worthy forever more. And friends, something more is with me which I thought to omit, but find I can't well do it, that is, concerning our children, that we be very careful while they are young, that we suffer them not to wear such things that truth allows not; and though it may be said, they are but little things and well enough for children, but we find, that when they are grown up, it is hard for them to leave off, which may be, if they had not been used when young, would not have been expected when grown up: So I desire we may all be clear in ourselves, and keep our children out of the fashions and customs of this world. And Oh! that we were all of one heart and mind in these and other things, then would the work of the Lord go on easily, which is the sincere desire of your friend,

HANNAH CARPENTER.

A Testimony from the Yearly-Meeting in Virginia, *concerning* ROBERT JORDAN.

HE was son of Thomas and Margaret Jordan, of Nancemond county in Virginia, born the 11th of the seventh month 1668, and carefully educated in the way of
truth

truth by his worthy parents, who lived to see the religion of his education become that of his choice and practice in his mature years, in which he was preserved to the last, without wavering, in great peace with the Lord and unity of his brethren.

He was an hospitable man, very ready to entertain strangers, especially the Lord's messengers, whom he treated with great respect and affection, honouring them for their work's sake; being also charitable to the poor, and as a man of trade and commerce, obtained a good reputation, having declared he had never wronged any man knowingly in all his life.

In the time of his illness, which continued about two weeks, he seemed very patient and resigned to the will of God, and much concerned for the everlasting welfare of his children, which he expressed in a lively manner; and often in fervent prayer, desired they might be preserved from the vanities and corruptions of this world, and that they might love and fear the Lord in their youth, saying at one time, " O Lord preserve my flock, let them never go astray, nor forget thee nor one another: O my God! hold them in thy arms that none of them be lost, let not the enemy prevail over them:" Being humbly thankful and blessed God, that he had been pleased to support him through every dispensation of his providence to that time. He died the 3d of the eighth

eighth month 1728, and on the 9th of the same month, after a large meeting held on the occasion, was interr'd in the family burying-ground.

A Testimony from Gwynedd *Monthly-Meeting in* Pennsylvania, *concerning* ROWLAND ELLIS.

OUR ancient and esteemed friend Rowland Ellis, was born in the year 1650, in Merionethshire North Wales, convinced of the truth about the twenty-second year of his age, suffered several years imprisonment with constancy on account of his testimony, it being then a time of sore persecution; the two judges who committed him with many others for refusing to take the oath of allegiance and supremacy, declared openly at the assizes, " That in case they refused a second time to take it, they should be proceeded against as traitors, the men hanged and quartered, and the women burned." In 1686 he came over into Pennsylvania to prepare for a settlement for his wife and family, with whom he return'd in 1697. He was endued with a gift in the ministry, and tho' not very frequent in appearance therein, his service was acceptable and to edification; being of sound judgment, ready and willing to assist his neighbours and friends in all cases civil or religious when desired.

desired. He was zealous for supporting our christian discipline, and exemplary in conducting himself agreeable therewith, sometimes saying "If the hedge of discipline was not kept up, the labour of the husbandman would soon be laid waste." He was careful in educating his children religiously, by timely endeavouring to inculcate in them the principles of piety and virtue; a practice of his tending thereto, was, having meetings frequently in his family, which he long continued. In the last monthly-meeting he attended he was taken unwell, but afterwards said to divers friends present, "I am glad I was here to day, for I had a lively meeting, and though I now feel much weakness and the infirmities attending my advanced age, yet I can say, truth is as dear and as sweet as ever." He also said, "Sa-
"tan sometimes lies in wait like a roaring
"lion to devour me, but I find he is chain-
"ed by a secret hand which limits his pow-
"er, so that he cannot harm me." His indisposition continued a few days, which he bore with christian patience, expressing "His sense of his near arrival at the haven of rest and quiet, where none could make him afraid." He expired at the house of his son-in-law John Evans, in the eightieth year of his age, and was interr'd in friends burying-ground at Plymouth, (to which particular meeting he belonged) in the seventh month 1729. Concerning whom we trust it may be said, *he rests, enjoying the reward of the righteous, and his works do follow.*

A Testimony

A Testimony from Newark *Monthly-Meeting in* New Castle *county on* Delaware, *concerning* Moses Mendenhall.

HE was born at Concord in Chester county Pennsylvania, about 1693, being the son of Benjamin Mendenhall, an early settler in that place; in his youth he was religiously inclined, loving the conversation of such, and choosing places of retirement to wait upon God. He married about the year 1719, and soon after settled at Kennet, where he continued his habitation the remainder of his life. As he grew in years he grew in religious experience, and in 1724 appeared in the ministry; first in a few words, but continuing faithful, he increased in his gift, and in time had a seasonable refreshing testimony, which often affected the minds of the hearers. He visited the meetings in Maryland, New-Jersey, and sometimes those near home; being also rightly gifted for the discipline, and serviceable therein. He had a clear discerning of a spirit of undue liberty that seemed at one time to prevail, which afterwards manifested itself to the exercise of the faithful.

Being sensible in his last sickness that his end was near, he signified " He was thankful to the Lord, that he was like to be taken from the troubles of this world;" exhorting friends to faithfulness; and died in a resigned

resigned frame, in the ninth month 1731, aged about thirty-eight, and a minister about 7 years, and was interr'd in Kennet burying-ground.

A Testimony from Duck-Creek *Monthly-Meeting in* Kent *county on* Delaware, *concerning* Joseph Booth.

HE was born at or near Scituate in New-England, and educated in the religion of the independants; leaving his native country when a young man, he came and settled early on Muspillion in Sussex county upon Delaware, where he filled the station of a magistrate many years, and was also chosen a member of the house of assembly, discharging the several trusts reposed in him, with reputation.

In the year 1699, he was convinced by the ministry of Thomas Story, who left this testimony respecting him, " That he was the most sober and knowing person in those parts." As he gave up faithfully to the manifestation of truth, it so operated upon him, as to bring the creaturely part into subjection, tho' much in the way of the cross, and the more so, by reason of the station and character he supported in the world; but thro' continued obedience, he witnessed love so to prevail in his heart, as to constrain him, livingly to declare to others what

what the Lord had done for him. Being rightly called and anointed for the work, his appearances were folemn and awful, miniftring in the power of truth. He was a nurfing father in the church, conftant in attending religious meetings, and exemplary in humbly waiting therein; having likewife been inftrumental in fettling the meeting at Murtherkiln where he belonged, as alfo that at Cold-Spring; and before any meeting was held at the latter, he frequently vifited the few families of friends adjacent thereto, and was in general good efteem amongft men. He died about the year 1732.

A Teſtimony from Wrights-Town *Monthly-Meeting in* Bucks *county* Pennfylvania, *concerning* ANN PARSON.

SHE appeared in the miniftry in her youthful days, and continuing faithful, fhe travelled on that account, feveral times through New-England, the Jerfeys, Pennfylvania, Maryland and Virginia in America, and through England, Ireland, Scotland and Wales in Europe; her miniftry being favoury and to edification. She was a good example, of an inoffenfive life, patient in affliction, and died in good unity with the church.

In

In her last illness, she said to her brother Abraham Chapman, "I have travelled a pretty deal in my time, and, according to my ability, have laboured in the love of God (in the service of truth, and good-will to all men) which springs in my bosom now as fresh as ever; blessed be his name. And I desire thee (if I go) by a few lines, to remember my kind love to friends, desiring they may stand in the counsel of God; for I have often rejoiced and been glad, to see friends stand in his counsel and keep their places in the truth; and on the contrary, it has often wounded my spirit, to see those that have made a profession of the truth, (and some of them children of good parents) take undue liberty, taking pleasure in vanity and folly, and neglecting that which would be to their everlasting peace. It is my advice to friends, that they stand in the counsel of God, which will be to them as a mighty rock in a weary land, and enable them to wade through the various exercises and troubles which may fall to their share to meet with in this troublesome world. I have found it by experience to be a sure help in every needful and difficult time, when exercises seemed to surround me on every hand like the billows of the main, then I found, to stand in the counsel of God, was the only place of refuge that I could retire unto, where I found safety, and was often refreshed,

"freshed, strengthened and comforted by
"the influence of the love of God in me;
"and I would counsel and advise, that all
"friends keep close to meetings, and pa-
"tiently wait to feel their strength renewed
"in God. And as it has been the desire
"and labour of my spirit, that friends
"should keep up their meetings in good
"order, and in the wisdom of truth; so I
"recommend it as my advice and counsel
"to friends, to be careful to keep to meet-
"ings, and patiently wait to feel the over-
"shadowing power of truth, to strengthen
"and renew their hope in God, which
"brings down and abases every thing that
"would exalt itself above the peaceable
"government of truth." After having lain sometime in great stillness, she, in fervent prayer, besought the Lord, " To carry on
"the work he had begun, so that many
"might flock unto his church, as doves
"unto the windows; and that sin and ini-
"quity might cease, and righteousness and
"truth cover the earth, as the waters cover
"the sea;" fervently beseeching the Lord,
"To bless his people and her near relations,
"and that her companion might be favor-
"ed with the visitation of divine love, and
"know his last days to be his best days;
"and that he might find admittance into
"rest and peace, when time to him in this
"life should be no more," with many more of the like expressions, at sundry times during her illness.

She died the 9*th* of the tenth month 1732, in the fifty-seventh year of her age, having been a minister 33 years.

A Testimony from Nottingham *Monthly-Meeting in* Pennsylvania, *concerning* Joseph Elgar.

HE was born (as we are informed) at Folkstone in Kent, Old England, the 30*th* of the fourth month 1690, of believing parents; and came into America about the year 1720, living some time near Philadelphia, and in 1728, removed within the limits of East Nottingham particular meeting. After his coming to this country, he was called to the work of the ministry, wherein he was not forward, yet his appearances being lively and edifying, friends had near unity therewith. A good example in attending meetings, a faithful labourer therein, and careful in keeping to the hour appointed. He was industrious in outward affairs, tho' cheerfully given up to answer the requirings of truth; visiting the meetings of friends in Pennsylvania, as also in New-Jersey and Maryland generally. He was gifted in discipline, and likewise qualified for the service of visiting families, wherein he was engaged the last time he was absent from home, within the limits of Bush-River and Deer-Creek particular meetings;

ings; in his return from whence, he told a friend, "There was an unusual weight over his spirit, and a cloud that he could not see beyond, which made him think his days work was nearly over." The night he return'd home, he was affected with sickness and much pain, which continued several days, bearing the same with exemplary patience. Afterwards growing weaker but remaining sensible, he often expressed, "He had done with the world, and was willing to leave it, for he had been faithful to what was made known to him, since he gave up to the requirings of truth."

Continuing in a sweet composure of mind, he departed on the 19th of the eleventh month 1733-4, in the forty-fourth year of his age, a minister about 12 years. His remains were interr'd in friends burying-ground at East-Nottingham; on which solemn occasion, our friend Mungo Bewley of Ireland, who was then on a religious visit in America, exercised his gift to the comfort of many friends.

A Testimony from the Yearly-Meeting of friends in Virginia, *concerning* JOSEPH JORDAN.

HE was born in Nancemond county in Virginia, in the year 1695, being the third son of Robert Jordan, as well as one of the third generation who have walked in the truth. He was of a sprightly genius, affable difpofition, and even temper, which, as he grew to manhood, gave him eafy accefs to company, efteemed the better fort. A vifitation of divine love being extended to him about the twenty-fecond year of his age, he like Zaccheus, made hafte, and with joy embraced, both the meffage and the meffenger of falvation: And being endued with a gift in the miniftry, acquitted himfelf "As a workman that need not be afhamed," and had great place in the minds of men. Altho' he had not much fchool literature, yet he might be faid to have had the tongue of the learned, being both correct and concife in fpeaking the word in feafon, infomuch that divers have confeffed to the truth and embraced the doctrine he preached. Being patient in tribulation, he was favour'd with that hope which affords content and folace of mind. After labouring in the gofpel in his own country and the adjacent provinces, he vifited moft parts of England, Ireland, and divers parts of Holland; being abfent on this fervice above three years, he returned with peace, and found his prefence neceffary at home; for his father being deceafed, and his brother Robert then abfent, the care of the family devolved upon him, which truft he difcharged with judgment, being a good œconomift, kind neighbour and fteady friend.

He

He often intimated that he should not continue long, and was therefore concern'd to use diligence. Not long before his decease, he visited friends in Virginia and North-Carolina, edifying them with his gift; and in the beginning of the month in which he died, (tho' very weak in body) attended their quarterly meeting, signifying at his return, his great satisfaction therein, believing it would be the last meeting of the kind he should ever be at, and accordingly he never afterwards went from home, except to a week-day meeting in the neighbourhood.

On the morning of the day of his dissolution, he uttered many favoury expressions, saying to some young ministers, " Mind
" your gifts and the Lord will bless you,
" and you will be a blessing to the church.
" Be humble and obedient; obedience brings
" sweet peace. I have a great desire there
" might be a right ministry continued in
" the church, for there are many not strict-
" ly of this fold, who in due time the Lord
" will bring in: And as you come to have
" an experience of the work of truth in
" your own hearts, you will be able to con-
" fute them who persuade themselves there
" is no living without sin in this world. I
" am not in a condition to speak much,
" neither is it, I hope, very needful; as you
" are thus taught of the Lord, you will
" have cause to rejoice in him on whom you
" have believed."

Thus

Thus having happily compleated his day's work, he laid down his head in much refignation and peace with the Lord, the 26*th* of the ninth month 1735, aged forty years, a minifter about 17.

A Teftimony from the Monthly-Meeting of Philadelphia, *concerning* RICHARD TOWNSEND.

HE was a meek and humble man, fincerely concerned for the promotion of piety and virtue; his miniftry being found, living, and tending to edification, was well accepted. He vifited friends in the fervice of truth in Great Britain, continued faithful to the end of his days, and departed this life about the 30*th* of the third month 1737.

A Teftimony from Newark *Monthly-Meeting in* New Caftle *county on* Delaware, *concerning* CHRISTOPHER WILSON.

HE was born in Yorkfhire Old England, of parents who were members of the church of England. In his youth he was inclined to vanity, but his mind being reached thro' the vifitation of divine grace. When he grew up, he joined in fellowfhip with friends; and came to America in 1712,
being

being well recommended by certificate, tho' then a servant. About 1728 he appeared in the ministry, first in a few words, but growing therein, his appearances were seasonable and savoury, and attended with a degree of that life that "Makes glad the heritage of God;" being likewise serviceable in the discipline of the church according to ability.

He began the world with little, but being industrious in the creation, and concern'd for truth's prosperity, the Lord blessed his labours, so that he lived comfortably and maintained his family reputably, supporting the character of an honest peaceable man, and was often instrumental in restoring peace amongst others. In his last sickness, being asked by a friend "How it was with him?" He answered, "If the messenger of death comes, I see nothing in my way." Keeping mostly still and quiet, he, in a resigned, composed frame of mind, finished his course the 11th of the seventh month 1740, in the fiftieth year of his age, a minister about 12 years, and was interr'd in Center burying-ground.

A Testimony from the Monthly-Meeting of Philadelphia, *concerning* Thomas Chalkley.

HE was a member of our monthly-meeting above forty years, so that some of us had opportunities of being intimately acquainted

quainted with him, and of knowing his fidelity and diligence in promoting the cause of truth, and the edification of the church of Christ; this having been the principal engagement and concern of his mind, and which he preferred to any other consideration; as will evidently appear to those, who, with an honest and unprejudiced intention, peruse his journal of his life and travels.

By which it will appear, that he was, in the early part of his life, sensibly affected with the visitation of divine life and grace, and, by adhering thereunto, was preserved from the vanities and follies, which often divert and alienate the minds of youth from the due remembrance and awful regard of their creator; so that he was enabled to bear a testimony of christian patience and self-denial in his youthful days, and, by keeping under that exercise, as he advanced in years, attained to further knowledge and experience in the work of religion, in which he had a sight of the necessity of keeping in a state of humility, and of bearing the cross of Christ, which mortified him to the world; so that the loss many sustain by the anxious pursuit of the lawful things thereof appearing to him, he was concerned to avoid it, and in obedience to the precept of Christ, to *seek first the kingdom of God, and his righteousness,* having faith in his promise, *that all these things* (necessary for him) *should be added.*

Thus the love of God influencing his mind, and opening his understanding, he
became

became concerned for the general good of mankind, and received a gift of the ministry of the gospel of Christ, before he had attained the age of twenty-one years; in the public exercise of which, he soon after travelled thro' many parts of England, and into Scotland, and the next year, being 1697, he came to visit friends in this and the adjacent provinces of America, where his ministry and conversation were to the comfort and edification of the faithful, (as some of us can with satisfaction declare, from our knowledge and remembrance of him at that time) and the near fellowship and union he then had with friends here (we believe) contributed to his more speedy determination of settling among us, which he afterwards thought it his duty to do, tho' the leaving his parents and relations (as he afterwards expressed) was no small cross to him, being of a dutiful and affectionate disposition.

After fixing his residence among us, he persever'd in his concern and labour for the edification of the churches, and gathering people to faith and dependance on the inward teachings of Christ, and for that purpose only he travelled many long journies and voyages through the several English colonies on this continent, and most of the islands in the West-Indies, and in Europe, through England, Wales, Scotland, Ireland, Holland, Frizeland, and several parts of Germany, and the adjacent northern kingdoms; and in many of these places his ministry

niſtry and religious labours were bleſſed with the deſired ſucceſs, of which there are yet ſome witneſſes living, and others, who were convinced of the principles of truth by his means, became ſerviceable members of the church, and continued therein to the end of their lives.

But as the wiſe king Solomon formerly obſerved, that *one event cometh to the righteous, and to the wicked,* ſo it happened to this good man, who met with various loſſes and diſappointments in his temporal eſtate; after which, the circumſtances of his affairs engaged him to undertake ſome buſineſs, in the management of which he was obliged to croſs the ſeas frequently: This, however, did not abate his zeal and religious care to make uſe of all opportunities of viſiting the meetings of friends when among them, and of calling, at other times, to ſuch who might be accounted as *the outcaſt of Iſrael, and the diſperſed of Judah, or as ſheep not yet of the fold of Chriſt*; and his ſervices of that kind are worthy to be commemorated, having been often productive of good effects.

His patience was remarkable in diſappointments and afflictions, of which he had a large ſhare; and his meekneſs, humility and circumſpection, in the general courſe of his life and converſation, were conſpicuous and exemplary; and as he frequently exhorted and admoniſhed others to the obſervation and practice of the many excellent precepts and rules of Chriſt, our Lord and lawgiver,

lawgiver, and more especially those expressed in his sermon on the mount (which contains the sum of our moral and religious duties) so he manifested himself to be one of that number, whom Christ compared to the wise builder, who laid a sure foundation; so that his building stood unshaken by the various floods and winds of tribulations and temptations he met with, both from within and without.

He was a lover of unity amongst brethren, and careful to promote and maintain it, shewing the example of a meek, courteous, and loving deportment, not only to friends, but to all others, with whom he had conversation or dealings; so that it may be truly said, that *few have lived so universally beloved and respected among us*: And it was manifest this did not proceed from a desire of being popular, or to be seen of man: For his love and regard to peace did not divert him from the discharge of his duty in a faithful testimony to those that professed the truth, that they ought to be careful to maintain good works; and he was often concern'd zealously to incite and press friends to the exercise of the good order and discipline established in the wisdom of truth, by admonishing, warning, and timely treating with such as fell short of their duty therein, and by testifying against those who, after loving and brotherly care and endeavours, could not be brought to

the

the sense and practice of their duty; and thereby he sometimes shar'd the ill-will and resentment of such persons.

The several Essays he wrote on religious subjects at sea, are further proofs that his mind was principally engaged in the great business and concern of religion; and as he continued under the same engagement to the end, we are fully persuaded the words with which he concluded his last public testimony on the island of Tortola, may be truly and properly applied to him, *that he had fought a good fight, and had kept the faith, and* we doubt not, *he now enjoys a crown of righteousness.*

Much more might be truly said of his integrity, faithfulness and worth, but we do not think it necessary; our chief intention being to express our respectful remembrance of him, and our unity with his labours and services; and we are sincerely desirous, that the glory of every good and perfect work may be attributed to that divine power alone, which can qualify others to supply the places of those faithful ministers and servants of Christ, who have been of late years removed from among us, and are of that number, of whom it is written, *blessed are the dead, which die in the Lord, from henceforth, yea, saith the spirit, that they may rest from their labours, and their works do follow them.*

He departed this life on the island of Tortola (where he was engaged on a religious visit) the 4*th* day of the ninth month 1741, aged upwards of sixty-six years.

A Testimony

A Testimony from the Monthly-Meeting of Philadelphia, *concerning* ESTHER CLARE.

SHE was a minister well qualified for the publication of the doctrine of the gospel, and visited friends in Great-Britain and Ireland in the service of truth. In the latter part of her life, when not prevented by bodily infirmities, we had the benefit of her labours much in this city; her testimony being frequently attended with demonstration of divine help, was well accepted and of good service. She departed this life the 3*d* of the eighth month 1742, in the sixty-eighth year of her age, in unity and good esteem among friends.

A Testimony from the Monthly-Meeting of Philadelphia, *concerning* ROBERT JORDAN.

IT appears, he was born in the county of Nancemond in Virginia, the 27*th* of the tenth month 1693, of parents in good esteem among friends, and that about the year 1718 he received a gift in the ministry, as did his brother Joseph about the same time; and to their first appearance in that weighty work the labours of Lydia Lancaster and her companion then on a religious visit from Great-Britain, were, under divine help, made instrumental.

Of his first travels in the service of truth, the following is an abstract from an account committed to writing by himself.

' I early found a concern on my mind
' to visit friends in Maryland, which I did
' on both sides of the bay (Cheasapeak) in
' fear and trembling, being young and
' weak, and the work very exercising by
' reason of an obvious declension, which
' occasioned me much exercise in speaking
' and writing against the spirit of liberty,
' superfluity, and conformity to the world,
' for a testimony against which, in many
' particulars, ancient friends suffered much;
' but now, with many is the offence of that
' cross ceased, and friend's sufferings tram-
' pled upon, to the great grief of my spirit,
' respecting tythes, apparel &c. And as the
' Lord hath been pleased to commit a part of
' the ministry to me, and of that part which is
' more necessary than desirable, in this age
' of the church, he hath been graciously
' pleased hitherto to furnish with a suitable
' ability for his honour, and my faithful
' discharge of duty; for, as before my ap-
' pearance I was long under the concern,
' being fully convinced it was required of
' me, but giving way to reasonings, the
' suggestions and buffetings of Satan, I was
' likely to lose my condition, had not the
' Lord been very gracious, who knew that
' I did not hold back obstinately, but thro'
' human weakness, and contempt of my-
' self for such a weighty service; so in a
' deep

'deep travail of soul once in a meeting, breathing for strength to bring forth, I desired, that the Lord would commit the hardest part of the work to my charge, which I think was granted, and a hard travail I had in my first appearance; but it fared otherwise with my brother, whom I prefer, he was not disobedient to the heavenly vision, submitting speedily to the call, and has been very prosperous hitherto; may the Lord preserve us steady and faithful to the end.

'After this, we travelled together in Maryland, visiting friends on each side of the bay, and at the yearly-meeting near Choptank, having meetings also in the way on our return, and were frequently employed and zealously concerned in the Lord's work; blessed be his name who hath called us out of darkness, and with the day spring from on high visited our souls, accounting us worthy of this high vocation, even to hold forth the glory of this gospel day, giving encouragement and enlargement of heart in the mysteries and doctrines of his kingdom, so that in the ability of divine faith, we frequently travelled about, both in Virginia and Carolina, while young; but as there is a diversity of gifts, so there is of operation, according to the good pleasure of our great benefactor, and the emergency of times and occasions; so let not us of the ministry, imitate one another in this respect,
'but

'but be careful, dear friends, to keep to our
'true guide, the holy spirit, for youth is
'warm, zealous, and without seasonable
'caution and watchfulness, apt to exceed
'ability and experience, and so may be over-
'strained, and sustain loss and injury.'

In the year 1722, he performed a religious visit as far as New-England, which employed him about ten months, and on his return home, he was sued in the beginning of the following year for priests wages, and for his refusal to comply with the demand, he offered to the magistrates in writing, sundry considerations, which being taken amiss, he was, after some time, indicted by the grand jury, and summoned before the governor and council; in this time of trial (he says) 'Some forsook me as being asham-
'ed of my testimony, and of my sufferings
'for it; at my first appearance the fierce-
'ness of the dragon was felt, his dark pow-
'er seeming to be great and terrible, as
'though he would have swallowed me up
'quick, and truth's adversaries seemed to
'rejoice, for I was made to stand like a fool
'for them to glory over me; however my
'mind being composed, and stayed in still-
'ness on the Lord, with earnest breathings
'for divine aid in this his cause, for which
'and myself, I found it safest to say little
'at that time, being greatly desirous that I
'might not give way one jot from my tes-
'timony, through fear even of death itself,
'for I thought I felt the bitterness of it strike
'at my natural life. 'On

'On the day when final judgment on the
' case was to be given, I was brought before
' them the third time, and they demanded
' what I had further to say before sentence
' was passed; I then desired liberty to make
' my defence, and to give my sense on the
' contents of my paper, the commissary or
' chief priest having perverted my meaning,
' which request the governor seemed dis-
' posed to allow, but it was afterwards de-
' nied, as I apprehend, through the influ-
' ence of the priest, howbeit I told them I
' remembred to have read a proviso of an
' act of parliament, that no man should be
' punished for any offence against the act,
' unless he was prosecuted within three
' months after the fact, but this, said I,
' was about seven months after; but some
' of the court resolving on severity to in-
' duce me to submit, they proceeded to give
' sentence of a years imprisonment, or bonds
' with security for good behaviour &c. when
' with a composed mind and an audible
' voice, I said, *this is an hard sentence and I
' pray God to forgive mine adversaries*, which
' affected divers of the bystanders with tears,
' and one in particular, a judge, and man
' of note, was much affected, made him-
' self acquainted, and conversed with me
' more than once, appears to be a tender
' man, and well convinced, having since
' gladly received meetings into his house,
' and as he has told me, laid down his
' commission.—

'Being

'Being committed to prison, I was first placed in the debtors apartment, but in a few days was removed into the common side, where condemned persons are kept, and for sometime had not the privilege of seeing any body, except a negro who once a day brought water to the prisoners; this place was so dark, that I could not see to read even at noon, without creeping to small holes in the door; being also very noisome, the infectious air brought on me the flux, that, had not the Lord been pleased to have sustained me by his invisible hand, I had there lost my life; the governor was made acquainted with my condition, and I believe used his endeavours for my liberty: The commissary visited me more than once under a shew of friendship, but with a view to ensnare me, and I was very weary of him. I wrote again to the governor, to acquaint him of my situation; so after a confinement of three weeks, I was discharged, without any acknowledgment or compliance, and this brought me into an acquaintance, and ready admittance to the governor, who said I was a meek man &c.—Thus I returned home with praise and thanksgiving in my heart to the Lord, who had caused his truth to triumph over the strong efforts of man and the powers of the earth.'

In the year 1725, accompanied by Thomas Pleasants, he again visited friends in Maryland, and the yearly-meeting near Choptank,

Choptank. My concern here (he says) 'Was principally to labour for the restoration of wholesome discipline, the neglect whereof I conceive has been a great cause of the disorder and undue liberty prevailing among the professors of truth there, and when the service of this meeting was over, we visited the meetings on the western shore, and returned home, having left an example of that useful and necessary practice of visiting families, joining friends therein for sometime; we are, thanks be to God, come and coming into the same in Virginia, which, with some assistance, I have pretty generally performed through our monthly-meeting, and never, I think, was more sensible of the company and ability of truth in any service, according to the dignity of it.'

A malicious person getting into his possession, the judgment obtained against him for the demand of tythes before mentioned, had seven of his cattle seized and appraised, but deferred taking them away until about two years after, when he procured a new action against him, alledging, but not proving, that Robert had converted at least a part of them to his own use, and so managed the matter in his absence, as to make the debt amount to twenty-pounds, tho' the demand was but eight-pounds, and serving the execution on his body, he was again committed to prison in the twelfth month 1727, where being confined fifteen weeks, he was at length difcharged, without any perfon paying any thing for him, which he would not fuffer.

Soon after he was brought under a trial, with others of his friends, by the operation of a militia-law, whereupon they addreffed governor Gooch on his arrival, reprefenting to him their fufferings by fpoil of goods and imprifonment, which, with the friends who attended on the occafion, he received with kindnefs.

' Having this year (he remarks) fuffered
' perfecution in body and eftate, as a pre-
' parative to a greater affliction, (all which
' doth and will work for good) my dear af-
' fectionate wife was called away.

The next year 1728, he embark'd for Great-Britain, with our friend Samuel Bownas, who had accomplifhed his journeys on this continent in the fervice of the gofpel; and after performing a religious vifit to the meetings of friends in England, Scotland, Wales and Ireland, he proceeded to Barbados, and arrived from thence in this city in 1730, then went to Virginia, and in the fame year performed a vifit as far eaftward as Rhode-Ifland, accompanied by his intimate friend Caleb Raper of Burlington.

The following year intermarrying with Mary the widow of Richard Hill, he became a member of our monthly-meeting, and after a vifit to the meetings of friends in Maryland and Virginia, he embark'd on a fecond vifit to Great-Britain, from whence he he returned in the summer of 1734, between which time and the year 1738, he performed another visit eastward, and three to the southern provinces, besides one to South-Carolina and Georgia, and from thence proceeded to Rhode-Island, and to Boston, and in 1740 he went on a second visit to Barbados, and in the succeeding year, accompanied by Caleb Raper, he accomplished his last visit eastward as far as Boston.

Hereby we may observe his unwearied application and exercise, to fulfill the ministry which he had received of the Lord. He was a member of this meeting above ten years, and tho' his time was much employed in his religious duties abroad, he did not omit the adjacent meetings, being industrious and laborious for the general welfare and prosperity of the churches; for the promotion whereof he was, through the divine anointing, eminently qualified.

His ministry being convincing and consolatory, his delivery graceful but unaffected; in prayer he was solemn and reverent; he delighted in meditation, recommending by example, religious retirement in his familiar visits among his friends; in his sentiments he was generous and charitable, yet a firm opposer of obstinate libertines in principles or practice, demonstrating his love to the cause of Religion and righteousness above all other considerations, being careful to adorn the doctrine of the gospel, by a life of piety and benevolence, and we have

have ground to hope and believe he was prepared for the sudden summons from his pilgrimage here, which was on the fifth day of the eighth month O. S. 1742, when being at the house of one of his most intimate friends on the third day of the week in the morning, waiting for the hour of meeting, he was seized with a fit of the apoplexy, which very soon deprived him of speech, and he died about midnight following, in the forty-ninth year of his age, being a minister about 24 years; his burial on the 7th of the same month was attended by a great number of his fellow-citizens, to our meeting-house in High-street, and thence to the grave-yard.

A Testimony from Abington *Monthly-Meeting in* Pennsylvania, *concerning* JOHN CADWALADER.

HE was convinced of the principle of truth when young, and underwent many deep baptizing seasons, by which, it is believed, he was in a good degree made an overcomer. He travelled much in the exercise of his gift in the ministry, having visited his brethren in truth's service, in most or all parts of this continent where friends then resided; and crossed the seas twice to Europe on the same account, and once to the island of Barbados. In which concern he was always careful to have the concurrence

concurrence of his brethren, and good accounts and credentials of his acceptable service were upon all those occasions communicated to this monthly-meeting. He was also serviceable amongst us in meetings of discipline. His last visit was to the island of Tortola, in company with our worthy friend John Estaugh. He was taken unwell on his passage thither, yet when he landed, proceeded in the service he went upon, to the satisfaction of friends there, as appears from accounts sent hither by a friend of that island. But his distemper increasing upon him, he departed this life in peace on said island, the 26*th* of the ninth month 1742, aged near sixty-six years.

A Testimony from Haddonfield *Monthly-Meeting in* New-Jersey, *concerning* JOHN ESTAUGH.

THE remembrance of our dear deceased friend John Estaugh, remains as a good favour on many of our minds. He was born in Keldevon in Essex in Great-Britain, on the 23*d* of the second month 1676. In the year 1700, he came over to America on a religious visit, which he performed to the great satisfaction of friends; after which, he settled at Haddonfield, in the county of Gloucester, and western division of New-Jersey. He has been heard to say, that when he first settled in our parts, he was
nearly

nearly united to a folid remnant of friends that then belonged to Newtown-meeting, and that he had been careful to feel the drawings of the father's love in vifiting neighbouring meetings, in many of which, he was favoured to minifter fuitably to the ftates and conditions of thofe that heard him; he being as a fcribe well inftructed, who brought forth out of the heavenly treafury, things both new and old.—Since his firft fettlement among us, he vifited friends in England, Ireland, New-England and fome of the Weft-India-Iflands, feveral times. He was an humble minded exemplary friend, folid and grave in his deportment, well becoming a minifter of Chrift, zealous for preferving good order in the church, and maintaining love and unity, that badge of true difciplefhip, remarkably careful in his converfation among men, his words being few and favoury. The laft vifit which he made was to the ifland of Tortola, where after his fervice was over, he was taken fick, and departed this life: And we doubt not but that he is in the fruition of that glory and happinefs which will never have an end.

An Abftract

An Abstract from Elizabeth Estaugh's *Testimony, concerning her beloved husband* JOHN ESTAUGH *deceased, prefixed to a treatise of his, entitled* " A call to the unfaithful professors of truth."

SINCE it pleased divine providence so highly to favour me, with being the near companion of this dear worthy, I cannot be altogether silent, but must give some small account of the early working of truth in him. He was born of religious parents, but grew uneasy with the religious professions of both father and mother who were of different persuasions, and being a seeker, fell in with the baptists, and liked them so well he was near joining them. But a neighbour who was a friend, being dead, he was invited to the burial, where that worthy minister of the gospel, Francis Stamper of London, being led to speak with life and power directly to his state, it made such deep impressions on his tender mind, that put him upon search into the principles of friends, and being fully satisfied, joined with them in the seventeenth year of his age.

About the eighteenth year of his age, he came forth in the ministry, and being faithful he grew in his gift, so that in some time he travelled to visit friends in the north of England, and Scotland, and in the year 1700 came over on a visit to friends in America. We were married on the first day of the tenth month

month 1702, and settled at Haddonfield in New-Jersey. In the fore part of his time he travelled pretty much; but in the latter part he was prevented therefrom by an infirmity of body; and his good master, who requires no impossibilities of his servants, favoured him with being easy at home; where thro' mercy, we lived very comfortably; few, if any, in a married state, ever lived in sweeter harmony than we did. He was a pattern of moderation in all things; not lifted up with any enjoyments, nor cast down at disappointments; a man endowed with many good gifts, which rendered him very agreeable to his friends, and much more to me, his wife.

After some years of indisposition, (as before is observed) it pleased the Lord to restore him to a state of health; and soon after he had a concern to visit friends at Tortola. This brought on him a deep exercise, but when he was confirmed it was really required of him, he gave up to it; and was then weaned from home, and the company there which used to be so pleasant to him. He first wrote to friends on that island; but finding that would not excuse him, he durst no longer delay; so, on the 13*th* of the eighth month 1742, we parted in the aboundings of love and affection. And now, the most acceptable account I can give of his service in Tortola, is extracted from two letters which I received from a friend of that place, directed to me, and to the following effect, viz.
' On

'On the eighth of the ninth month 1742, he arrived at the house of John Pickering with his companion John Cadwalader, where they were received with much love and great joy, being made to rejoice together in the tender mercies and love of God, which was greatly manifested that day, to the honour and praise of his great name, and also to the comforting of his poor people. The testimonies of these servants of the Lord were with life and power, and were as clouds fill'd with rain upon a thirsty land.—

'But to be more particular concerning thy dear husband, whose memory is dear and precious to me, and many more whose hearts were open to receive the glad-tidings which he brought. His godly life and conversation spoke him to be a true follower of the the Lamb, and minister of Jesus Christ, whom he freely preached, and by the effectual power of whose divine love, was he called forth to our assistance, for which we bless, praise and magnify the God of all our mercies: And as a faithful messenger, with much love, in a tender frame of spirit, would he invite all to the fountain which had healed him. O! the deep humility that appeared in him in the time of his public testimony; and when in private conversation with his near and dear friends, as he often said we were to him, how cheerful and pleasant would he be, in that blessed freedom

'dom wherein Chrift had made him free.
'Innocent, harmlefs, of a cheerful coun-
'tenance, yet not without a chriftian gra-
'vity well becoming the doctrine he preach-
'ed. He was valiant for the truth to the
'laft, and tho' he is gone to his grave, his
'memory is fweet and precious.

'He had his health very well until the
'death of his dear companion; but going
'to his burial, we were caught in a fhower
'of rain, which we and he believed was
'the occafion of his illnefs. However, he
'was mightily favoured with the divine
'prefence, which enabled him to anfwer
'the fervice of that day; and the next, be-
'ing the firft day of the week, we had a
'bleffed meeting, the Lord's prefence ac-
'companying us; and tho' thy dear huf-
'band was fo near his end, his candle fhin'd
'as bright as ever, and many that beheld
'it were made to glorify God on his behalf.
'This was the laft opportunity on this ifland,
'fave his farewell upon his dying bed,
'where he both preached and prayed, a lit-
'tle before his departure.

'On the next day, being the fecond day
'of the week, he went to a little ifland call-
'ed Jos Vandicks, accompanied with feve-
'ral friends; but on the 3d day in the
'morning he complained very much, yet
'was enabled to go to meeting, where a
'pretty many people were affembled, and
'a bleffed opportunity we had together, to
'the tendring and melting our hearts into
'a heavenly frame. 'But

'But he who never spared his labour
' whilst amongst us, extending his voice as
' a trumpet of the Lord's own sounding,
' was so inwardly spent he was ready to
' faint. However, he went on board the
' sloop that afternoon, and next morning
' came ashore at our house; where he had
' not been long before a shivering fit seized
' him, and a fever soon followed, which
' kept its constant course every day. This
' being the 1*st* day of the tenth month, he
' took great notice that it ended forty years
' since his marriage with thee; that during
' that time you had lived in much love, and
' parted in the same; and that thou wast
' his greatest concern of all outward enjoy-
' ments. And tho' the last two days he was
' in much pain, yet he was preserved under
' it in much patience and resignation, and
' had his perfect senses to the last, exhort-
' ing friends to faithfulness, &c. And on
' the 6*th* day of the tenth month, about
' six-o'clock at night, he went away like a
' lamb, with praises and thanksgivings in
' his lips but about two minutes before.'
Thus far from the said letters.

And thus finished this dear worthy in the sixty-seventh year of his age; highly favoured by his great and good master in the very extreme moments; the consideration whereof, and the account given of his service, afford me, at times, some relief. And I have a secret satisfaction in that I was enabled to give him up (tho' so dear to me) unto the service into which he was called. This is a hint for those who may be under the like exercise and trial, that they may not hold back, but submit, and freely give up their all, leaving the consequence to the wise disposing hand, who knows for what cause it is, he is pleased so nearly to try his people.

A Testimony from the Monthly-Meeting of Philadelphia, *concerning* SAMUEL PRESTON.

HE was born in Maryland, but removing to settle in and near this city, he became and continued a member of this meeting; being an elder circumspect in his conduct, and carefully concern'd for the good of the church, active and serviceable in the maintenance of our christian discipline; and by his attention to the dictates of divine grace, he became well qualified for this service. He filled some stations in the government, wherein he acquitted himself with justice and uprightness; and being endued with a clear judgment and good understanding, his integrity to what he believed to be his duty, became conspicuous and instructive; being a lover of truth, and extensive in his charity to mankind. In his last illness he discovered great resignation of mind, and much love and fellowship with his brethren, with whom he lived and died in good unity.

He departed this life on the 10th of the seventh month 1743, in the seventy-ninth year of his age.

His first wife Rachel, was one of the daughters of our worthy friend Thomas Lloyd, and was said to have been a very serviceable, judicious, and valuable woman.

His second wife, was Margaret the widow of Josiah Langdale (a worthy minister who lived in Yorkshire in Great-Britain, and had formerly visited friends in America, but concluding afterwards to remove with his family to Pennsylvania, he died on his passage in the year 1723.)—Concerning the said Margaret, the aforesaid monthly-meeting of Philadelphia thus testify.

" She was endued with an excellent gift in the ministry, and travelled much in the service of truth through this and the neighbouring provinces; her testimony being lively, sound and edifying, was well received among friends; being likewise well qualified for the maintenance of our discipline, she became an useful instrument for the promotion and support of our christian testimony. She died the 23d of the sixth month 1742, in the fifty-eighth year of her age."

According to John Rutty's account, she went from Yorkshire on a religious visit to Ireland in 1715.

A Testimony

A Testimony from friends in Virginia, concerning Thomas Pleasants.

HE was the eldest son of John and Dorothy Pleasants, and born the 3d of the ninth month 1695; being a youth of good natural parts, and well instructed in school-learning. His father dying whilst he was young, he was deprived of the additional advantage of the admonitions and restraints of a worthy parent, so beneficial to the forming the minds of youth: Nevertheless he had an eye to the recompence of reward, and about the twenty-ninth year of his age was called to the work of the ministry, in which he laboured both amongst friends and other people much to satisfaction, having meetings where none had been held before. Once, in company with his brother Robert Jordan, he visited friends on the western shore of Maryland, and also attended the yearly-meeting at Choptank, on the eastern shore. His services seemed much confined to his own country, where, tho' the number of friends was small, he was not discouraged thereat, but endeavoured to discharge his duty amongst them, not only at the adjacent meetings but those more at a distance, and was made instrumental in convincing several in the upper parts of the colony, as well as in settling two or three meetings. A few years before his decease, he wrote an epistle, directed to friends in every station, but more particularly to the ministers, thereby further demonstrating that his diligence and labours proceeded from an earnest concern for the promotion of truth and a right gospel ministry. He was indeed a man much devoted to the service of truth, and a considerable sufferer for bearing his testimony against priests-wages, having once been a prisoner on that account. He married Mary the daughter of Robert Jordan of Nancemond county, and left a numerous offspring, some of them young, for whose eternal welfare he was particularly solicitous; being once on a visit to friends at some distance from home, he was taken very ill, and seemed desirous that he might finish his course among his dear children, in order that he might have an opportunity at that awful period, of enforcing his experienced advices to them, and promoting the cause of God to which he was much devoted to the last. Accordingly he departed this life at his own house the 24*th* of the eleventh month 1744, and on the 28*th* of the same month was interr'd in the family burying-ground at Curles, attended by a numerous company of friends and neighbours.

A Testimony

A Testimony from Gwynedd *Monthly-Meeting in* Pennsylvania, *concerning* CADWALLADER EVANS.

HE was a native of the principality of Wales, and arrived in Pennsylvania in the year 1698. And altho' he was not then in profession with friends, yet he soon after entered into close fellowship with them, and continued stedfast to his end. He was a diligent and seasonable attender of our religious meetings: On first days particularly, he was ready an hour before the time appointed, and then read several chapters in the bible or some religious book: As the time approached, he would frequently observe the time of day, and by means of such watchful care, he was seated in meetings one of the first, and scarcely ever after the time appointed. The gravity and composure of his countenance as he sat in silence, was no less remarkable than his punctual attendance, and bespoke such inward recollection and divine engagement of mind, as often attracted the eyes and affected the hearts of others.

He received a gift in the ministry, in the exercise whereof, he was generally led to speak of his own experience in religion and the christian warfare; and his testimony, tho' short, was instructive, lively, and manifestly attended with divine sweetness: Notwithstanding it was always acceptable, he he was very cautious of appearing, left any, as he often said, should be drawn from a right concern of mind, to place their dependance on words.

He was zealously concerned for the honour and promotion of truth, and support of our christian discipline; and being endued with discerning, and clear judgment tempered with charity, he was very useful in many services of the church, especially that weighty one of visiting friends in their families. And altho' he was naturally of a warm disposition, yet a tender regard to the service of truth, and a continual awe of the divine presence presided in his heart, insomuch that meekness and condescention were conspicuous in his conduct.

There was a freedom and affability in his behaviour and conversation, which indicated a benevolence of heart, and endeared him, not only to the *houshold of faith*, but also to the profligate and vain; rendering him serviceable in composing differences, and in comforting the sick and afflicted; and particularly in that skilful and tender office of healing discord in private families, wherein his endeavours were remarkably successful. In such services, he spent much of the latter part of his life, riding about from one house to another; and where no cause of reprehension appeared, he intersperfed his discourse on common affairs, with useful hints, solid remarks, and lessons of instruction. But where admonition or comfort were necessary,

cessary, the propriety of his advice and the uprightness of his life, added weight to his labours, and seldom failed of good effects.

In private life, few had a better claim to the virtues of temperance, justice, industry and frugality, and as he well knew how advantageous it was, " To train up a child in the way he should walk," he took frequent opportunities to drop his experienced advice among those under his care. It was his practice, in winter evenings especially, to read the holy scriptures in his family, and was particularly careful that neither child nor servant should be from home at unseasonable hours; being highly sensible how slippery the paths of youth are, and how numerous the snares which attend them.

He was greatly favoured in the use of his natural abilities, and enjoyed an uncommon share of health until his last illness, which was short; during that time, very many came to see him, who shewed great marks of esteem and affection; and even libertines whom he had often rebuked and treated with, were deeply affected with sorrow: Indeed it was rare to see so many tears shed at a sick bed, more especially of one of his years, which gave a proof that he had not outlived his services. His soul overflowed with love to God and man, and being favoured in his last moments, with a blessed hope and confidence, he was going to that place which God had prepared for those that love

love him; he had a happy exit from time to eternity, the 30*th* of the third month 1745, aged eighty-one.

A Testimony from Kennet *Monthly-Meeting in* Pennsylvania, *concerning* WILLIAM LEVIS.

WILLIAM LEVIS, of Kennet in Chester county Pennsylvania, son of Samuel Levis an early settler in Springfield in said county, was born in Springfield aforesaid, about the year 1688, and removed to Kennet about 1718. By giving heed to the measure of grace bestowed upon him, he became a serviceable friend in the society in divers respects; was a good neighbour, kind and open hearted to his friends, and has left a good report.

His last sickness was the small pox, which was heavy upon him, but he bore it with much patience and resignation of mind to the last; saying, that when the distemper came into the house, it was no surprize to him, for he was freely resigned, and thankful he was so, for he could not of himself. The same evening he was taken sick, he signed his will, and remark'd how good it was to be contented to bear affliction. One night, as those that watched with him were preparing something for him to take, he said, ' You shall see your endeavours for me will avail

avail nothing.' He continued in a state of resignation and appeared cheerful in the time of his illness. When nearer his end, he was concern'd that others might do their duty faithfully according to the best of their understanding, saying, ' I have often
' thought at other times as at this, of the
' shortness of our lives and time here, and
' the uncertainty thereof, which ought to
' engage us to circumspection and faith-
' fulness to the Lord, and I charge you here
' that are elders, to discharge your trust
' faithfully in the sight of the Lord, having
' your eye single to him, and let nothing of
' self rule, and then his work will be car-
' ried on in love and patience. I could be
' glad to have an opportunity once more
' with my friends, but if I should not, I
' would have those present, to acquaint
' them with what I have to say, and press
' it home to the elders, that they may faith-
' fully discharge their duty, and acquit
' themselves of that charge wherewith they
' are entrusted; and also that parents of
' children and heads of families, may faith-
' fully discharge that great duty which is
' laid upon them, not only in being good
' examples to their children and families,
' but also to be concerned that they follow
' their footsteps, adding, it was a noble
' testimony that God gave of Abraham, *I*
' *know him, that he will command his chil-*
' *dren and his houshold after him.* And if
' parents were concerned to teach their chil-
' dren

'dren and bring them up in the way of
'their duty to God, and lefs concern'd to
'deck and fet them off, and provide things
'to make them look great in the world, it
'would be of far more benefit to them.
'And my defire is, that elders may walk
'faithfully as good ftewards, not only in
'their own families, but to the flock which
'they have the overfight of; that fo they
'may leave a good favour to the rifing and
'fucceeding generation. I am fenfible that
'all thofe who are rightly concerned for the
'difcipline and promotion of truth, will
'meet with trials from that libertine fpirit
'which would lay all wafte; thefe will fay,
'that religion confifts not in fuch fmall
'things; but I have obferved, that one
'fmall thing makes way for another, and
'greater things will take place; and if there
'is not a careful watching againft thefe
'fmall things, the eye that fhould be kept
'open to fee the evil of them, will become
'darkened. But keep ye your places, and
'labour in faithfulnefs with fuch, if poffi-
'ble to gain them; but if after friends la-
'bour, they will not be gathered, friends
'will be clear and have peace in themfelves;
'but a blaft will come on fuch troublefome
'fpirits. And as friends faithfully main-
'tain this their difcipline, the Lord will
'preferve them, but if they neglect it they
'will furely fuffer lofs.' To fome prefent
who had been engaged in the fervice of vifiting families, he faid 'It was a good work
'and

'and desired it might not be forgotten.' At another time, being in a weighty frame of mind, he said, 'There is an enemy bu-'sy to accuse the innocent, and prompts 'on the wicked in their wickedness.' Seeing his affectionate wife and sister with some neighbours weeping, he said, 'Don't weep 'for me, but be you faithful, and we shall 'meet again, for it is the hardest of all to 'see you weep.'

The morning before he died, he desired to be helped to the chamber where his eldest son lay ill of the same disorder, and sitting down by him, he charged his children to be dutiful to their mother, and have a care of doing any thing that would be a trouble to her, but mind to take her advice, and desired a blessing might attend them; adding, 'My race is almost run, and I shall 'lay down my head in peace with the Lord; 'and if you are faithful (meaning his wife 'and children) and live in the fear of God, 'he will bless you.' After some time of silence, he said, 'Farewell my son, the Lord 'bless thee my child, and thine after thee.' Being then helped down stairs, he sat in his chair, and after a time of silence, clasped his hands together, saying with a composed countenance, 'I bless thee O Lord.' Afterwards laying still in a quiet composed frame of mind, he grew weaker and weaker, and about the ninth hour in the evening, departed without sigh or groan, like
one

one going to sleep, and we believe in peace with God and unity with faithful friends.

He died the 17*th* of the second month 1747, in the fifty-ninth year of his age, and was interr'd in Kennet burying-ground, the 19*th* of the same month.

A Testimony from Gwynedd *Monthly-Meeing in* Pennsylvania, *concerning* EVAN EVANS.

HE was born in Merionethshire, in the principality of Wales, in the year 1684, and came to Pennsylvania with his parents in 1698; under whom he received a sober religious education; but, being early in life convinced, that a form of godliness, without the real enjoyment of the quickening principle of grace and truth, would not afford solid and lasting peace to his soul, he therefore sought earnestly after it, and resigned his heart to the baptizing power of God, which fitted him for eminent services in the church.

In his constant attendance at our religious meetings, he was a remarkable example of unaffected piety; for whilst he sat in silence, the earnestness wherewith his soul " wrestled for a blessing," was obvious in the steady engaged appearance of his countenance. He was favoured with an excellent gift in the ministry, which he exercised in solemn dread and reverence; and as he always

ways retained an awful sense of appearing in public testimony, he was particularly cautious and watchful, not to presume to speak without assurance of a necessity being laid upon him, and equally careful to attend to the continuance of it: And therefore his " Preaching was not with enticing words of man's wisdom, but in the demonstration of the spirit and of power." His service was rendered more effectual, by the distinguishing marks which he bore, of " An Israelite indeed, in whom was no guile," a plainness and simplicity of manner in word and deed, with a zeal seasoned with divine love; and as he had large experience in the work of regeneration and the mysteries of the heavenly kingdom, as well as the snares of the world, he was thereby well qualified to administer to the states of the people.

He travelled through many of these colonies in the service of the ministry, in company with his relation and dear friend John Evans. Their friendship was pure, fervent, and lasting as their lives, and their separation a wound to the latter, the remembrance of which he never wholly survived. He also frequently visited the several counties in this province, and more particularly many of the adjacent meetings in their infancy; wherein his unwearied labours of love, tended much to their comfort, growth, and establishment in the truth.

He

He was religiously concerned for the support of our christian discipline; and as he was always diffident of himself, he laboured faithfully for the discovery of truth and a disposition of mind to embrace it; whereby he was often enabled to lay " Judgment to the line, and righteousness to the plummet," whether in reproof to the obdurate, or instruction and comfort to the penitent. In visiting friends families his service was great; for being endued with a spirit of discerning and the authority of truth, his advice was adapted with great propriety and advantage, to the particular states and conditions of persons and families. His conduct and conversation in common life, adorned the doctrine he preached, being a good example of plainness, moderation, and uprightness of heart.

He was abroad in the service of truth when attacked with his last illness; and as the disorder was slow and tedious, he attended several meetings in the forepart thereof; in some of which, his lively powerful testimonies clearly manifested, that the God of his youth who had raised him up an instrument in his hand, and on whom he had relied all his life, continued to be his shield and support in the evening of his days and period of life; which was on the 24*th* of the fifth month 1747. He was buried at Gwynedd.

A Testimony

A Testimony from Buckingham *Monthly-Meeting in* Pennsylvania, *concerning* JACOB HOLCOMBE.

HE was born at or near Tiverton in Old England, being a descendant of friends: His father died while he was young, and his mother brought him up to useful learning, being naturally of a quick and cheerful disposition, and his capacity large and extensive. The prime and strength of his days, was, much of it, spent in folly and vanity, until it pleased the Lord effectually to touch his heart, and favour him with a close visitation of his blessed truth, which wrought a willingness in him to take up the cross, and submit to the Lord's righteous judgments, whereby he came to witness a being redeemed from his former conversation, and was often zealously concerned to tell others, what the Lord had done for his soul. He was frequent and diligent in the exercise of his gift in the ministry, which was acceptable; often signifying he was as one born out of due time: He was zealous in maintaining the discipline of the church, wherein he was clear and his labour very helpful and serviceable; very diligent in attending meetings for worship and discipline, wherein he was exemplary by his steady waiting and lively labour that life might be witnessed.

In his last illness, which was short, he appeared cheerful, patient and resigned; saying, 'There was no cloud in his way, that 'he was thankful he had known his re- 'deemer to live, and redeem him from all 'iniquity, and that he was well assured he 'should see a happy eternity.'

He died the 30*th* of the sixth month 1748, and was buried at Buckingham. A minister upwards of 18 years.

A Testimony from Gwynedd *Monthly-Meeting in* Pennsylvania, *concerning* ALICE GRIFFITH.

ALICE GRIFFITH, late wife of Hugh Griffith, of North Wales in the county of Philadelphia in Pennsylvania, was one that feared the Lord from her youth, remarkable for her modesty and plainness. When she was married and settled, she demonstrated a religious concern for the advancement of truth and welfare of the professors thereof; and being a woman of great integrity and uprightness of heart, became very serviceable in divers respects; zealous for maintaining good order and christian discipline in the church.

She was well qualified for that weighty service of visiting families, having, at such opportunities, to communicate of her own experience, and tell what God had done for her soul; and under a good degree of divine influence, would often be drawn forth in opening divine mysteries, as if she had been in a large assembly, as many witnesses can testify, that have been sensibly reached, yea baptized by her religious visits; at which she was mostly full of good matter, well adapted and suitable to the different circumstances of individuals and families.

She was often concern'd to stir up her friends, to a close attendance of meetings, both on first and other days, as also to observe the hour appointed, being herself a good example therein, until, by old age and infirmity of body she was disabled, which was about three years before her removal. And notwithstanding the circumspect life and watchful state she was observed to be in, yet in the time of her weakness, she was visited with great discouragements and dejections, as may appear by her following expressions.

At a certain time she was heard to say, ' Lord how long wilt thou withdraw thyself ' from me, and not shew for what cause ' I am thus afflicted; I have been ac- ' quainted with thy righteous judgments, ' which were ever mixed with mercy; but ' now, my trouble is more than I am well ' able to bear, being almost ready to sink.' Again was heard to say, ' Lord, where- ' in have I offended thee; what part of my ' duty have I neglected, that thou shouldst ' thus hide thy face from me? Time was,
' when

'when my hope in full affurance was to
' reft in thee, but now I fear I fhall become
' a caft-away.' At another time fhe faid,
' What have I done that I fhould be thus
' afflicted, Lord fhall there be any end of
' my forrow? Many fweet times and op-
' portunities I have had when alone, but
' now am left as in the dark, fearing to make
' one ftep forward left I ftumble, he that
' once was my guide has now left me.'
Again faid, ' I ftill defire to be willing to
' fuffer whilft in this body, any thing thou
' mayeft pleafe to bring upon me, be the
' exercife of what kind foever, if thou wilt
' favour me with thy living prefence; then
' Lord, fhall not any thing be too near or
' dear to part with, or to fuffer for thy name-
' fake. Yea Lord, if thou fhould fee meet
' to deprive me of my fight or hearing,
' health or fpeech, let me never murmur,
' but Oh! give patience to bear this inex-
' preffible exercife to the end.' One morning, after calling her two daughters, fhe faid,
' Put by your work my children, for I
' have to tell you of a glorious vifitation the
' Lord was pleafed to favour me with. As
' I was making my fupplication to him for
' deliverance and redemption from my fore
' exercife, and to obtain fome refrefhment
' to my poor diftreffed foul, the Lord was
' gracioufly pleafed to anfwer my requeft in
' a fatisfactory manner: He opened the eye
' of my mind, to fee him coming in his
' glory to relieve me from my long diftrefs.

' May

'May my whole truft and confidence ever
' abide in him, who has fo filled my heart
' with joy, that pain and grief vanifhed
' away. This glorious feafon furpaffed all
' that ever I had known before: At which
' time, the Lord gave me a fure promife,
' that, altho' my afflictions were many,
' and more I had yet to go through, yet I
' fhould in the end, be rewarded with a
' crown of righteoufnefs in the kingdom of
' reft and peace;' with more to the fame
effect.

It was obferv'd, that a certain change appeared in her countenance from that time forward; fhe being cheerful and pleafant and never fad as before.

Her deceafe was on the firft day of the fecond month 1749, and was buried on the 3d of the fame.

A Teftimony from friends in Virginia, *concerning* Sarah Pleasants.

SARAH PLEASANTS, fourth daughter of Thomas and Mary Pleafants, was taken ill the 26th of the feventh month, and departed this life the 7th of the eighth month 1749, in the feventeenth year of her age. In the time of her illnefs, fhe called to feveral perfons then prefent, to view her blooming youth, how changed, and likely in a fhort time to bid adieu to the world and

and all its enjoyments; praying that the moment she was prepared she might go; but in a particular manner, she desired the physician who attended her, to observe the frailty of poor mortals, as well as the uncertainty of time in this life, saying, ' Look
' on me doctor, I am like a bud cropt from
' the vine before it is fully blown, yet young
' as I am, I have something to repent of,
' which in health and strength we are apt
' to overlook, and flatter ourselves is no
' crime, which is, I have been too much giv-
' en to laughter and jesting with those of my
' companions who fondly embraced and re-
' turned the same,' naming one in particular, whom she expressed a great desire to see before she died, that she might warn her of the weight she now felt, not only in these two things, but in a third, which was, taking too much delight in dress. Then directing her discourse to the doctor, she said,
' Nothing else have I to charge myself with,
' yet, dear doctor, I find it enough, there-
' fore let me prevail with thee to take warn-
' ing by me; I am sensible that some things
' thou art in the practice of, are full as dan-
' gerous, if not more so, than those which
' now lay so heavy on me; that of drink-
' ing to excess to oblige company, as thy
' excuse and many others is, yet thou wilt
' find it of greater weight when thou comes
' to lay in the condition I now am in, than
' now thou may think possible, thou wilt
' surely wish it had been left undone, with
' all

'all other unprofitable things.' The doctor replied weeping, 'I take it very kind 'and hope I shall observe it.' Many more good expressions and advice she dropt to him and others then about her.—She one day called her brother Thomas to her bed-side, and said to him, 'Dear brother, I know 'thy situation to be very lonesome, and 'destitute of suitable company, notwith- 'standing, I pray thee, keep as much as pos- 'sible out of low company, not the poor 'do I mean, because they are poor, but 'the loose and vulgar, whether poor or rich, 'which are of a corrupting spirit, and 'will tend to the hurt of those who asso- 'ciate with them; but keep thy place and 'thou wilt be like a light set on a hill, as a 'guide to others, who will praise God on 'thy behalf.'

A Testimony from Gwynedd *Monthly-Meeting in* Pennsylvania, *concerning* WILLIAM TROTTER.

OUR friend William Trotter, late of Plymouth in the county of Philadelphia, son of William Trotter, was born in the fourth month 1695, of religious parents, and was educated amongst friends; as he grew in years, he was blessed, in that he grew in grace, and in the fear and knowledge of our blessed Lord and Saviour Jesus Christ.

About the twenty-firſt year of his age, he received a gift in the miniſtry, in which he was frequently exerciſed during the courſe of his life. His miniſtry was ſound and favoury, attended with a good degree of that life and power " By which the dead are raiſed, and without which all preaching is vain." He was not tedious or burdenſome, but often very reaching and edifying to his hearers. In his life and converſation he was grave, yet innocently cheerful, and ſtrictly juſt in his dealings, alſo a lover and promoter of peace, unity, and brotherly love amongſt friends, of which himſelf was a good pattern. He was generally beloved during his life, and at his death left a good favour. His removal from time to a happy eternity, though certainly his greateſt gain, was a conſiderable loſs to the meeting where he belonged. He departed this life on the 19*th* of the tenth month 1749, aged about fifty-three years and ſix months, and was interr'd on the 21ſt of the ſame month, in friends burying-ground at Plymouth; and we believe is gone from his laborious ſervice here, to receive a heavenly reward of peace, " Where the wicked ceaſe from troubling, and the weary be at reſt."

A Teſtimony

A Testimony from Salem Monthly-Meeting in New-Jersey, concerning ELIZABETH WYATT.

ELIZABETH WYATT (wife of Bartholomew Wyatt) a minister, removed by marriage, within the limits of our monthly-meeting, in the year 1730, as appears by her certificate from Haddonfield monthly-meeting. Her testimony was large and edifying, found in word and doctrine, to the comfort of the humble minded amongst us; yet she was a sharp threshing instrument in the hand of the Lord, against the backsliders and unfaithful professors of truth.

Her labours were not confined to this meeting, but it pleased the great Lord of the harvest, to send her forth in his service into other provinces on this continent, as Pennsylvania, Maryland, Virginia, North-Carolina, New-England, Rhode-Island, Long-Island, &c. in all which she had good service for truth, as appears by certificates produced to this meeting. She was exemplary in life and conversation, adorning the doctrine she had to deliver; and was in good esteem amongst her friends and neighbours. It pleased God to take her off the stage of this world, on the 20*th* of the eleventh month 1749-50, aged forty-three years. It may be observed, that about three years of her time, her residence with her husband

band and family was at Philadelphia, to the satisfaction of friends there, as appears by certificate from thence.

Her name before marriage was Tomlinson, she first appeared in public testimony at Evesham-meeting in New-Jersey, while she lived at the house of our friends William and Elizabeth Evans, which was about four years before her marriage. Besides what is truly said of her above, it may be justly added, that her capacity, qualifications and improvements were superior to most, and that she possessed a cheerfulness of temper, joined with great discretion, which rendered her company very desirable and profitable.

A Testimony from Gwynedd *Monthly-Meeting in* Pennsylvania, *concerning* Ann Roberts.

SHE was convinced of the truth in her native country, Wales, when young, which incurred her father's heavy displeasure, but in time he became reconciled to her. Some years after her convincement, she came over into this country, where she received a gift in the ministry, and by a diligent improvement thereof, together with the influence of a pious life, she was made
useful

useful in her generation and a blessing to many. Her love and compassion for the widow, the fatherless, and others in affliction, appeared by her often visiting them: She was one of the wise in heart, who was favoured to foresee the enemy in his approaches, and would rouse and excite her fellow-soldiers to use their utmost endeavours to repel his attempts, which was often done with desirable success. She was also zealously concern'd for maintaining christian discipline in the church.

She was rightly qualified for the weighty service of visiting friends families, and at those opportunities was frequently favoured with something suitable to every state and condition, which was attended with beneficial effects, especially on the youth. But such indeed was the divine favour which usually accompanied her discourse and conversation, one could rarely be an hour with her without sensible edification.

Her first coming to reside among us was seasonable, for we having but few ministers, the field before her was extensive, in which she laboured fervently, tenderly inviting those afar off to draw nigh, and querying with them, whether they knew what the Lord had for them to do. By the visitations of heaven and a blessing on her labours, many came to have their mouths opened to speak of God's goodness to their souls; whereby was verified, what she had declared at our meeting before she came to dwell among

among us, though it then seemed improbable, and some doubted the accomplishment thereof. To these babes in the ministry, she who had a large share of experience in the work, was not wanting to administer suitable precaution and advice.

She went pretty much abroad, visiting friends in this and the adjacent provinces, to wit, the Jerseys, Maryland, Virginia and Carolina, accompanied to the remotest parts by her near and dear friend Susanna Morris. In her more advanced years she visited Great-Britain, accompanied by our esteemed friend Mary Pennel, between whom a near and strict union was preserved throughout their travels; and she brought home very clear and comfortable accounts of her acceptable service in the gospel ministry, and her godly conversation in Christ.

After her return from Great-Britain, she met with great difficulties in respect to her outward circumstances, which she sustained with christian fortitude. A near friend of hers asking her how she felt under it, she replied, ' While I keep my eye steadily di-
' rected to the object worthy of our chief
' regard, it seems as if a wall was on each
' side; all is calm, and nothing hurts or
' annoys: But if I suffer my eye to wander
' to the right hand or the left, the enemy
' breaks in upon me like a torrent, which
' hurries me away, and it is with great
' difficulty I recover myself.' After this, she met with a very heavy affliction in the

loss of her husband, which she likewise bore with becoming resignation and composure of mind. In a few months afterwards, she fell into a lingering disorder; (the dropsy) and as in time of health she preferred the prosperity of truth to her chief joy, so in her illness she rejoiced much to hear of any young people appearing hopeful in the ministry. On the other hand, she would, even in time of great weakness, lament with anxiety of mind the low situation of the seed, and say, Oh! what will become of us? Will this dark cloud which hangs over our assemblies, terminate in a boisterous storm to try the foundations of the children of men?

By the long continuance of her disorder, she was reduced to great weakness sometime before her end; yet it was evident, that charity, (to wit) Love to God and his people, continued with her to the last.

She died on the 9*th* day of the fourth month 1750, in the seventy-third year of her age, having been a minister 50 years, and was buried at Gwynedd aforesaid; on which solemn occasion we had a good meeting, the extendings of divine love being witnessed.

A Testimony

A Testimony from Wilmington *Monthly-Meeting in the county of* New-Castle *on* Delaware, *concerning* LYDIA DEAN.

SHE was the daughter of Joseph Gilpin, of Birmingham in Chester county Pennsylvania; was born the 11*th* of the eleventh month 1698, and married to William Dean of the aforesaid place in 1722. In the year 1728 she appeared in the ministry, much in the cross, which was manifest by her brokenness of heart and contrition of spirit under the weight thereof. And as she became willing to give up all for the cause of truth, the Lord in his own time made her a living minister of the everlasting gospel; in the exercise whereof, she was drawn to visit friends in New-England, Jersey and Maryland. Her ministry was plain and powerful, often speaking particularly to the states of meetings where her lot was cast; her conversation solid, weighty and grave, becoming the gospel of Christ; and very helpful to those who stood in need. Her place of abode was at Birmingham aforesaid, until about a year before her decease, when the family removed to Wilmington; where she had the exercise of parting with several of her children, who were taken away by death; which she bore with patience and great resignation to the will of divine providence, expressing a sense she had of her own dissolution being nigh: And being

ing engaged with friends who were visiting families belonging to this monthly-meeting, she was taken sick, and her illness increasing, she said, the day before she died, 'It was the joyfullest day she ever had.'

Thus having passed the time of her sojourning here, in a good degree of godly fear, she finished her course, and is gone (we doubt not) into the mansions of undisturbed rest.

She departed this life the 2d of the tenth month 1750, and was interr'd in friends burying-ground at Wilmington, aged fifty-two, a minister 22 years.

A Testimony from Richland *Monthly-Meeting in* Pennsylvania, *concerning* THOMAS LANCASTER.

ABOUT ten years of the latter part of his time, he was a member of this meeting, he was found in the ministry, and exercised his gift therein with great fervency and zeal, his life and conversation corresponding therewith. In the second month 1750, he laid before our meeting his concern to visit friends on the islands of Barbados and Tortola, which the meeting approved of, and gave him a certificate in order thereto: Towards the latter end of the same year he perform'd said visit, and had good service there, as appeared by certificates

cates from friends on each of the said islands; on his return homewards, it pleased divine providence to visit him with sickness, of which he died at sea; his removal being deeply felt and lamented by his family and friends at home.

A Testimony from friends in Virginia, concerning WILLIAM LADD.

WILLIAM LADD, son of John and Mary Ladd, both from Old-England, was born near Curles in Virginia, in the sixth month 1679, and about the time of his marriage he removed to Wainoak, became a member of that meeting, and resided there the remainder of his days. He had an acceptable gift in the ministry, and was a great sufferer for bearing a testimony against the hireling ministers. In one instance, a very exorbitant seizure was made upon his effects, yet he lived to see the officer who made it reduced to such low circumstances, that he charitably contributed to supply his necessities.—He continued a faithful sufferer to the end of his days, encouraging his children to faithfulness, saying, ' The truth is more to me, than my ' all in this world.'—The night of his decease, one of the family saying, ' This was ' to be a night of great sorrow to them,' he replied, ' It was a night of great joy to him,'
which

which was one of the laft of his expreffions.—He died the 27*th* of the ninth month 1751, and was buried in the family burying-ground near his own houfe, aged feventy-two, and a minifter about 25 years.

A Teftimony from the Monthly-Meeting of Philadelphia, *concerning* Israel Pemberton.

HE was born in the county of Bucks in Pennfylvania, in the year 1684, being defcended of pious parents, well efteemed among friends in the firft fettlement of this province. He ferved his apprenticefhip and fettled in this city. Having chofen the fear of the Lord in his youth, and being preferved therein, he eftablifhed and fupported an unblemifhed character, by his juftice, integrity, and uprightnefs in his dealings amongft men, and his mild, fteady and prudent conduct through life. He was a member of this meeting near fifty years, and being well grounded in the principles of truth, of found judgment and underftanding, he approved himfelf a faithful elder; adorning our holy profeffion by a life of meeknefs, humility, circumfpection, and a difinterefted regard to the honour of truth; of great ufe in the exercife of our difcipline, being a lover of peace and unity in the church, careful to promote and maintain

tain it; conftant in the attendance of meetings, and his deportment therein, grave, folid and reverent, and a true fympathizer with thofe who were honeftly concerned in the miniftry; a confpicuous example of moderation and plainnefs; extenfive in his charity and of great benevolence. In converfation cheerful, attended with a peculiar fweetnefs of difpofition, which rendered his company both agreeable and inftructive.

A few days before his deceafe, being in a free converfe with two of his friends whom he much loved and refpected, he took occafion to recount many occurrences of his life, and with a great fenfe of gratitude, to exprefs the lively remembrance he retained of the merciful extendings of divine love towards him in his youth, by the continuance whereof he had been enabled to perfevere in a confcientious difcharge of his religious duties to the beft of his knowledge; and that being ftill favoured with a degree of the fame love, it was his greateft comfort in his declining years.

His death was fudden, tho' not altogether unexpected, having been at intervals, frequently affected with a dizzinefs in his head; and feveral times fo as to deprive him of his fpeech.

He was very lively and pleafant the morning before his departure, and in the afternoon went to the burial of an acquaintance, and accompanied the corps to the graveyard, where he was feized with a fit, fuppofed posed to be of the apoplectick kind, and expired in about an hour; being the 19th of the first month 1754, and was buried on the 22d of the same month, in the sixty-ninth year of his age.

A Testimony from Haddonfield *Monthly-Meeting in* New-Jersey, *concerning* HANNAH COOPER.

OUR well esteemed friend Hannah Cooper, was born in Wensleydale in Yorkshire Great-Britain, and arrived at Philadelphia in the year 1732, on a religious visit to friends in America, and performing that service, was afterwards married to our friend Joseph Cooper, a member of this monthly-meeting, where she resided the most of the remaining part of her life, except when she was called abroad in truth's service, in which she travelled much in the fore part of her time; but as she grew in years, she was under great indisposition of body, and so continued the most of her time, which unfitted her for travelling.

She was indeed a living minister, an humble tender hearted friend, a true sympathizer with those in affliction, and as a nursing mother to those that were young in the ministry, her service was truly very acceptable, and her memory still remains as a sweet favour.

Near

Near the conclusion of her time, she desired those then present, 'Not to mourn for her, for that she had nothing to do but to die.' She departed this life, the 11th of the second month 1754, and we hope enjoys that unmixed felicity which will never have an end.

Her name before marriage was Dent. She received a gift in the ministry when young, and travelled in that service in several parts of England before she came to America. In 1739, having our friend Mary Foulke for a companion, she took shipping for Barbados, and after visiting friends and others on that island, went from thence to Rhode-Island, from whence she returned home.—The following testimony concerning her husband, whom she survived several years, is from the same monthly-meeting, of which he was divers years an elder, viz.

Our well esteemed friend Joseph Cooper deceased, was born in Newtown in the county of Gloucester New-Jersey. He was an exemplary friend, and serviceable amongst us in many respects; was generally well respected, careful to rule well his own house. He departed this life, about the 1st of the eighth month 1749, having express'd a little before, 'That he had done justly, loved mercy, and hoped he had been careful to walk humbly.'

A Testimony

A Testimony from the Monthly-Meeting of Philadelphia, *concerning* Michael Lightfoot.

HE came over from Ireland with his family and settled in this province, in the beginning of the year 1712, and was called to the ministry about the year 1725, and the forty-second year of his age. Being faithful in the exercise of his gift, he became zealously concern'd for the honour of truth and promotion thereof; and in this service performed a religious visit to friends in Great-Britain and Ireland; from whence we received very satisfactory and comfortable accounts of his labours. He likewise visited friends in New-England; and in the year 1753, he travelled on the same account in the southern provinces.

He was a member of this meeting the last eleven years of his life; being of a grave and solid deportment, and an example of plainness and temperance, was much esteemed amongst us. His ministry was deep and penetrating, attended with the demonstration of the spirit and power; under the influence whereof he was frequently led to unfold the mysteries of the kingdom, and eminently qualified to set forth the excellencies of the gospel dispensation, with the benefit and advantage of inward and spiritual worship; recommending diligent attendance on the spirit of truth, for instruction and

and assistance therein. His delivery was clear, distinct and intelligible, and in supplication humble and reverent. He was likewise well gifted in discipline, and often concerned to speak in those meetings to our edification and comfort.

He departed this life, on the 3*d* day of the twelfth month 1754, after a short sickness, in the seventy-first year of his age, and 29*th* of his ministry.

A Testimony from Hopewell *Monthly-Meeting in* Virginia, *concerning* EVAN THOMAS.

HE was born in Wales, and educated in profession with the church of England; but in his tender years, joined in society with friends; and proving faithful to the gift and measure of grace bestowed upon him, by the great giver of every good and perfect gift, he came to be early engaged in the work of the ministry, and was a serviceable instrument; being also a preacher in life and conversation, remarkably meek, humble and grave in his deportment. He was zealous for the honour of God and promotion of his blessed truth, and serviceable among friends, being one of the first settlers in these parts, and a constant attender of our meetings whilst in health. He died in a very serene frame of spirit, on the 4*th* day of the second month 1755, aged about seventy years.

A Testimony from Duck-Creek *Monthly-meeting in* Kent *county on* Delaware, *concerning* WILLIAM HAMMANS.

HE was born in Old-England, in the year 1683, and educated in the profession of the church of England; but as he grew up, he became uneasy with the ways and ceremonies thereof; and being a diligent seeker after the true way of worship, in a short time joined with friends; soon after which, he left his native country, being but a young man altho' married, and coming over to Pennsylvania, settled in Chester county, and after some time, received a gift in the ministry; by keeping low and humble, and attending thereto, he became an able minister, having a particular gift in quoting the scriptures and explaining them clearly to the understandings of the people. About the year 1738, he removed within the limits of our monthly-meeting, where his service was very considerable, being well qualified for the discipline of the church, and very exemplary in attending meetings both for worship and discipline, and an humble waiter therein. Divers within the bounds of our monthly-meeting, were convinced by his ministry, and others who had been convinced before, were thereby further confirmed in the truth of the gospel.

Living in a public place, he had much of friends company, whom he was very hearty in entertaining, and so continued to the end of his time; and departed this life, the 8*th* day of the fourth month 1755, in the seventy-second year of his age. On the 11*th* of the said month, was interr'd in friends burying-ground at Duck-Creek.

A Testimony from Richland *Monthly-Meeting in* Pennsylvania, *concerning* SUSANNA MORRIS.

AS the reviving and transmitting to posterity, the memory of the righteous and faithful servants of God, especially those worthy elders who are to be highly esteemed and loved for their work's sake, may be conducive to the promotion of truth, the comfort and edification of the living, and to encourage the imitation of their pious examples.

We are concerned to give forth this testimony concerning our ancient and worthy deceased friend Susanna Morris, late wife of Morris Morris, who was a member of our monthly-meeting near fifteen years of the latter part of her time: Her memory still lives, and yields a precious favour to those who are measurably sharers of that divine love and life with which she in an eminent degree was endowed, and was frequently made an instrument to communicate it to others, by a living and powerful ministry, in which she faithfully laboured with unwearied diligence both at home and abroad, for the space of forty years and upwards, having travelled much in the service of the gospel both in America and Europe, made three voyages over the seas to visit the meetings of friends in Great-Britain, and twice through Ireland and Holland; in which voyages and travels, the gracious arm of divine providence was evidently manifested, in preserving and supporting her through divers remarkable perils and dangers, which she ever reverently remembred and gratefully acknowledged.

Her life and conversation was innocent and agreeable, seasoned with christian gravity; was a bright example of plainness, temperance, and self-denial; devoted to the service of truth and the propagating of religion and piety amongst mankind: In which ardent love and zeal she continued, until it pleased her great Lord and master in his wisdom to put a period to all her pious labours and travels, and to take her to himself, as a shock of corn gathered in due season, after a short illness of nine days continuance, within which time, on a first day of the week, friends at her request, held an evening meeting in her room, wherein she was wonderfully strengthened to bear a lively testimony to the everlasting truth, setting forth, the ground work of true religion and divine worship, concluding with a fervent prayer to the father of all our mercies, for the continuance of his

his love and favours to his children and people. After which, her weakneſs increaſing, ſhe lay in a calm and quiet frame, without much appearance of pain, until ſhe died, which was on the 28*th* day of the fourth month 1755, in the ſeventy-third year of her age.

The Teſtimony of the Quarterly-Meeting of Sandwich *in* New-England, *concerning* NICHOLAS DAVIS.

HE was born at Sandwich, the 28*th* of the eighth month 1690, but lived the greateſt part of his days in Dartmouth and Rocheſter. He came forth with a living teſtimony in the miniſtry, before he was twenty years old, in which he grew very faſt, and ſoon became an able ſkilful miniſter of the goſpel, dividing the word of truth aright; zealous againſt obſtinate offenders, but to thoſe under affliction, his words were as healing balſam, and his ſpeech as dew on the tender graſs. He ſtrove to live in peace with all men, and was generally well beloved by his acquaintance and neighbours, more eſpecially his brethren of the ſame religious denomination. He travelled much in viſiting friends in New-England, was very ſerviceable in ſtrengthening them, and alſo made inſtrumental in convincing ſome of the bleſſed truth. A diligent

diligent and seasonable attender of meetings, and a lover of the honest hearted, but always hated hypocrisy in any. He twice visited friends in the western parts of America, going once as far as North-Carolina.—Before he proceeded on his last journey into those parts, he appeared resigned to the will of God, and much weaned from the things of this world; his kinsman Adam Mott accompanied him, and by testimonials receiv'd from several meetings, their service was well accepted. On his way homeward, he was taken sick at Oblong in New-York government, bearing his pain with great patience to the last; and whilst his understanding was clear, often mention'd his concern for the prosperity of truth. In the time of his sickness he wrote a letter to his wife, wherein he express'd his submission to the will of God whether in life or death, desiring she might experience the same; and in an especial manner requested her care in the education of their children, to bring them up in the nurture and admonition of the Lord; keep them from hurtful and unprofitable company, and endeavour to instil into their minds the christian principles of patience, temperance, meekness and sobriety, that so they might be made fit vessels for the holiest to dwell in. In another letter wrote to his children, in the time of his sickness, we find these words, ' I hereby let you know, that as I
' am doubtful whether I shall ever see you
' more, there rests something on my mind
' to

'to write to you by way of advice, which
'I greatly defire may not be forgotten, and
'that is, as you have a tender affectionate
'mother, who is defirous you may do well,
'therefore dear children, be obedient to her
'in all things in the Lord, and fubmit to
'her counfel and advice at all times in love
'to her, and alfo endeavour to live in love
'and peace one with another at all times,
'and let not any contentions or hard
'thoughts arife one againft another by any
'means, but be helpful one to another, and
'be exceeding careful to attend week-day
'meetings, and encourage others alfo, and
'endeavour to let all things be in good or-
'der in the church.' He would fometimes
defire thofe about him to be ftill and quiet,
that they might have a time to wait on the
Lord in filence, and feveral times opened
his mouth in prayer and fupplication in a
living and powerful manner; alfo exhorted
the by-ftanders in the fame life and power.
Thus he finifhed his courfe at Oblong aforefaid, on the 7th of the tenth month 1755,
in the fixty-fifth year of his age; and we
believe he is admitted "Where the weary
"are at reft." He bore a public teftimony
above forty-fix years, and hath left an unblemifhed character.

A Teftimony

A Testimony from Burlington *Monthly-Meeting in* New-Jersey, *concerning* PETER ANDREWS.

IT having pleased the Lord to bestow on him a gift in the ministry, he was faithful thereto, and made helpful to many; being so devoted to the service of God, that when any religious duty was required of him, he was fervently engaged to perform it, as strength was afforded.

He was careful to attend meetings for worship and discipline, and when there, manifested a real concern to wait upon God for strength and wisdom, that so our meetings might be truly profitable. Amongst his neighbours he was serviceable, his example having a tendency to strengthen the good in them and others, and to discourage that which was wrong.

His engagements in the exercise of the ministry, occasioned him to be much from home, yet his regard to his family was becoming his station both as a husband and a father; it was his frequent practice to sit down with them to wait upon the Lord, and we believe his faithfulness therein, was of considerable service.

In the year 1755, he, in a weighty manner laid before us, a concern that had sometime rested on him to visit friends in England. And having obtained the concurrence of friends here, and settled his temporal affairs, he embark'd about the 29*th* of the fourth month the same year.

For an account of his services in that nation, we refer to the following testimony of the monthly-meeting of friends in Norwich, at which place he departed this life, aged about forty-nine, and a minister about 14 years.

A Testimony from Norwich Monthly-Meeting concerning PETER ANDRWS.

OUR dear friend Peter Andrews, from West-Jersey in North-America, being on a religious visit to friends in this nation, deceased in this city; and the lively sense of his services, and the regard we bear to his memory, engages us to trasmit the following testimony concerning him.

His first visit to us was in the eleventh month 1755, and his service and exemplary deportment will remain as a lasting testimony for him, and to the truth he preached, in the minds of many; and we have good reason to believe he was made instrumental, in a very particular manner, to the help and furtherance of some amongst us, whom it had pleased the Lord to visit with a fresh visitation of his love. And by the information of other friends, who well knew him, and particularly our friend Edmund Peckover, who frequently accompanied him, as well as from our own knowledge, we are enabled to give the following brief account of his labours and travels, from the time of his arrival to his death.

He

He landed in the south part of England, in or about the sixth month 1755, and came directly up to London, where he was kindly received by friends, and had very good service during a short stay there; but being desirous of being at the quarterly-meeting to be held at York, in company with several friends of London, he went as directly to the said city as he could well do, being near two hundred miles, and reached there by the 24*th* of the sixth month, at which time began the quarterly-meeting; and this our dear friend had a very memorable and weighty opportunity in ministry, in the meeting of ministers and elders at the opening thereof; but, in the succeeding meetings for worship, was mostly silent; yet in those for discipline, was divinely led to set forth the nature, good end and tendency of the same, and very zealously pressed to the keeping them up, in the same wisdom and power in which they were first established; evidently setting forth, ' that they proceeded from that which ' gathered our fore-fathers to be as a pecu- ' liar people unto God;' to the no small edification and comfort of many sincere hearts, who rejoiced greatly in having his company, which remains fresh in their remembrance; his services being as bread cast upon the waters, which, according to the wise man's observation, *shall be found after many days.*

After the quarterly-meeting was ended he went to Pickering, where a very large meeting is kept annually for worship, and had seasonable

seasonable and profitable service. He travelled to many other places in that county, and friends were greatly refreshed and edified by his christian visit, though not always attended by public declarations in their religious meetings appointed on his account, which were mostly very large, and expectations high, yet his eye was to his great master's putting forth. He often was led to famish that too eager desire after words; and in several public meetings he had nothing to say amongst them; which tho' a great disappointment to many for the present, yet there afterwards appeared a signal service in it.

He was at Yarm, Stockton, Bainbrig, and several other meetings in and about the Dales; then came to Leeds, Bradford, Wakefield, Doncaster, and so into Lincolnshire; which county he visited pretty generally, also the isle of Ely, and came into Norfolk, and to this place in the eleventh month 1755, as afore-mentioned; was at most, if not all, of friends meetings in our county; then went into Suffolk and Essex, and returned to London the latter end of the first month 1756, where he remained a few weeks, being exceeding ill; yet was at most of the meetings in that city, and was very serviceable, with many other friends, in affairs particularly relating to the society in Pennsylvania at that time.

He went back again into Essex, and so for Hertfordshire, some parts of Buckinghamshire,

shire, Oxfordshire, Gloucestershire, and to the yearly-meeting at Bristol in the fifth month 1756; and had good service both in meetings for worship and discipline, which was well received, and, it is hoped, made lasting impressions on the minds of many who had the opportunity of being present.

His indisposition still continued, but did not hinder him from travelling: From Bristol he passed through some part of Gloucestershire, Wiltshire, and Oxfordshire, and got to the yearly-meeting at London in the sixth month, and altho' his illness continued upon him, was enabled to bear several living testimonies, in the demonstration of the spirit and of power.

After the said yearly-meeting was ended, he came down to the yearly-meetings at Colchester and Woodbridge, where he was eminently supported to be serviceable in the churches. At Woodbridge he was strengthened to bear a large, powerful and affecting testimony in the last meeting of worship, to the tendering of many hearts, whose states were so effectually spoken to, as that it may be fitly compared to the excellency, and glorious situation which the Psalmist described, when he says, " How " good, and how pleasant a thing it is, for " brethren to dwell together in unity! It is " like the precious ointment upon the head, " that ran down upon the beard, even Aa- " ron's beard, that went down to the skirts " of his garments: As the dew of Hermon,
" and

"and as the dew that defcended upon the mountains of Zion; for there the Lord commanded the bleffing, even life for evermore," Pfalm cxxxiii. 1, 2, 3. It was indeed a moft heavenly, precious, baptizing feafon, (this being the laft public opportunity our dear friend had) in which he was wonderfully led to fet forth the progreffive fteps the Almighty was pleafed to make ufe of, in appearing to Gideon, confirming him in the certainty of his requirings, condefcending to grant his requefts in a very peculiar manner, and fealing them with his prefence, and giving him victory over his enemies, as he was faithful to follow the bleffed author that pointed forth the beginning as well as finifhing that great work, to which that extraordinary fervant of God, Gideon, in his day was called; which memorable fervice of our dear friend, there is great reafon to believe the great Lord, who prepared him for the fame, was gracioufly pleafed to fix as a nail in a fure place; and may it fo continue in the remembrance of thofe then prefent, who are left for a fmall fpace yet in mutability.

He continued very weak in body all his ftay in Woodbridge, being above five days, and no perfuafions could prevail with him to hinder his fetting forward for his journey, having ftrong defires in his mind to fee friends in this place again; and to a particular friend he expreffed his love fo great to us, 'That he thought he could willingly
'die

'die with us.' He was favoured to accomplish it in two days after he left Woodbridge, though with great difficulty, and lodged at the house of our friend John Oxley, as he had done before, but took to his bed soon after he got in, to which, the remaining part of his time, he was mostly confined.

It being the time of our yearly-meeting, many friends went often to visit him, and he expressed to some, 'That he was satisfied
'he was in his place, in giving up to follow
'the requirings of the Lord, in leaving his
'outward habitation, and those near bles-
'sings of a most tender affectionate wife
'and dutiful children.'

The severity of his illness kept him mostly delirious, yet he was favour'd with some clear intervals; in one of which, being in a sweet heavenly frame of mind, he broke forth in the following fervent supplication, viz. 'Oh! this poor soul hath been for many
'days on the brink of the pit of distress;
'but thou, dear father, dost not afflict thy
'children willingly, but for some great and
'good cause known only to thyself: Dear
'father! suffer not thy children ever to de-
'spair of thy mercies, but that we may be
'helpful, as much as may be in our pow-
'er, to one another in all such times of
'trouble. Dearest father! thou hast been
'pleased to open, and to favour with thy
'goodness; my soul is thankful, and can
'say, thou art worthy of glory and praise
'for evermore.'

He continued to the 13*th* of the seventh month 1756, and then departed this life, and was interr'd in friends burying-ground the 18*th* of the same, after an awful meeting, (his corps being attended by a very large number of friends and others) and no doubt he rests, with the spirits of the just made perfect, in those glorious mansions prepared for all those that hold out in faithfuness to the end. His memory is very precious and dear to many who are yet surviving, and we believe it may truly be said, that few friends who have travelled in this nation, have been more approved, or had more general service in so short a space of time.

A Testimony from Gwynedd *Monthly-Meeting in* Pennsylvania, *concerning* JOHN EVANS.

HE was born in Denbighshire, in the principality of Wales, in the year 1689, and arrived in Pennsylvania with his parents in 1698, under whom he received a pious education.—He was a man of good natural understanding and favoured early in life to see the necessity of a diligent attention to the voice of divine wisdom, to establish and preserve him in peace with God; and by a steady adherence to it, he became honourable in society and eminently serviceable in the church of Christ.—In the twenty-third year of his age he appeared in the ministry of of the gospel, his deportment therein was reverent as became a mind sensible of the awful importance of the service. He had a clear engaging manner of delivery, was deep in heavenly mysteries, and plain in declaring them; being well acquainted with the holy scriptures, he was made skilful in opening the doctrines therein contain'd, and was often led to draw lively and instructive similitudes from the visible creation. He travelled through most of the northern colonies in the service of truth, and several times thro' this province.—He was often drawn to attend general meetings, funerals and other public occasions, particularly the adjacent meetings after their first establishment, over which he had a tender fatherly care, as a good shepherd taking heed to the flock;—and the great shepherd of Israel blessed his labours, and afforded him at times great satisfaction and comfort.—The latter part of his time, the visible declension of many from the life and power of truth, frequently made sorrow and deep lamentation his portion.—His labours were fervent with the youth, in much love and zeal, that they might come to know God for themselves, bow their necks to the yoke, and lay their shoulders to the work, saying, " That their remembering their creator in " the days of their youth, would be as mar- " row to his bones." It was indeed his great joy to behold the peaceable fruits of righteousness, and his labours for the promotion

motion thereof made him honourable amongst men of various ranks and professions, and his testimony generally acceptable to them.

In the support of our christian discipline, he was zealous, active and unwearied, and favoured with qualification to advise in difficult cases, which seldom failed of succeeding. His testimony was close against hypocrisy and an outside shew of religion only, but full of parternal tenderness to the afflicted, weak, or diffident in spirit; of sound judgment, and deep in divine experience, yet modest and condescending, and being favoured with the descendings of the father's love, that at times appeared to clothe him as with a mantle; he had an open-door in the hearts of his friends, and an ascendency over the spirits of gainsayers.—He was a zealous promoter of visiting friends in their families, was many times engaged therein, and his labours were awakening and useful; often employ'd in visiting the sick, the widow, and the fatherless and others in affliction; on these occasions he was seldom large in expression, but his silent sympathy and secret breathing for their relief, were more consolatory than many words; a considerable part of his time was spent in assisting widows, and the guardianship of orphans, which, though laborious to him, was of much advantage to them.

The importance of love and peace to civil and religious society he was deeply sensible

sible of, diligent in promoting them both by precept and example, and successful in restoring harmony where any violation of it appear'd.—His conduct and conversation in private life was exemplary, and such as implied an inward close inspection into the secret operations of his own heart.

He was apprehensive of his approaching end for sometime before his last illness, and told a friend, 'He should not survive one 'year,' who admir'd he was so positive; but he made no further reply than, 'See what 'will follow.' In his public testimony also, he frequently said, 'He had but an inch of 'time to treat with us.' In the first part of his illness, he went to some meetings, one whereof was large, and he was favour'd with strength to speak in a powerful and instructive manner to the youth, for whose welfare his desires were ardent.—His disorder was slow and lingering, wherein he was favour'd with his understanding almost to the last; and altho', at some seasons, he was much concern'd on account of the gloominess of the times in religious and civil respects, yet in general he possess'd a very great degree of calmness and serenity of mind, with a perfect resignation to the will of God, whether life or death should be his portion. On the day of his departure, observing his wife troubled, he said with a cheerful countenance, 'I am easy, I am ea-' fy, and desir'd her to be easy also;' indeed it appear'd that the Lord had strengthened
him

him on the bed of languishing, and made all his bed in his sickness. And thus having served God in his generation, he departed the 23*d* day of the ninth month 1756, aged sixty-seven years; having, we hope, shaken himself from the dust, put on his beautiful garments, and enter'd the wedding chamber of the bridegroom of his soul, and enjoys the reward of his faithful labours; was buried on the 25*th* day of the same month, in friends burying-ground at Gwynedd.

A Testimony from the Monthly-Meeting of Philadelphia, *concerning* THOMAS BROWN.

HE was born in Barking, in the county of Essex, Great-Britain, on the 1*st* of the ninth month 1696, came whilst young with his parents into this province, and lived some time in this city, from whence he removed with them to Plumstead in Bucks county, where he first appeared in the ministry; some years after which, he settled in this city. His gift in the ministry was living, deep, and very edifying; and in the exercise thereof, he was remarkable for an awful care, not to appear without clear and renewed evidence of the motion of life for that service: And though not a man of literature, was often led into sublime matter, which was convincing and persuasive, in setting forth the dignity and excellence of the chriftian religion, yet was very attentive that thofe heighths fhould not detain him beyond his proper gift, but to clofe in and with the life, which made his miniftry always acceptable to the living and judicious. Although he was not led to vifit the churches in diftant parts, yet was fometimes concern'd to attend fome of the neighbouring meetings, of two of which he has preferv'd fome minutes, which being a lively defcription of his concern of mind for the promotion of the caufe of truth, it is thought well to fubjoin them here in his own words.

'1756, eighth month 9*th*, I went to Con-
' cord quarterly-meeting, but found no
' caufe to efpoufe the caufe of God in a
' public manner that day. The next day
' went to the youth's meeting at Kennet,
' which was to great fatisfaction; my foul
' was fo bended towards the people, that I
' could fcarcely leave them, being engaged
' in a ftream of the miniftry, to extol the
' divinity of that religion that is breathed
' from heaven, and which arrays the foul
' of its poffeffor with degrees of the divini-
' ty of Chrift, and entitles them to an eter-
' nal inheritance; alfo introduces a lan-
' guage, intelligible only to the converted
' fouls which have accefs to a celeftial foun-
' tain, which is no lefs than a foretafte of
' eternal joy, to fupport them in their jour-
' ney towards the regions above, where re-
' ligion has room to breathe in its divine
' excellencies

'excellencies in the foul; here it is inftruct-
'ed in the melody of that harmonious fong
'of the redeemed, where the morning ftars
'fing together, and the fons of God fhout
'for joy.—

'1756, the 29*th* of the eighth month, I
'vifited Gwynedd-meeting, where in wait-
'ing in nothingnefs before God, without
'feeking or ftriving to awake my beloved
'before the time, by degrees my foul be-
'came invefted with that concern that the
'gofpel introduces, with an opening in
"thefe words; I think it may conduce to
"my peace, to ftand up, and engage in a
"caufe dignified with immortality and
"crowned with eternal life." The fubject
'raifed higher and brighter until my foul
'was tranfported on the mount of God
'in degree, and beheld his glory; where I
'was favoured to treat on the exalted ftati-
'on of the redeemed church, which ftands
'in the election of grace, where my foul
'rejoiced with tranfcendent joy and adored
'God. Returned home in peace.'

His conduct and converfation was innocent and edifying, being much weaned from
the world and the fpirit of it. He was careful not to engage in worldly concerns fo as
to encumber his mind, and draw it off from
that religious contemplation, in which was
his chief delight; which happy ftate of
mind he maintained to the laft, as evidently appeared to thofe friends who were with
him

him towards his conclusion; to some of whom he expressed himself in the following manner, viz.

'I am fine and easy, and don't know but 'what I may recover; but if I should, I 'expect to see many a gloomy day, but 'nevertheless I am willing to live longer, if 'I might be a means of exalting religion, 'that the gift bestowed on me, might shine 'brighter than it hath ever yet done, or else 'I had abundance better go now; for I 'think I have shone but glimmeringly to 'what I might have done, had I been still 'more faithful; tho' I cannot charge my- 'self with a presumptuous temper, nor wil- 'ful disobedience; but I can say, it has of- 'ten happened with me, as with the poor 'man at the pool of Bethesda, whilst I was 'making ready another has stepped in. I 'am sensible that my gift has been different 'from some of my brethren, I have not 'been led so much into little things, but I 'am far from judging them.

'I have often to pass through the valley 'of the shadow of death, and have experi- 'enced the possibility of a soul's subsisting 'the full space of forty days without re- 'ceiving any thing, only living by faith 'and not by sight, provided they keep up- 'on the foundation of convincement and 'conviction, and not turn aside to take a 'prospect of the world, and desire to draw 'their comfort from visibles; they will be 'supported by an invisible yet invincible
'power;

' power; for he will be sure to appear, and
' when he doth appear at times, doth rend
' the vail from the top to the bottom, with
' an invitation, as Samuel used to say (mean-
' ing Samuel Fothergill) " Come up hither,
" and behold the bride the lamb's wife;"
' then the soul will have to enjoy, and see
' things beyond expressing; my tongue can
' do little or nothing at setting it forth.
' The soul will be filled with holy admirati-
' on, and say, " Who is she that looketh
" forth as the morning, fair as the moon,
" clear as the sun, and terrible as an army
" with banners."

' Although the soul has at times to be-
' hold the glory, splendor and magnitude of
' the true church or spouse of Christ, yet
' those extraordinary sights are but seldom,
' not often: Though I have had at times,
' cause to espouse the cause of God, yet
' there are times that the soul is so veiled,
' and surrounded with temptations and fiery
' trials, and all out of sight, that I have
' wondered that I was made choice of; but
' I have experienced, that they that would
' reign with Christ must suffer with him; I
' never expect to get beyond it, while I am
' cloathed with this clog of mortality.

' People may have a regular outside, and
' be diligent in attending meetings, and yet
' know little or nothing of it; for formality
' and externals are nothing; religion is an in-
' ternal subject, subsisting between Christ and
' the soul: I don't confine it to our name,
' but

'but amongst the different names there are, that my soul is nearly united to, who are in a good degree, I do believe, in possession of that religion which is revealed from heaven: And I am in the faith, that there will be them raised up, that will shine as bright stars, and religion will grow and prosper, and the holy flame rise to a greater height than it hath ever yet done. I can say with the holy apostle, "I have nothing to boast of, save my infirmities," yet thus much I venture to say, that if I die now, I die a lover of God and religion.' And after expressing a compassionate sympathy with the poor afflicted churches up and down, concluded with this saying, "Be of good cheer little flock, for greater is he that is in you, than he that is in the world."

In the sixty-first year of his age, he was seized with an apoplectick disorder, which gradually increasing, deprived him of life, on the 21st of the sixth month 1757, and was interr'd in this city the next day.

A Testimony from Newark *Monthly-Meeting in* New-Castle *county on* Delaware, *concerning* Betty Caldwell.

SHE was the daughter of George Pierce, of Thornbury in Chester county, was born in Gloucestershire in Old-England, and came into Pennsylvania with her parents,
about

about the year 1683, who settled in Thornbury aforesaid. She was married to Vincent Caldwell in 1703, and soon after they settled in Marlborough, Chester county, where she continued, and belonged to Kennet meeting, till a few years before her death, when she removed to Wilmington. She was from her youth, remarkably exemplary for plainness and sobriety, much concern'd for peace in the church and amongst neighbours, labouring to restore it according to ability as occasions required, often with the desired success. She was very serviceable in that weighty work of visiting friends families, in which she had at times to impart to others, of her own experience in the work of religion, and to exhort to faithfulness and obedience to what the Lord requires; was a constant attender of meetings, and exemplary for solid and humble waiting therein, and much concern'd that her children might walk in the truth. After the death of her husband in 1720, she had the care of the family upon herself, remaining in a state of widowhood upwards of 37 years, in which station she behaved with such prudence and circumspection, that her conduct, in bringing up her children without much correction, is worthy of imitation; which together with her pious concern for the welfare of the church, entitled her to be accounted of the number of the " Widows indeed." She had many years been in the station of an elder for Kennet meeting, and several years before

fore her death, had a few words in testimony in meetings, which was generally well received, being seasonable and weighty.

Her last sickness was a fever, which brought her very low, often 'Praying the 'Lord to be near her, and by his support-'ing hand to bear up her spirits now in this 'pinching time;' and finished her course here, we believe in peace with the Lord and in unity with friends, the 27th of the tenth month 1757, and was interr'd in Kennet burying-ground the 29th of the same month, in the seventy-seventh year of her age.

A Testimony from Burlington *Monthly-Meeting in* New-Jersey, *concerning* ABRAHAM FARRINGTON.

HE was born in Bucks county, Pennsylvania, of parents professing the truth as held by us the people called Quakers. About nine months after his birth his father dying, and his mother sometime after marrying from among friends, exposed him to a loose irregular education; about ten years of age being put apprentice, where through eleven years servitude, he suffered great bodily hardship, and much greater danger as to the better part; yet (says he in a manuscript left for the use of his children) 'I 'took delight in my bible, and believe the 'good hand was with me, that inclined my 'mind

'mind thereto.—Tho' I followed lying va‑
'nities, and so forsook my own mercies,
'yet I could say my prayers every night,
'till I grew afraid to say them any more,
'and seemed like one abandoned from good
'for several years.' Having served his time
out, he providentially became a resident in
Benjamin Clark's family at Stony-brook, who
were exemplary and kind to him; 'I thought
'(says he) they were the best people in the
'world, careful in their words, yet cheer‑
'ful and pleasant, so that I thought I must
'be a Quaker.' And Edward Andrews,
from Eggharbour, being at a quarterly meet‑
ing at Crosswicks, 'He came (adds he) with
'power to give me my awakening call; I
'was much reached, but after the manner
'of the world, looking at the man, gave
'him the praise, viz. he is a brave man,
'he preaches well, I wish I lived near him,
'I would go to hear him every first day;
'at same time not minding what he direct‑
'ed to, Christ in ourselves, the true teach‑
'er, that will not be removed till we re‑
'move from him; in us is the place he has
'ordained to reveal himself.—I afterwards
'went more to friends meetings than I had
'done before, and read much in friends
'books, but was yet in the dark, the time
'of my deliverance was not come, the sins
'of the Amorites were not full; I was un‑
'der Moses in the wilderness, come out of
'Egypt, but Joshua's time was not come,
'the Saviour, the warrior that brings
                                      'through

' through judgment, and makes war with
' the old inhabitants; yet I sometimes long-
' ed for something which I could not find,
' a lot in the good land. I think this year
' Thomas Willson and James Dickenson,
' came into the country, and sometime af-
' terwards to visit the meeting of friends at
' Crosswicks, I happened to be at the meeting
' before they came in; the sight of them
' struck me, the heavenly frame of mind
' which their countenances manifested, and
' the awe they seemed to sit under, brought
' a stillness over my mind, and I was as
' ground prepared to receive the seed: James
' stood up in the authority of the gospel,
' and in it he was led to unravel me and all
' my works from top to bottom, so that
' I looked on myself like a man dissected
' or pulled to pieces, all my religion as
' well as all my sins were set forth in such a
' light that I thought myself undone: Af-
' ter he sat down, Thomas stood up and
' brought me together again, I mean what
' was to be raised, bone to his bone, with
' the sinews and strength that would con-
' stitute a christian; I almost thought
' myself new born, the old man destroyed
' and the new man made up, concluding I
' should never be bad again, that my sins
' were forgiven, and I should have nothing
' to do but to do good; I thought I had got-
' ten my lot in the good land, and might
' sit now under my own vine and fig tree,
' and nothing more should make me afraid.
                                         ' Poor

'Poor creature! I had only a fight, I did
' not yet think what powerful adversaries I
' had to war with; this has been the mise-
' rable case of many, they have sat down
' under a convincement, and in a form of
' religion, some depending on former expe-
' rience or former openings, some on their
' education, some a bare belief, and know-
' ledge historical of the scriptures and prin-
' ciple of truth.—Thus tho' I received the
' truth, yet I was like the stony ground;
' I received it with joy, but had not root in
' myself, my heart grew hard again, for
' when tribulations, persecutions, tempta-
' tions and trials came upon me, I fell. Oh!
' how I moped at times and wandered about
' as a prisoner at large, I would have run,
' but I could not, my offended judge, my
' accuser was in me, I could not fly from
' him; yet, great goodness was near, and
' his power kept me from gross evils in a
' great degree.—I kept pretty much to meet-
' ings, but there was such a mixture of un-
' digested matter in me, it was not to be
' soon separated. Oh! the necessity there
' was, and still is of a continual watch
' against our soul's enemies both within
' and without.'

Having passed thro' various probations, he had considerable openings of the divine sense of the scriptures, and also saw that the Lord had a work for him to do, to which he at length gave up, and being faithful therein, was made helpful to many, being enlarged

enlarged and found in teftimony, and at times very particularly led to explain paffages in the fcriptures, to the comfort and information of hearers.

He was an affectionate hufband and parent, diligent in attending meetings for worfhip and difcipline, and manifefted therein a zealous concern for the promotion and honour of truth, waiting for wifdom to fee his duty, and ftrength to perform it.—He divers times travelled abroad on this continent in the fervice of truth, and frequently to the neighbouring meetings to fatisfaction; his outward circumftances being at times difficult, gave him an opportunity to fhew an example of chriftian refignation, and to fee its effects in divers providential affiftances.

In 1756 he laid before this meeting a religious concern to vifit friends in Great-Britain, which had been on his mind upwards of ten years, wherewith the meeting concurring, he had our certificate, and embarking, landed in Ireland; and after vifiting the meetings in that country, arrived in England and performed his religious vifit in feveral counties, but was taken ill, and died in London the 26th of the firft month 1758; finifhing his days work with a firm affurance that the gates of Heaven were opened to him; very acceptable accounts of his fervices both in England and Ireland have been received, as are more fully fet forth in the annexed teftimony of Devonfhire-houfe monthly-meeting concerning him.

He died aged about sixty-seven, was in the profession of the truth near 44, and an acceptable minister upwards of 30 years.

A Testimony from Devonshire-house *Monthly-Meeting in* London, *concerning* ABRAHAM FARRINGTON.

THIS worthy minister and elder, having had drawings in spirit for several years, as we are informed, to visit the churches of Christ in this nation and Ireland, in the service of the gospel; when he apprehended the time approached wherein he was to enter upon this weighty engagement, he settled his outward affairs; and having the concurrence and unity of the brethren, embark'd in a vessel bound from Philadelphia to Dublin, in company with three friends from Europe, who had performed a religious visit to the churches in America.—After a favoured voyage of about four weeks, landing at Dublin, he visited the meetings of friends in Ireland, and by the accounts from thence, had very weighty and acceptable service there: Having laboured faithfully in that nation to strengthen the brethren and assist in building up the waste places in Zion, he embark'd for England, visited the churches in some of the northern counties, attended the yearly-meeting at Penrith, and afterwards that in this city, his labour of love in the work of the miniſtry, being to edification and comfort, was truly acceptable.—After attending the yearly-meetings of Colcheſter, Woodbridge, Norwich and the quarterly-meeting of York, he viſited many meetings in the northern and midland counties, from whence good accounts have been received of his weighty and affecting labours. He returned to London the lattter end of the twelfth month 1757. Having travelled with great diligence and laboured fervently, his health was impaired; neverthelefs he attended meetings till his diforder increafed fo as to render him incapable of further fervice.

As this our dear friend ſpent but little time in this city, we cannot from knowledge and experience give fuch a teſtimony concerning him as might be thought requifite; yet, as fome of us partook of the benefit of his religious labours, we find ourfelves engaged to give forth this teſtimony concerning him.

His converfation was innocently cheerful, yet grave and inſtructive; he was a man of a weighty fpirit, a valiant in Ifrael; a fharp reprover of libertine and loofe profeffors; but tender to the contrite and humble; and a lover of good order in the church.

He was ſtrong in judgment, found in doctrine, deep in divine things; often explaining, in a clear and lively manner, the hidden mifteries wrapt up in the fayings of Chriſt, the prophets and apoſtles; and it may

may truly be said, he was well instructed in the kingdom, bringing forth, out of his treasure, things new and old.

His ministry was in plainness of speech, and attended with divine authority, reaching the witness of God in man, and to the habitation of the mourners in Zion; frequently pointing out, in a lively manner, the paths of the exercised travellers, and the steps of heavenly pilgrims; by which he was made helpful to such as are seeking the true rest, which the Lord hath prepared for his people. It may truly be said, he was eminently gifted for the work of the present day, remarkably qualified to expose the mystery of iniquity, and to point out wherein true godliness consisted.

His distemper increasing, he was confined to his bed, at the house of our friend Thomas Jackson, in Devonshire-square, where all necessary care was taken of him. During his illness, he was very sweet and tender in his spirit, and remarkably patient. He uttered many comfortable and heavenly expressions, and several times said, ' He ' apprehended his time in this world would ' be but short;' and seemed fully resigned to quit mortality, having an evidence, ' That ' he should be clothed upon with immorta- ' lity, and be united to the heavenly host.'

He had frequently been heard to say, in time of health, ' That he thought he should ' lay down his body in this nation, and not ' see his friends in America more;' to which he he appeared freely given up. He often expressed his desire, 'That he might be favoured with an easy passage,' which was graciously granted.

He departed this life, the 26th of the first month 1758, like a lamb, without either sigh or groan, as one falling into a sweet sleep, aged about sixty-six years; and on the 30th of the same, his body was carried to Devonshire-house, where a large and solemn meeting was held, which was owned by him whose presence is the life of our meetings; and from thence his body was carried, by friends, to their burying-ground in Bunhill-fields, a large concourse accompanying it, and was there decently interr'd among the remains of many of our primitive worthies, and valiant soldiers in the lamb's war, who loved not their lives unto death, for the word of God and testimony of Jesus.

A Testimony from Kennet *Monthly-Meeting in* Pennsylvania, *concerning* HANNAH CARLETON.

HANNAH CARLETON, late wife of Thomas Carleton, of Kennet, in Chester county Pennsylvania, was born at Haverford in the said county, about the 5th month 1689; she was sensible of the Lord's visitation of love to her in her young years, and as she gave heed thereto, was preserved in a
good

good degree from the vanities and evil conversation of the world; as she grew in years she grew in the truth, was a serviceable friend in the society and her neighbourhood in divers respects; and of latter years was helpful in that weighty work of visiting friends families, having at times to impart (not only in such opportunities, but in our more public meetings) of her experience of the work of truth in her young years, and urging to others the necessity of the same work in them; which was well receiv'd by friends. Being taken with an excess of bleeding at the nose, she was thereby so weakened that for some months before her decease, she did not go from home nor much out of doors; she apprehended her end was near, and when it was proposed to send to a doctor for help, she said, 'It seemed needless, for I am in the hands of the great physician who knows what is best for me.' A neighbour signifying she hoped to see her better, she answered, ' Better I shall be in ' a little time.' The friend replied, ' In a ' better state of health I mean;' she answered, ' I neither expect nor desire it,' admiring the kindness of the almighty in favouring her so, that she felt neither sickness nor pain. Another time she said, ' As I have laboured ' for peace and love, so now I see nothing but ' peace before me,' with several other sentences which manifested, that the peace and quietness she was favoured with, came from the father of mercies to her in her last moments.

She departed this life, the 6*th* of the fifth month 1758, about the 3*d* hour in the afternoon, and was buried in friends burying-ground in Kennet, the 8*th* of the same month, in the sixty-ninth year of her age.

A Testimony from Gwynedd *Monthly-Meeting in* Pennsylvania, *concerning* JANE JONES.

JANE JONES, wife of John Jones of Montgomery township, was educated amongst friends, and as she grew in years, she increased in divine knowledge, and became a serviceable member of the church. The affability and sweetness of her disposition, and her love to all, render'd her very near, not only to the faithful, but many others also. As a parent, she was much more concern'd for her children's eternal welfare, than for their acquiring of wealth or preferments in this world. And as she possessed affluence and plenty herself, the sensibility of her heart towards the needy, would not permit her to eat her morsel alone. She sought for the poor, and distributed bountifully to their wants. As she advanced to old age, she became frail, and subject to pain and disorders, which disabled her from attending meetings as duly as she desired; nevertheless her love to truth and the prosperity of Zion brightened and increased, and she bore her weakness with patience, as a dispensation permitted for her probation. She

She departed this life, the 11*th* of the fifth month 1758, and was interr'd the 14*th* of the same month in friends burying-ground at Gwynedd, in the seventieth year of her age.

A Testimony from Haddonfield *Monthly-Meeting in* New-Jersey, *concerning* JOSEPH TOMLINSON.

OUR well esteemed friend Joseph Tomlinson deceased, was convinced of the truth in the early part of his life. His zeal for attending religious meetings when but young, was such, that he frequently travelled many miles on foot to them, and continued remarkably diligent in attending all our religious meetings. As he grew in years, he became more and more serviceable amongst friends, being several years an overseer of Haddonfield meeting, and likewise an elder; careful to maintain the discipline. His life seemed to be unblameable. He was nearly united unto his friends, and their love to him was very great.

He died the 3*d* of the ninth month 1758, and we believe he was prepared to receive the answer of " Well done, &c."

A Testimony

A Testimony from Wrights Town *Monthly-Meeting in* Bucks *county* Pennsylvania, *concerning our ancient friend and sister* Agnes Penquite, *who departed this life, the 20th day of the eleventh month 1758, being upwards of one hundred years old.*

SHE brought a certificate with her from Europe, dated the 6th day of the second month 1686. She was of an innocent pious life and conversation, a good example in attending meetings both on first and week-days, until a few years before her death. She was a minister above seventy years; her testimony, tho' generally short, was mostly to satisfaction and edification; and in her declining age, when nature seemed almost spent, she appeared more divinely favoured than common, to the admiration of some. When she could no longer attend meetings, she would often, at meal times, appear in prayer, with praises to the Lord, to the comfort and satisfaction of those present; and frequently signified, ' She had ' the evidence of divine peace.' Not long before her departure she said, ' That her ' sweet Lord had not forsaken her, but was ' still with her to comfort and refresh her in ' her old age.' Thus she was removed from time to eternity, like a shock of corn fully ripe.

A Testimony from Goshen *Monthly-Meeting in* Chester *county,* Pennsylvania, *concerning* CADWALLADER JONES.

HE was born the 27*th* of the first month 1687, near Bala, in Merionethshire, in the principality of Wales, and removed with his parents into Pennsylvania about the year 1697; soon after their arrival, he was placed with a friend until he came of age, in this time of his youth, he was naturally very wild and airy, and delighted much in vain company, until by convictions he broke off from his companions. In the year 1710 he married, and soon after settled at Uwchlan in Chester county, where he remained until his decease. A meeting being established at that place shortly after his removal thither, he duly attended the same both on the first and other days of the week; sometimes remarking, ' That he knew the bene-
' fit of leaving the hurry of the world to
' attend meeting,' where he was a good example, both in keeping to the time appointed, and his solid sitting in silence. He was zealous for the support of our christian discipline and active therein, as well as in overseeing the flock and other services in the church.

He served in the station of an elder about 28 years, diligently attending those meetings even until old age and under bodily weaknesses. In his sickness, he often express'd press'd much concern and sorrow for some of the professors of truth, saying, 'They are on the decline, what will become of them?' And further said, 'This thing had often been a burden to him, and he thought he had discharged his part, and it would now soon become the burden of others;' expressing a concern for the right management of the discipline, and remarking the remissness of some herein. He frequently expressed his resignation to the will of God; and on the 21*st* of the eleventh month 1758, quietly departed this life, and was buried the 23*d* in friends burying-ground at Uwchlan aforesaid.

A Testimony from Woodbridge *Monthly-Meeting in* New-Jersey, *concerning* SARAH SHOTWELL.

SARAH SHOTWELL departed this life, in the eighth month 1759, in the forty-fourth year of her age. She was educated amongst friends on Long-Island, and was early engaged in a public testimony. In the twenty-seventh year of her age, she was married to Joseph Shotwell of Rahway; was a woman much beloved, of a sweet, free and hospitable spirit, guarded in her expressions, careful to give no just occasion of offence, a prudent loving wife, a tender exemplary parent, an affectionate and kind neighbour;

neighbour; often sympathizing with those in affliction, especially such as were religious and virtuous; the rich and poor of those were equally near to her, and nearer than natural kindred where truth had not united in spirit: She gladly received strangers; and her carriage and behaviour to young ministers and burden-bearers, manifested her concern for and sympathy with them, often dropping seasonable hints for their encouragement. Although she did not travel much abroad, yet she was diligent in attending meetings at and about home, being endued with a sound and living ministry, clear and distinct in her testimony, whereby many were alarmed, some convinced, strengthened and confirmed in the faith through a blessing on her labours. She was much engaged in silent humble waiting on the Lord, who was pleased to own her, and often raise in her memorials and songs of thanksgiving to the God of all mercies, who never forsook his people in the deep, nor left them to perish in the wilderness, but was faithful and true, and failed not to bring to the promised land. The gospel truths she was enabled to open, were so affecting to many, that some who were prejudiced against women's preaching, have been heard to say, ' If such a thing could be, she was a true ' gospel minister.'

She was a pattern of humility, not seeking applause, nor forward in her public appearances, and tho' sometimes large, was
generally

generally careful not to stand long; fervent and living in prayer, wherein, we believe, she had access to the father. She frequently exhorted all to come up in faithfulness, signifying, 'That God would have a people 'that would serve him in uprightness and 'integrity of heart.'

Having had a sight sometime before her last sickness, that her time here was nearly accomplished, she departed this life, after about four days illness, in a resigned frame of mind.

A Testimony from Hopewell *Monthly-Meeting in* Virginia, *concerning* Isaac Hollingsworth.

IN his youthful days he was deeply affected with the visitation of the love of God, and by adhering and carefully waiting in his counsel, he was preserved from the deluding vanities of the world, which are too apt to draw and divert the minds of young people, from an awful regard to him who created them. He received a gift in the ministry when about twenty-one years of age, and was, we believe, a faithful labourer in his master's work, being much concern'd for the promotion of truth and the eternal well-being of mankind: Of a sober and grave deportment, diligent in attending religious meetings, and exemplary in humble

ble waiting therein. He visited the churches in divers parts of the neighbouring colonies; and we find by accounts from thence, that his services and labours of love were well accepted among them. In the year 1757 he removed with his family within the limits of Fairfax monthly-meeting, so that we cannot give a very particular account of him, towards the latter part of his time, which we refer to that meeting.

A Supplement to the foregoing Testimony, from Fairfax *Monthly-Meeting in* Virginia.

THE foregoing testimony concerning our worthy friend Isaac Hollingsworth, was read in this meeting, to which we are free to add, that the few years he resided among us, he was a diligent attender of our religious meetings, and also a promoter of opportunities for retirement in families. He greatly desired, ' That truth might pros-
' per in the hearts of the youth,' being frequently concern'd in meetings, to speak to and encourage them, ' To come up in their
' duty,' and also to warn the disobedient, ' To forsake the evil of their ways;' A degree of the holy anointing accompanying his ministry, it tended to the encouragement and edification of the sincere in heart.

His last illness was a nervous disorder, which continued on him nineteen days; within which time he attended our meeting on a first day, and bore a living testimony
much

much to the satisfaction of friends, whereby he seemed much spent; and on going home he immediately took his bed, uttering but few words, and departed this life, easy and quiet, on the 10th of the ninth month 1759, and on the 12th of the same month, was interr'd in friends burying-ground at Fairfax, aged about thirty-seven years; and we doubt not he is a partaker of that joy which crowns the labours of the faithful.

A Testimony from Buckingham *Monthly-meeting in* Bucks *county* Pennsylvania, *concerning* EDMUND KINSEY.

HE was born in Philadelphia, in the year 1683, and it pleased the Lord to make him acquainted with truth, which he embraced in a good degree, and became sober, grave and steady in his deportment. In his early days he received a gift in the ministry, wherewith friends had unity; being also serviceable and exemplary to the particular meeting of Buckingham when it was small, by his diligence in attending it, his humble waiting therein, and lively ministry to the refreshing and encouraging of the little flock. Though his understanding as a man was not very extensive, yet that was abundantly supplied by his meek, innocent, loving and inoffensive deportment to all people. He was very diligent and industrious

dustrious in his outward affairs, a good example in his family, and affectionate to friends. His latter days were attended with great affliction of body, which he bore with patience and resignation, frequently signifying his ' Dependance on the Lord, the great ' physician of value;' saying, " He was " travelling towards the city of rest, whose " builder and maker God is." Having attained to the age of seventy-six years, he departed this life, the 24*th* of the twelfth month 1759, in great peace and good will to all men. A minister upwards of 40 years.

A Testimony from Salem *Monthly-Meeting in* New-Jersey, *concerning* ELIZABETH DANIEL, *wife of* James Daniel.

SHE was born in the year 1709, was a woman endowed with a lively gift in the ministry, and by yielding in obedience to the heavenly call and following the paths of true wisdom, it became as a crown and royal diadem on her head; for the truth was her chief adorning, and by it she was advanced from a poor, low, despised girl, to be as a mother in our Israel; and by wisdom was enabled to stand in the midst of the congregation, with reputation and honour for the cause of our God, and to plead with gainsayers and the lukewarm, to join in with the glorious truth that had made her free,

free, in the demonstration of the power of pure love; and in the stream thereof she was often led forth, to comfort the mournful travellers in Zion, and in the line of experience could tell what great things the Lord had done for her soul, thro' her obedience and trust in him, to whom she freely attributed all she received as from his bountiful hand, and thereby gave the glory to God, and administred comfort to weary travelling souls. But being of a backward spirit, from a sense of her own weakness, was loath to give up to travel in truth's service, which often brought her very low under such exercises. She sometimes travelled in Pennsylvania and Maryland, of which service we had comfortable accounts, and was also useful in building up the church within the limits of our monthly-meeting.

She was very lively to the last, and her testimonies were accompanied with power that made them truly seasonable to the auditory, the divine presence being sensibly with her, under a sense whereof she was very much resigned, and rather desirous to depart and be at rest with the Lord. On being asked how she was, she answered with much calmness, 'I am in great pain of bo-
' dy, but quite easy in mind, free to depart
' and be releafed from my various exercifes;
' and feel as if my day's work was done,
' and that I might lay down this tabernacle
' in peace. But Oh! the pain at times is fo
' great, nature is ready to shrink, and am
'afraid

' afraid I shall not be able to bear it with
' that patience I ought, tho' I strive for it,
' for my mind is quite easy and resigned.'

Her pain was great under the extremity of a sharp pleurisy, and after seven days, this servant of the Lord quietly departed in peace, on the 30*th* of the tenth month 1760, in the fifty-first year of her age, and the 26*th* of her public ministry.

A Testimony from Haddonfield *Monthly-Meeting in* New-Jersey, *concerning* JOSHUA LORD.

HE was born the first day of the eleventh month 1698, near Woodberry, in the county of Gloucester West-New-Jersey, of parents professing with friends, and appeared in the ministry about the year 1727, being early favoured to experience a growth therein, becoming a useful member in society. The forepart of his time he travelled pretty much, having twice visited friends in New-England and Long-Island, as also Maryland, Virginia and North-Carolina; of which services we had satisfactory accounts by certificates; he also frequently visited the neighbouring meetings in Pennsylvania and the Jerseys; the latter part of his time he spent mostly at home.

His

His laft illnefs was of fhort continuance, in which he was favoured with a quiet and refigned mind; expreffing, 'That he had 'gone through a feries of trouble, but had 'been fupported by the beft of fupport;' and we believe he is gone to enjoy that unmixed felicity that will never have an end.

He departed this life, the 19*th* of the eleventh month 1760, aged about fixty-two years, and on the 22*d* of the fame month was interr'd in friends burying-ground at Woodberry Creek.

A Teftimony from Chefterfield *Monthly-Meeting in* New-Jerfey, *concerning* ISAAC HORNOR.

HE was fon of John and Mary Hornor, born the 17*th* of the fecond month 1678, in the town of Tadcafter, in Yorkfhire Old-England. In 1683, he came with his parents to America, and fettled within the limits of this meeting. After his father's deceafe, it pleafed the Lord to vifit him with his bleffed truth in his young years, which he received in the love of it, and being obedient thereto, as he grew in years he grew in grace, and in the faving knowledge thereof, whereby he became a ferviceable member amongft friends, both as an overfeer and elder. Although he did not appear in public teftimony, he had a fenfe of the true miniftry, and was particularly

larly qualified to administer counsel and admonition; often advising to a steady course of life, and setting forth the way and leadings of truth in a very informing and encouraging manner, to the edification and comfort of many, which render'd his conversation agreeable, not only amongst those of our society, but others also; being likewise useful in settling differences. His sitting and waiting in meetings was grave and solid becoming a true worshipper; was a nursing father and a faithful elder, serving in that station divers years. He departed this life, after a short illness, on the 24*th* of the eleventh month 1760, and was interr'd in a burying-ground on his own plantation, aged eighty-two years and six months.

A Testimony from Evesham *Monthly-Meeting in* New-Jersey, *concerning* OBADIAH BORTON.

HE was born in the township of Evesham, in New-Jersey, in the year 1708, and the influence of divine grace made early impressions on his mind whilst young in years, which led him to love solitude and sobriety, and to shun those vices incident to youth. About the twenty-second year of his age, a dispensation of gospel ministry was committed to him. He was very awful at times in his public approach before the

the divine majesty in prayer, and often engaged to exhort friends to humility, and to shun arrogancy and pride, being a good example herein himself; so that his upright innocent deportment, gained him the good esteem of his friends and others. He departed this life, the 7th of the seventh month 1761, aged fifty-three, a minister 31 years, and was buried at Evesham.

A Testimony from Haddonfield *Monthly-Meeting in* New-Jersey, *concerning* ELIZABETH ESTAUGH.

SHE was daughter of John and Elizabeth Haddon, friends of London; born in the year 1682, her parents gave her a liberal education; who having an estate in lands in this province, proposed coming over to settle; and in order thereto, sent persons over to make suitable preparation for their reception; but they being prevented from coming, this our friend with her father's consent, came over, and fixed her habitation where he proposed if he had come; she being then about twenty years of age, in a single state of life, and exemplary therein.

In the year 1702, she was married to our worthy friend John Estaugh, who settled with her where she then dwelt, the place being called Haddonfield, in allusion to her maiden name; there they lived together,
near

near forty years (except in that space, her several times crossing the sea to Europe, to visit her aged parents, and when he was called abroad on truth's service, to which she freely gave him up.) She was endowed with great natural abilities, which being sanctified by the spirit of Christ were much improved, whereby she became qualified to act in the affairs of the church, and was a serviceable member, having been clerk to the women's meeting near 50 years, greatly to satisfaction. She was a sincere sympathizer with the afflicted, of a benevolent disposition, and in distributing to the poor, was desirous to do it in a way most profitable and durable to them, and if possible, not to let the " Right hand know what the " left did;" and tho' in a state of affluence as to this world's wealth, was an example of plainness and moderation; zealously concern'd for maintaining good order in the church, diligent in attending meetings at home, where her service seemed principally to be, and from her awful sitting, we have good cause to believe she was an humble waiter therein, which administered edification to the solid beholder. Her heart and house was open to her friends, whom to entertain, seemed one of her greatest pleasures; was prudently cheerful, and well knowing the value of friendship, was careful not to wound it herself, nor encourage others in whispering and publishing their failings or supposed weaknesses.

Her last illness confined her about three months, being often in great bodily pain, but favoured with much calmness of mind and sweetness of spirit, which render'd her confinement more easy to herself and those with her, which affords matter of encouragement to survivors, to press after the mark of the high calling in Christ Jesus. She departed this life, the 30th of the third month 1762, as one falling asleep, full of days, like unto a shock of corn fully ripe. Her body was interr'd on the 1st of the fourth month following, in friends burying-ground at Haddonfield, being accompanied by many friends and others, where a solid meeting was held; aged about eighty-two years.

A Testimony from Woodbridge *Monthly-Meeting in* New-Jersey, *concerning* ANNA WEBSTER.

ANNA WEBSTER, an elder, wife of John Webster of Plainfield, departed this life, the 20th day of the fifth month 1762, in the thirty-sixth year of her age. She was favoured when young, to have her mind turned to him who is able to preserve all that put their trust in him; and by her obedience to the manifestations of divine light, she was enabled to conduct herself in a steady and upright manner; and in the time of her last sickness, gave much useful and

and inſtructive advice, to her huſband, children and friends. She divers times entreated her huſband, 'To give up to the Lord's 'diſpoſings, and not to be over troubled 'about her,' expreſſing, 'Her dependance 'on the Lord and reſignation to his will,' with deſires, 'That the Lord would be with 'and comfort him, and that he might ſeek 'for heavenly wiſdom, and thereby be di-'rected how to walk before the Lord, and 'bring up their children in his fear, that 'they may have a portion in heaven;' charging her children, 'To conſider the poor and 'adminiſter to their neceſſities.'

At a time, ſpeaking to her eldeſt ſon, ſhe ſaid, 'My dear child, let it never be ſaid 'of thee, "The foxes have holes, and the "birds of the air have neſts, but the ſon "of man hath not whereon to lay his head." She earneſtly importuned friends, 'To keep, 'not only themſelves, but their offspring, 'to week-day meetings, and teach them to 'wait on the Lord, that he might merci-'fully bleſs them.' Alſo recommended, 'Unity amongſt friends,' expreſſing, 'Her 'ſorrow in the breach thereof,' and urged cloſely, 'The neceſſity of living in love;' entreating friends, 'To notice her huſband 'and children in their diſtreſs, and watch 'over and adviſe her children, not ſparing 'to tell them their faults.'

She adviſed her children, 'In all their 'undertakings to ſeek the Lord for counſel, 'eſpecially in that of chooſing companions,' and

and exprefs'd her experience of favours received thereby, faying, 'She had often 'magnified that gracious hand which was 'with her when a poor orphan child; and 'preffed them to ferve the Lord in their 'youth, which would draw divine bleffings 'on them;' adding, 'There are excellent 'accounts of God's love to fuch as give up 'all in their youth;' and charged them, 'To avoid bad company, and keep to plain-'nefs;' ftrongly advifing, 'Againft difobe-'dience to parents.'

At a time when feveral young people were prefent, one of whom was light and airy, fhe teftified againft her vain practices in very moving expreffions, and informed her, 'That 'the enemy would incline the mind in 'meetings, to fuch vanities as were prac-'tifed out of meetings.'

She was divers times concern'd in fervent prayer and fupplication to the almighty, 'That fhe might have fure hope before her 'change, and bear patiently her diftrefs; 'and for the poor afflicted feed, that the 'Lord's work might be carried on in the 'earth, and that he would deftroy all the 'inventions of the enemy, which lead peo-'ple to fin againft him.' Many more deep and weighty expreffions fhe uttered, which for brevity fake are omitted.

May the dying penetrating language of one whofe general conduct was virtuous, have a proper impreffion on our minds, and ftir us up to prepare for our great and final change, is our fincere defire.

A Teftimony

A Testimony from Chesterfield Monthly-Meeting in New-Jersey, concerning SARAH MURFIN.

THIS worthy woman was one whom it pleased the Lord, to call out of the broad way and vanities of the world, and make acquainted with his blessed truth; and as she abode under the cross, it pleased the almighty to manifest unto her, that she was a chosen vessel or instrument for his service, to preach the gospel. She was fervent in prayer, serviceable in visiting families, and her godly example in life and conversation, great humility and self-denial, much adorned her ministry; careful to bring up her family in the fear of the Lord, and in plainness of speech and apparel; being indeed a mother in Israel.

We fervently desire that the great Lord of the harvest, may be pleased to continue to his church and people, a living ministry; and that many may be made willing to run his errands and be serviceable in his hand, as was this our worthy friend, who departed this life, the 26th of the seventh month 1762, aged about seventy-six years.

A Testimony

A Testimony from Rahway *Monthly-Meeting in* New-Jersey, *concerning* ELEANOR SHOTWELL.

ELEANOR SHOTWELL, late wife of Jacob Shotwell of Rahway, was a tender hearted friend, and encouraged such as sought the Lord. She was an elder of sound judgment, concern'd for the church's welfare, and that Zion might be restored to her primitive beauty, and was a pattern of plainness and self-denial. In the ninth month 1762, being on her journey to attend the yearly-meeting at Philadelphia, a friend mentioned the danger of going to said city, on account of an infectious distemper then prevalent there; to which she replied, ' She had no
' fear on that account, and that it was no
' matter where we departed the world, so
' that we were in our duty.' She accordingly went to the meeting and attended the sittings of it, until she was suddenly seized with a violent disorder, attended with extreme pain near three days, which she bore with a calm and even mind. To a friend who visited her, she said, ' She was almost
' gone, and in great pain of body, but ex-
' ceeding peace of mind.' At another time said, ' It was satisfactory that her peace was
' made with the Lord, and that it would be
' terrible to have a wounded conscience at
' such a time to struggle with.' Concerning her husband and children whom she dearly loved,

loved, she said, 'Though she was not like to
'see them more, she was glad in the Lord,
'that she had given up to attend the yearly-
'meeting;' expressing her desire, 'That her
'offspring should be brought up in plain-
'ness, and that friends watchful care might
'be over them; and that her husband might
'be preserved in self-denial, and humble re-
'signation to the Lord's will in all his trials.'

She departed this life, on the 2d day of the tenth month 1762, in the forty-sixth year of her age, and was interr'd in friends burying-ground at Philadelphia.

A Testimony from Burlington *Monthly-Meeting in* New-Jersey, *concerning* PETER FEARON.

HE was the son of John and Elizabeth Fearon, of Great-Broughton, in Cumberland, and born in or about the year 1683. He came amongst friends on a principle of convincement, during his apprenticeship with his uncle Peter Fearon, and appeared in a few words in meetings before he was twenty years of age. In the latter end of 1703, with the concurrence of friends, he left England, and landed in Virginia, where he staid about three months, then came to Burlington in the second month 1704, and from that time until his decease, he was a useful member of this meeting.

Between

Between the years 1704 and 1730, he travelled in the service of the gospel, through most parts of this continent where meetings were then settled, and to some provinces several times; and employed above two years in visiting friends in England, Scotland and Ireland; returning with satisfactory certificates of the approbation and unity of friends with his religious labours.

After those travels, his worldly circumstances being attended with difficulties, and his desires earnest that he might get through them with credit, he went many voyages to sea as a factor, chiefly to Boston and the island of Barbados; and thro' many difficulties, he was enabled to pay his debts, and to save sufficient, with industry and care, to yield a comfortable subsistance in old age, and to be helpful to some others. In those undertakings he took certificates, and returned such as were very satisfactory, both of his diligence in his outward business, and of his care to edify the churches with the gift of ministry which had been committed to him. Whilst in Barbados in the beginning of 1746, a concern came upon him to visit friends on Tortola, which by their large and full certificate, appears to have been very seasonable; and was the first after our worthy friends Thomas Chalkley, John Cadwallader and John Estaugh, had laid down their heads in peace among them. They say, ' He came in a needful time, as
' a cloud

' a cloud full of rain upon a thirfty land,
' greatly to our mutual comfort and joy in
' the Lord, and in one another.'

One of his laft voyages by fea, was in 1750, and on purpofe to perform a religious vifit to friends in Barbados and Tortola, having our friend Thomas Lancafter for his companion; and when they had performed their fervice, the faid friend was, after a fharp ficknefs, removed by death at fea. Befides this, he met with other fore trials in his pilgrimage through life, particularly in the long confinement of his wife, who was feized with the palfy five years before her death, and lay moft of that time entirely helplefs. His behaviour towards her, was as an affectionate hufband, with much tendernefs and care; and indeed his frequent practice of vifiting the fick and afflicted, evidenced a fympathizing heart, and was very becoming his ftation.

He was preferved in the exercife of his miniftry, in much love and gofpel fimplicity. And his fenfe of the nature and fpirit in which the difcipline fhould be managed, is thus exprefs'd in an epiftle which he wrote to friends on Tortola, viz. ' That you may
' grow up together a fpiritual houfe that
' holinefs becomes, and a care according to
' gofpel order may be kept to amongft you,
' and that no harfhnefs be ufed one towards
' another, but tender and helpful, and not
' apt to judge or cenfure one another, that
' you may be kept in that univerfal fpirit
                                        ' of

'of love, that seeks the good of all and hurt of none, and yet gives all their due, and what is right and just.'

His diligence in attending religious meetings was remarkable, for though he lived three miles from the particular meeting of Burlington to which he belonged, it was very uncommon for bodily infirmities, or any extremities of weather to keep him at home on meeting days; and the year before his decease, he visited several general meetings both in this and the neighbouring provinces.

A life so spent in fervent endeavours to promote truth and righteousness among mankind, was, we have cause to hope, in a suitable preparation to be closed at a short warning. He was seized with a fit by his own fire side, which quickly deprived him of understanding, and about three days after he breathed his last, on the 21st of the twelfth month 1762, in the seventy-ninth year of his age, having been a minister about 60 years. He was interr'd on the 23d in friends burying-ground at Burlington, after a solid meeting held on the occasion.

Having observed strict temperance and moderation, he finished his course in a good old age; being an example of prudence and steadiness, which we desire may be often remembred, and usefully improved to the advantage of such as are left behind.

A Testimony

A Testimony from Shrewsbury *Monthly-Meeting in* New-Jersey, *concerning* Thomas Tilton.

ON the 4*th* day of the first month 1763, died our friend Thomas Tilton, in the seventy-ninth year of his age. Some of whose last expressions were as follows, viz.

'That his passage was very long and
' hard, and many times prayed God to car-
' ry him through, that his poor wife's trou-
' ble was greater for him than she could
' well endure, and that he was not insensi-
' ble, she laboured for him both in body
' and mind.' Some time after he said, ' It
' was a comfort to him to see his children
' concerned for themselves,' and desired them, ' To keep to their duties, for there
' was a falling away of some, but that they
' might not neglect theirs; that they would
' live in love and in the fear of the Lord,
' which would be to their advantage, but
' to live loose and wanton would make hard
' work on a dying bed;' observing, ' That
' people thought too little of their latter end,
' although they think of it sometimes, it
' soon goes out of their minds.' Then prayed, ' That the Lord would carry him
' through,' saying, ' His passage was very
' hard, and his pain and affliction great;
' yet his peace was steady, for the Lord did
' not charge him with any thing.'

A Testimony

A Testimony from Rahway *Monthly-Meeting in* New-Jersey, *concerning* Elizabeth Haydock.

OUR friend Elizabeth Haydock, late wife of James Haydock, of Rahway, was religiously inclined from her youth, and an early pattern of self-denial and plainness to those of her age and sex. Being called to the work of the ministry, it became a trial to her, and such a cross to her own will to give up to the Lord's work, that she was ready to give way to consultations, and on account of her own incapacity and frailties, to question its being his call; so that (as she expressed) could she have found peace, she would rather have chosen death than obedience; but finding the love of God, as it is abode in, to be stronger than the world, she yielded thereto; and confiding in the Lord alone, came forth an instrument of his own preparing; and continuing to walk in the way of self-denial, she grew in her gift, increasing both in understanding and utterance to the close of her days.

In her last illness, she signified, ' She had ' near done with time, and was fully resign- ' ed;' and departed this life, in the seventh month 1763, in the twenty-seventh year of her age, and the 4*th* of her ministry.

A Testimony

A Testimony from Exeter *Monthly-Meeting in* Pennsylvania, *concerning* Ellis Hugh.

THOUGH few of us were personally acquainted with this our dear ancient friend in the early part of his life, yet as we have information by good authorities, of some things remarkable therein, we think it not amiss to transmit some hints of them, with what hath fallen out within the compass of our knowledge concerning him.

He was born in Merionethshire, in the principality of Wales, and came over with his parents into Pennsylvania, when about twelve years of age.

He was naturally of a very cheerful disposition, and for some time indulged himself in keeping company with such, whose conversation and conduct were unprofitable and vain, for which, though we do not understand he was guilty of immoral practices, he was closely reproved by the witness of God in secret, and his condition being thereby plainly manifested to him, as likewise the danger of pursuing such courses, he did not dare to go any longer in vanity; but submitting to the reproofs of instruction, was brought under great exercise and godly sorrow; in which state, the conversation of his former companions, once his delight, became a burden and increased his distress; but avoiding to feed their light airy dispositions, keeping his mind retired, and reading

ing the holy scriptures, when they sought to entice him, had such an effect, that they forsook him, which was a great ease to his mind, in that it afforded him opportunity for a further search after the will of him, who in mercy had called him to glory and virtue. As he was thus engaged, after many deep baptisms and trials, it pleased the Lord, about the thirty-fourth year of his age, to call him to the work of the ministry; which was an exceeding humbling exercise to him, and many sore conflicts he had therein, through the buffetings of Satan; but by endeavouring to follow the Lord in the way of his requirings, help was administred, so that he at times, had to experience, that he gives "The oil of joy for mourning, and " the garment of praise for the spirit of " heaviness."

His chief inducement to come and settle in these parts, was a strong draught of love attending his mind, which however he did not hastily give way to, having felt drawings hither near eight years before he came; of so great moment did the removing himself and family appear to him.

He was a diligent attender of first and week day meetings for worship, as also of our monthly, quarterly and yearly meetings, even when age and infirmity of body rendered travelling very difficult to him. He likewise visited some of the neighbouring provinces on truth's service, with the unity of friends; and by accounts which

we

we have had from the places he vifited, his labours of love were well received and ferviceable.

From the time of his coming amongft us, he was always one of the number, who went on the vifit to friends families; which weighty work he undertook in much diffidence of himfelf, and fear of a forward fpirit, often faying, ' That former appoint-
' ments and engagements thereto, were of
' no account for future fervices; but that
' fuch as went, muft wait for renewed
' qualifications to enter upon that work,' which he ufed to fay, ' He thought muft
' be a good one, fince it occafioned greater
' nearnefs, and was a renewal of love, both
' among vifitors and vifited:' And by accounts received, it was fo in a good degree.

In meetings for worfhip he was a good example in filent patient waiting upon the Lord, and when raifed to bear a public teftimony, it was with that power and authority, which accompanies a true gofpel minifter, and hath made lafting impreffions upon fome minds. Though he was of an exceeding tender difpofition, yet being a lover of good order in the church, and well knowing the dangerous tendency of undue liberty, he both by precept and example, endeavoured to promote the former and difcourage the latter; in which he gave repeated proofs, that the near connections of natural kindred did not bias his judgment.

His deportment being meek and loving, and his converfation familiar and inftructively cheerful, gained him the efteem of moft who knew him, of different ranks and religious perfuafions. He was a nurfing father in the church, and particularly fo to divers whom the Lord had vifited that were under affliction, whether of body or mind; nor was his charity in this refpect confined to the members of our fociety.

He was an affectionate hufband, a tender parent, a kind mafter; and having, by the bleffing of divine providence on his honeft induftry, obtained a competency of the neceffaries of life, was very hofpitable, entertaining both friends and others freely and kindly, not with oftentation or for applaufe, but for the promotion of piety and virtue, and the good of mankind.

As his natural ftrength abated in the laft years of his life, he appeared more bright and lively in his public miniftry, both at home and abroad; and the day he was taken ill of his laft ficknefs, at the funeral of one of his fons, which was the laft meeting he was at, he was remarkably favoured in his public teftimony to a large gathering of people; and in fupplication at the fame meeting, his great Lord and mafter was pleafed to favour him with a tranfcendent view into the beauty of holinefs, crowning a life, a great part of which had been, according to the meafure received, devoted to his honour, with evident tokens of his being near to to the kingdom of rest and peace everlasting. And the same evening he was taken ill at his own house in Exeter aforesaid, and continued for about eleven days, mostly in extreme pain, yet bore it with patience and resignation to the divine will; and though he inclined much to be still and quiet, uttered many comfortable expressions, some of which were taken down in writing. At one time he said, ' It is a fine thing to have a ' clear conscience.' And one morning, ' Here is another day, Lord so preserve me ' through it, that I may do nothing to of- ' fend thee.' In the evening he said, ' Lord ' bless this night to me.' And taking something to give him ease, he said. ' He that ' turned water into wine is able to give a ' blessing.' After laying still some time, said, ' Sorrow at night, but joy cometh in the ' morning.' And in the morning he said, ' I remember a dream I had about fifty ' years ago, I thought I was in a room alone, ' just going to die, and as I was much con- ' cerned and troubled because there was no ' one present to see me die, I thought the ' great physician of value stood by me and ' said, *I will be with thee;* and I have a lit- ' tle faith, that he will be with me, and if ' I am favoured with my senses, hope I shall ' not give over wrestling for a blessing.' A little before noon he said, ' Lord, this is ' the way of mortal men, when they come ' to lie on a sick bed, they crave thy favour, ' though at other times many are forgetful 'of thee.' At another time he said, 'Though affliction may not seem pleasant during its continuance, yet it worketh an exceeding great joy to them that love and fear God.' And in the evening, being in great bodily pain, said, 'Lord give me ease if it be thy blessed will.' The next day being the first day of the week, several friends came to see him before meeting, to whom he said, 'Fear God and serve him, and his regard will be unto you, but if you neglect to worship him, he will cast you off forever,' or words nearly to that import. And being fearful they would over stay the time for meeting, inquired what hour, saying to them, 'Don't neglect the business of the Lord:' And when they were going, desired, 'They would remember him when it was well with them.' In the evening inquiring what sort of a meeting they had that day, and being answered, a good meeting; he said with seeming joy, 'The Lord is not limited to persons, but all that worship him aright shall be accepted of him,' or words to that effect. A little after midnight, being in great bodily pain, and from the symptoms, it was thought for about an hour he was departing, during which he appeared to have his mind retired to the Lord, and then reviving a little said, 'This has been a blessed meeting.' The next morning taking leave of a neighbour, he said, 'Farewell, and if we never meet again in this world, I hope we shall meet in a 'more

' more glorious place among the righteous.' The day before his departure his speech failed much, tho' he remained very sensible; and the last words he was heard to say, were, ' Lord in heaven receive my soul.' Then growing weaker until the third hour next morning, being the 11th of the first month 1764, he departed this life, in a quiet frame of mind, aged seventy-six years and some months. His corps was interr'd in friends burying-ground at Exeter aforesaid, accompanied by a large number of his friends and neighbours.

A Testimony from Bradford *Monthly-Meeting in* Pennsylvania, *concerning* MARY PENNEL.

SHE was born in Radnorshire, in Wales, and educated by her parents in the profession of the church of England. About the thirteenth year of her age, going with her elder sister to a meeting of friends, who were sitting in awful silence, with tears dropping down the cheeks of divers, it made such religious impression on her tender mind, that she thereby became in some degree, convinced of the truth. About the sixteenth year of her age, she arrived in Pennsylvania, where living in a friend's family, and experiencing the renewed visits of truth, she became willing to come more closely under the discipline of the cross, and

joined

joined with friends; was married to John Pennel, and resided within the compass of Concord meeting many years. Being divers years under a weighty exercise to appear in public ministry, about the year 1722, she gave up thereto, and increasing in her gift, had in time, a refreshing edifying testimony; being well approved by her friends at home, and frequently led into the states of meetings where her lot was cast; in the exercise of the ministry she travelled into the eastern provinces, also into Great-Britain and Ireland, where in divers places, she had acceptable service, to the strengthening some tender minds in the way and work of truth. Afterwards removing with her husband to East Caln, they resided there the remainder of their time; and several years before her decease, her understanding by reason of age, became weak, yet she was preserv'd in much innocency, having a love and regard to friends, and was always pleased with their visits.

She died the 10th day of the fifth month 1764, and was interr'd in friends burying-ground at East Caln aforesaid, aged eighty-six years.

An additional Testimony concerning MARY PENNEL, *by a friend from* Great-Britain.

HAVING read the preceeding memorial, concerning our worthy deceased friend Mary Pennel, it is in my heart to make a
small

small addition thereto. In the course of her travels in England, she visited friends at Ipswich in Suffolk, and had good and acceptable service there, among a number of young persons who were newly convinced of the truth. Her conversation was solid and instructive, accompanied with sweetness of spirit, and having obtained to a considerable growth in experimental religion, she spoke in a feeling effectual manner to our inward states. At a certain time giving some account of her own convincement, she said, 'In her very young days, she was a watch- ful observer of the conduct of friends at markets and public places, that she might see whether in their dealings they kept to the principle of truth, of which she was convinced; and seeing their words were few and savoury, their countenances and behaviour weighty, and that they were just and upright in their commerce amongst men, it had a great tendency to confirm and establish her mind in the truth she had embraced.'

I. H.

A Testimony from the Monthly-Meeting of Philadelphia, *concerning* RACHEL PEMBERTON.

SHE was born at Burlington, in West-New-Jersey, in the year 1691, being the daughter of Charles Read, who was one of the early settlers of Pennsylvania under the

the grant to William Penn. It pleased the Lord to extend his gracious visitation to her in her tender age, which as she submitted to and abode under, she happily experienced to lead her into a life of righteousness and great circumspection. About the eighteenth year of her age, she was married to our worthy friend Israel Pemberton, who united with her in a pious concern for the prosperity and prevalence of the cause of truth, her sincere love to which and the friends thereof, she uniformly manifested by her kind sympathetic care as a "Mother in Israel." She usefully filled the station of an overseer and elder, being carefully concerned to rule her own family well, and that her offspring might have a portion in that treasure which faileth not. She was a true sympathizer with those under affliction of body or mind, demonstrating her sensibility herein, by her frequent visits to such, which were weighty and comforting, her conversation being solid and instructive.

In the first month 1754, it pleased divine providence to deprive her of her beloved husband, in whom was removed, a father, a friend, and counsellor to her and the church; which close trial (after 40 years living together in much harmony) she was enabled to bear with christian calmness and resignation; having often to experience the reality of that truth left upon record, " A father " to the fatherless, and a judge for the wi- " dow, is God in his holy habitation."

She

She continued her houfe open for the reception of friends near and from remote parts, as it had been in her hufband's time, particularly for the entertainment of thofe who came from Europe on religious vifits to America, with whom fhe was often dipt into much feeling fympathy under their weighty travel and exercife.

Few have been more zealoufly concerned, and diligent in the attendance of religious meetings, feldom allowing the inclemency of weather to prevent her; and continued to manifeft the like concern when very feeble; which diligence, was, in the time of her confinement and languifhing ftate, a fatisfactory reflection to her, as her attendance had been from a real fenfe and perfuafion of duty.

On the 22d day of the tenth month 1764, fhe attended the fecond day's meeting of minifters and elders, which was the laft meeting fhe was at, her feeble ftate requiring her confinement to her chamber the 25th, and gradually weakened; yet love to the caufe of truth continued, and her concern was great, that the profeffors thereof might live under its preferving influence.

She uttered many lively expreffions at different times in the courfe of her illnefs, in acknowledgement of the goodnefs and mercy of the Lord, ' In preferving her in ' patience under great bodily pain, and ' with an evidence of her future well-being.

She departed this life, on the 24th day of the second month 1765, and was interr'd in our burial ground in this city, on the 27th of the same month.

A Testimony from Gwynedd *Monthly-Meeting in* Pennsylvania, *concerning* ELLEN EVANS, *an elder of said meeting.*

SHE was the daughter of Rowland and Margaret Ellis, born near Dollegelle, in the principality of Wales, in the year 1685. She was favoured with a good understanding, which being improved by a religious education and strict attention to the dictates of divine grace, soon distinguished her as one seeking after heavenly treasure, which made her in riper years, an honourable member of society.

She married our worthy and much esteemed friend John Evans, of this place, to whom she was truly a help-meet, more especially in public religious services; for whenever she discovered the least inclination in him, to visit the meetings of friends whether far or near, she did all in her power to cherish and encourage the motion; she was also a great support and comfort to him under his spiritual conflicts about the time of his appearing first in a public testimony.

In her family, she was an example of piety and industry, rising early in the morning, and encouraging others so to do, often observing that those who lay late, lost the youthful beauty of the day, and wasted the most precious part of their time; that the sun was the candle of the world, which called upon us to arise and apply to our several duties. ‘ When the affairs of the morning were transacted it was almost her invariable practice, except on meeting days, to retire about noon, with the bible or some religious book; where a portion of her time was spent alone; from which retirement she often returned with evident tokens, that her eyes had been bathed in tears.

She was remarkably well acquainted with the holy scriptures, as also the writings and characters of our ancient worthy friends, together with those of her own time; frequently expressing, ‘ The many advantages
‘ she reaped from often conversing with the
‘ dead and absent; endeavouring to cultivate
‘ the same disposition in her family, by often
‘ calling them together in the winter even-
‘ ings, and requiring one of her children to
‘ read audibly in the bible or some other reli-
‘ gious book;' repeatedly observing to them,
‘ The benefit which attended preserving the
‘ characters of those faithful ministers and
‘ elders in the church, whose pious lives and
‘ happy dissolution, if held up to the view
‘ of posterity, might be a likely means of
‘ kindling the same holy zeal, and resoluti-
‘ on to tread in their footsteps.' And as ministring friends (whom she truly loved
from

from her infancy as brethren and sisters in gospel fellowship) in the course of their visits came this way, generally lodged at their house, at which times she seldom missed to prepare her family, and inform the neighbourhood of an intention to sit a while together in the evening; which select opportunities, many can yet remember, were often singularly blessed with divine comfort and edification.

Her diligence in attending meetings for religious worship, was no less manifest than her steady zeal for supporting our christian discipline, and that we might adorn the doctrine of God our Saviour in all things: Yet was her zeal mixed with charity, for having long experienced how few were qualified to lay justice precisely to the line and righteousness to the plumbline, she thought it safest rather to incline to the merciful side; firmly believing that the grace of God which bringeth salvation, had appeared unto all men; delighting to converse with our uninstructed Indians about their sentiments of the supreme being; and often said, ' She discovered evident traces of divine ' goodness in their uncultivated minds.'

In her friendships she was warm and steady, and on her death bed earnestly pressed her children, ' Not to forget the friends of ' their father and mother;' and the sensibility of her heart, made her very attentive to the wants of the poor in her neighbourhood.

Some

Some years before her decease she lost in the husband of her youth, a bosom friend, and the great support of her age, which proved so great a trial, she said, 'That if 'God whom she loved all her life long, had 'not enabled her to sustain it, she must 'have sunk under it.' This dispensation of providence weaned her from all temporal enjoyments. She continued attending meetings, and frequently visiting the sick and afflicted while her strength permitted, and when that failed, much of her time was spent in reading the holy scriptures and in meditation.

The early state of religion in this province was a grateful subject of conversation to her in the evening of her day, but upon turning her eye to the present time, she would say with a deep sigh, 'Oh! what 'is become of the morning dew and celesti- 'al rain, that used to fall and rest upon our 'assemblies.' For herself, she often prayed, 'That she might possess a lively relish of 'truth to the last, and retain the greenness 'of youth in old age, which God was gra- 'ciously pleased to favour her with.

Her last illness began about a year before her decease, in the forepart thereof she felt a lowness and depression of mind, that caused her to cry, 'Tell me, Oh! thou whom 'my soul loveth, where thou feedest, where 'thou makest thy flocks to rest at noon.' But after some time, this cloud was removed,

ed, and she was enabled to say, 'He brought me to the banqueting house, and his banner over me was love.'

And thus, by remembring her creator in the days of her youth, and a steady perseverance therein, she was enabled to meet the king of terrors with a serene countenance, and resigned her breath without a sigh or groan, the 29*th* day of the fourth month, and was buried at Gwynedd, the 2*d* of the fifth month 1765; being, we trust, admitted to the general assembly and church of the first born, which are written in heaven.

A Testimony from Kingwood *Monthly-Meeting in* New-Jersey, *concerning* SAMUEL LARGE.

OUR ancient friend Samuel Large, departed this life, the 9*th* of the sixth month 1765, and was buried the 11*th* of said month, in friends burying-ground at Kingwood, aged about seventy-seven years, having been a minister upwards of 40 years. He was religiously inclined when young, insomuch (as he related) that at times he thought he could freely declare to others of the goodness and merciful dealings of God to his soul; but for want of giving diligent heed to the inshinings of that divine light which had measurably
redeemed

redeemed him, he suffered a loss of that sweet and heavenly communion which he had been made a sharer of, and began to join with folly and vanity, which youth are apt to do; but in process of time, being revisited by an all-merciful God, he gave up to bear the cross; and about the thirtieth year of his age, was made willing to bear a public testimony, and declare to others what God had done for him; which testimony was living and powerful, and tended to the refreshing and watering the Lord's heritage and people; being often concern'd where his lot was cast, to invite and persuade people to seek the Lord for themselves, that they might know the work of regeneration wrought and compleated in and for themselves. He freely gave up to spend both time and substance on truth's account when called thereto, having visited several provinces on this continent, and some of them divers times. He was a generous kind friend, ready to do good to all, especially the household of faith, very ready in assisting the servants and messengers of Christ when travelling on that account; bringing up his children in the principles of the christian religion, and in plainness of speech and apparel, a great encourager of his family and others in attending meetings, that they might discharge their duties which they owed to their maker. In the latter part of his days, when old and infirm, he met with exercises and difficulties,

ties, yet we have good reason to believe, he was carried through them all, and died in peace with the Lord and goodwill to all mankind, and is enter'd into rest, and reaps the reward of the faithful, where trouble and exercise are at an end. He had a sight of his approaching exit, and gave orders that his burial should be plain. Some of the last words he utter'd, were to his wife, a few hours before he expired, when he said, 'All is done that is needful, now I must 'leave thee.'

A Testimony from New-Garden *Monthly-Meeting in* Pennsylvania, *concerning* WILLIAM MOTT.

OUR worthy friend William Mott, of Mamaroneck in New-York government, being on a religious visit to friends in this province; after attending our yearly-meeting at Philadelphia, intended proceeding to Nottingham, and on his way thither, was at our monthly-meeting in the tenth month 1765; where, after a time of silence, he appeared in a short yet satisfactory testimony; but being much indisposed, left the meeting in a few minutes afterwards, and went to a friend's house, where his disorder, which proved to be the small pox, increased and lay heavy upon him. Two days afterwards, some friends going to visit him, he mention'd mention'd his defire of having a time of retirement together, in which opportunity he exprefs'd in a lively and fenfible manner, his refignation to the will of God refpecting his indifpofition, and fpoke of the great advantage it would be to the members of our fociety, if they were more drawn from the fpirit and friendfhip of the world, and the eager purfuit after the riches and grandeur thereof; faying, that the profeffors of truth fuffered great lofs in a fpiritual fenfe, for want of being often deeply inward, when about their lawful callings, labouring to have their minds retired, where true comfort and inftruction is to be witneffed; and that friends who are heads of families, ought to wait for the movings of truth, to make way for them to call their children and fervants together; and if this was but the engagement of their minds, way would be made for fuch opportunities beyond their expectation. On which and fome other fubjects, he, at that time, fpoke in a fenfible humble manner.

At other times he frequently mention'd his uneafinefs in beholding, that many of the profeffors of truth did not keep within the bounds of true moderation refpecting cloathing and furniture, but rather pleafed the natural difpofition, to no real advantage, and confumed much precious time that might be profitably fpent in doing good among mankind; faying, that if friends lived near enough to the inward teacher that difcovers things to be as they really are; there are many things amongft us termed fmall or trifling, which would appear inconfiftent with the pure truth.

Notwithftanding his affliction was great, yet he bore it with remarkable patience, appearing more concern'd for the glory of God and the good of his church and people, than any temporal confiderations: And frequently exprefs'd his refignation to the divine will, being freely given up either for life or death. The retired frame of mind he generally appeared in, was inftructive; often faying he felt eafy in mind, having witneffed a comfortable refrefhing feafon, and exprefs'd his thankfulnefs for fuch peculiar favour in fo trying a difpenfation: Yet he had no other profpect but that he fhould recover, until a few hours before his deceafe, when he fignified, ' He had almoft ' done with time.' And changing faft, he quietly departed, the 15*th* of the tenth month 1765, in a fenfible compofed frame of fpirit. On the 17*th* his corpfe, accompanied by many friends, was interr'd in friends burying-ground in New-Garden, after a folid meeting.

A Teftimony

A Testimony from the Quarterly-Meeting of Philadelphia, *concerning our esteemed friend* MARGARET ELLIS, *late of* Radnor *meeting, deceased.*

SHE was born in the principality of Wales, of parents professing episcopacy, and religious in that way. By a short memorial she hath left, of some occurrences in her life, we find, she was early visited by the almighty, which she expresses in this manner. 'At fourteen years of age, the 'call of the Lord was to me, when seeing 'some of my companions carried to the 'grave, a concern came over my mind, 'with a consideration, whither their souls 'were gone, and where mine would be, if 'I should then be taken away; and that 'followed and remained with me for many 'days:' But being young and not willing to bear the cross, the witness for God was so far suppressed, that she gave way to follow the vanities and diversions of the world; yet the Lord did not forget her; but some years after, the visitation was renewed, and then, she says, 'I returned in earnest 'to look within, to my own state and con- 'dition, and to the anointing mentioned 'by the apostle John, which opened clearly 'in my mind.' This brought her to a close exercise, and often in secret prayer, that the Lord would be pleased to manifest her duty. Soon after this, she went to visit a brother

brother at Dolobran, who had a short time before joined in communion with friends; and being at a meeting, she was further reached unto, and the thoughts of her heart declared by a worthy minister then present. Her father took pains to dissuade her from joining friends, and got several priests to assist him with their endeavours, but being enlightened to see the formality and deadness of the profession of religion in which she had been educated, and the blindness and emptiness of their priests, she aquainted her father, 'She would never come more 'to their church, unless it was to his and her 'mother's burial.'

In a few years after this, she found a concern to appear in public testimony in friends meetings, and soon afterwards removed to this province; in which she apprehended a divine direction, believing the Lord would go along with her, which she experienced to her comfort, and was cordially received by friends; increasing in the gift bestowed on her.

She passed through various baptisms and trials in her young years in her native land, and many conflicts and exercises afterwards, yet experienced the arm of the Lord revealed for her help and support.

She was a sincere hearted woman, diligent in the exercise of her gift, which was in much plainness and simplicity. She visited the meetings frequently in some parts of this province and New-Jersey; and in the

year

year 1752, with the concurrence of friends, embarked in order to vifit friends in fome parts of Great-Britain, which fhe performed, and was in feveral places engaged to vifit many of the families of friends; which as we have underftood, were acceptable and ferviceable. She was favoured to return, and continued lively in the exercife of her gift.

Being taken ill in Philadelphia, in the eleventh month 1765, immediately after our quarterly-meeting which fhe attended, after a few days illnefs, fhe departed this life. She had divers times, to her particular friends, expreffed her defire, if it was the Lord's will, to finifh her days in this city; and in her ficknefs expreffed her willingnefs to depart, but requefted fhe might be favoured with fome interval of eafe from extreme pain, that fhe might take her leave of her friends, which was granted her. She uttered many lively and favoury expreffions in her ficknefs, was favoured with an evidence of her future well-being, and as fhe lived in the fear of God, we doubt not fhe was accepted of him, and enjoys the reward of her faithfulnefs.

She died the 13*th* of the eleventh month 1765, in a good old age; her body was carried to our meeting-houfe in High-Street, and after a folid meeting, buried the 15*th* in friends grave-yard.

A Teftimony

A Testimony from Nottingham *Monthly-Meeting in* Pennsylvania, *concerning* DINAH JAMES.

SHE was born the 7*th* of the sixth month 1699, near Chester, in the county of Chester in Pennsylvania. When she was about five years old, her parents John and Hannah Churchman, removed and settled at Nottingham, in the county aforesaid; and she being religiously educated by them, soon became inwardly sensible of the blessed truth; and taking heed to its teaching, was early adorned thereby with a meek and quiet spirit; was a great lover of meetings for the worship of God, and a humble exemplary waiter therein. About the thirty-fourth year of her age she appeared in the ministry, and being faithful in her gift, though she did not increase in many words, and but seldom appeared therein, being rather a pattern of awful silence, yet her testimony when she did appear, was remarkably seasoned with the baptising power of the spirit, which made it truly acceptable to friends. She was often heard to express her apprehension of the danger of words increasing in the church, without sufficient weight and awfulness; and at different times, especially in the latter years of her life, both in public testimony and in private, she spoke of a winnowing time at hand, wherein she apprehended the chaff was to be blown away, and

and the church reftored to as great, if not a greater degree of purity than heretofore; which is now frefh in the memory of divers perfons.

She was an example of plainnefs herfelf, and careful prudently to fupprefs the contrary in her children, as long as they remained under her immediate care, meekly diffuading in a moving manner, againft any appearance of corruption in converfation, as well as the world's vain fafhions and fuperfluity in drefs; firmly maintaining parental authority in this fteady refolution which fhe never departed from, viz. that while her children were clothed at her expence, they fhould fubmit to have their clothes fafhioned agreeable to her mind. She was no lefs remarkable for humility and charity, a promoter of good order in the church, and of true peace upon the right foundation; for which virtues fhe gained the general efteem of her friends and others.

Between the years 1742 and 1754, fhe vifited moft of the meetings of friends in Pennfylvania, New-Jerfey, Long-Ifland and the Eaftern-fhore of Maryland. Her care to attend meetings was memorable and worthy of imitation, even when under great bodily weaknefs and infirmity, as fhe was for many years in the latter part of her life, feveral of her joints being greatly affected with the violence of rheumatic pains; all which fhe bore with fuch patience and humble refignation of mind, as truly becomes a

chriftian

christian, and bespoke a well grounded hope of a lasting habitation at the end of a weary pilgrimage in this world.

She was at meeting a few weeks before her decease, but feeling much bodily weakness, she expressed her doubt of ever coming again; having at divers times before manifested a sense of her end being near. About five days before her decease she was seized with a fever and inward pains, which weakened her very fast. The night before she died she had several refreshing naps of sleep, and on awaking was often heard quietly to repeat these words, 'A happy change, a happy change;' and about the 8*th* hour on the 1*st* of the first month 1766, she quietly departed, as one falling asleep, being cheerful and sensible almost to the last moments of life; in the sixty-seventh year of her age, a minister about 33 years; and on the 3*d* of the same month, was interr'd in the burying-ground of friends at East-Nottingham.

A Testimony from Sadsbury *Monthly-Meeting in* Pennsylvania, *concerning* MARY MOORE.

OUR well esteemed friend Mary Moore, late wife of James Moore, and daughter of Joseph and Sarah Wildman, of Bucks county, was born the 8*th* day of the eighth month 1720, she was adorn'd with a meek and

and quiet spirit, favour'd with a gift in the ministry, whose testimony was generally well received, her words being few and savoury, and her awful deportment and exemplary conduct both at home and abroad, worthy of imitation. About a year before her decease she was taken with a lingering disorder, in which time of weakness she was often tenderly affected, advising her children and others, 'To prepare for their latter end, 'and not leave their work behind hand;' observing, in an humble manner, what an awful bowed people we ought to be.

About four hours before her departure many friends came to see her, whom she earnestly beholding, desired they would sit down, that they might truly wait in God's fear, and that those who knew how to wait would get deep in true silence: At which time, notwithstanding her great weakness, she was divinely favoured, and her tongue loosed to leave her last testimony, saying, 'Friends, if you love God, he will love you, 'and if you do not love God, how can you 'expect to be beloved of him?' Adding, 'If you would gather your families more 'often together, and sit down in his fear, 'and wait in true silence, to have your 'minds drawn from this world, you would 'grow in the truth,' with more to the same effect, desiring they might remember her words. After which she desired her husband would freely give her up and not mourn after her, at the same time encouraged

raged him to faithfulness, and defired friends would be ftill and quiet until her departure. Being fenfible to the laft, fhe quietly expired the 13th of the feventh month 1766, and was interr'd in friends burying-ground at Sadfbury, aged forty-five years.

A Teftimony from Haddonfield *Monthly-Meeting in* New-Jerfey, *concerning* THOMAS REDMAN.

HE was born in the city of Philadelphia, the 31ft of the third month 1714, and being ftripped of his parents when young, was placed apprentice in faid city, after which he removed and fettled at Haddonfield aforefaid. About the twenty-fecond year of his age, he appeared in the miniftry, and we believe laboured faithfully until the conclufion of his days. He travelled into New-England on a religious vifit, in company with Edmund Peckover, of Great-Britain, who was here on a vifit to the churches in America, from whence, at his return, we received a good account of his fervices, which, with his company, was very acceptable to us. He was often deeply exercifed for the growth and profperity of truth, which we believe he truly loved. In family vifits he was much favoured with divine ability, and had to deliver fuitable advice to the benefit and refrefhment of many:

His

His teftimony was plain, found and edifying; a lowly minded feeker of divine help, which made him very ufeful in the carrying on the affairs of the church. He ruled well in his own family, bringing them up in moderation and plainnefs, and was a good example therein himfelf. Although he did not travel much in diftant parts, yet he vifited moft of the meetings in New-Jerfey and Pennfylvania. He was fometimes fervently engaged to call to the youth, for whom he was much concerned; he was prudent, charitable and benevolent, whofe houfe was open freely to receive his friends. And altho' we fenfibly feel the lofs of fo worthy a friend and member, we defire to fubmit, believing our lofs is his great gain, and that he now inherits a place prepared for the righteous.

He departed this life, at his own houfe in Haddonfield, the 23d day of the ninth month 1766, in the fifty-third year of his age, and was interr'd the 25th in friends burying-ground at Haddonfield, after a large and folid meeting on the occafion.

A Teftimony from Uwchlan *Monthly-Meeting in* Pennfylvania, *concerning* SAMUEL JOHN.

HE was born in Pembrokefhire, in the principality of Wales, in the year 1680, and educated in profeffion with the church of England, being (as we have been inform'd inform'd by those who then knew him) a sober youth, religiously inclined, and concern'd for an inward acquaintance with the Lord, who had touched his heart with a sense of his own state and condition, whence desires being raised after that which is substantial, he continued seeking for many years, and among divers professions.

He came over to Pennsylvania, in the year 1709, and some time after settled at Uwchlan aforesaid, and soon joined in society with friends, having for divers years before been under some convincement of the principle of truth as held by us; and being measurably faithful to the manifestation of grace received, the Lord was pleased to bestow upon him a dispensation of the gospel to preach, in which we believe he laboured faithfully, and became a sound and able minister: His sitting in meetings for divine worship was solid and exemplary, often in silence, tho' at times when moved thereto, doctrine hath dropped from him as the dew, and his speech distilled as the small rain, to the refreshing the hungry and thirsty soul.

He was an example of plainness and moderation, his conversation weighty and instructive, also very encouraging to such as were well minded; and divers small pieces found among his papers, which appear as the produce of his private meditations, manifest that his conversation was often in heaven, and his meditation on heavenly things.

It

It was his lot to pass through divers baptising and afflicting circumstances (occasioned by the conduct of some who ought to have been a comfort to him in his declining years) which he bore with becoming patience, and retained his greenness to the last, appearing in a sweet comfortable frame of mind; he often express'd himself in a deep, sensible and affecting manner, to some who visited him during his last weakness which continued a considerable time, being confined at home thro' bodily infirmity and old age, for near two years before his decease.

He quietly departed this life, on the 16th of the tenth month 1766, in the eighty-seventh year of his age, having been a minister about 54 years, and was buried the 18th of the said month; when a solemn meeting was held, wherein the overshadowing of truth was measurably felt, under the influence whereof the unruly were warned, and the feeble minded comforted and encouraged to persevere in the way which leads to peace.

A Testimony from New-Garden *Monthly-Meeting in* Pennsylvania, *concerning* JOHN SMITH.

HE was born at Dartmouth, in New-England, the 3d of the fourth month 1681; his parents were Presbyterians, but joined with friends in their latter years. As he he grew to years of underſtanding, the Lord was pleaſed to favour him with the knowledge of his bleſſed truth, through the divine light ſhining in his heart, whereby he became acquainted with the diſcipline of the croſs, and was, whilſt young, in a good degree weaned from the vanities and periſhing enjoyments of this world.

About the twenty-ſecond year of his age, he bore a teſtimony againſt wars and fightings, for which he was fined and ſuffered ſeven months impriſonment. In the twenty-fourth year of his age, he embark'd for England, and on his arrival there, was preſſed on board a veſſel of war, where he was kept about ſix weeks; and for refuſing to fight or be an aſſiſtant therein, he underwent ſufferings, trials and many exerciſes, but thro' the Lord's mercy and goodneſs, he was preſerved ſteady in his teſtimony, and found peace and the preſence of the Lord to be with him in a large degree, rejoicing that he was accounted worthy to ſuffer for the teſtimony of truth. He came over to Pennſylvania ſoon after, and when married, reſided ſeveral years at or near Cheſter, and about the year 1713, he removed with his family into Eaſt-Marlborough in Cheſter county, where he dwelt upwards of 40 years. About the year 1714, a meeting for worſhip was ſettled at his houſe, which continued until a meeting-houſe was built in London-Grove townſhip not far diſtant.

He

He was one whom we think dwelt near the truth, having received the fame in the love of it. His miniftry was favoury tho' not very eloquent, zealous for good order and ferviceable in the difcipline of the church. He often fpoke of the degeneracy from the primitive plainnefs confpicuous amongft friends, both in drefs and addrefs, and the great need of a reformation; expreffing his fervent defires for the reftoration of ancient purity; and being himfelf an example of plainnefs, and in converfation cheerful, inftructive and edifying; was often concern'd to ftir up the negligent to their duty, both in refpect to attendance of meetings and humble waiting therein.

He cheerfully entertained his friends, whofe company and converfation he greatly defired; and tho' in the decline of life, he met with fome afflicting occurrences, yet he bore them with a good degree of chriftian fortitude, looking over them to that which is invifible, having an eye to the recompence of reward.

The laft place of his refidence, was within the limits of New-Garden particular meeting, which he carefully attended when able; the Lord being pleafed to preferve him as a fruitful branch, frefh and green, which was manifefted by his converfation, folid deportment in meetings, and particularly in his miniftry; a fweetnefs of fpirit and lively fenfe of truth apparently attending him to the laft.

His bodily infirmities gradually increasing, he departed this life, the 24*th* of the tenth month 1766, and was buried at London-Grove aforesaid, in the eighty-sixth year of his age; and we trust he is at rest, receiving the reward of the faithful.

A Testimony from Warrington *Monthly-Meeting in* Pennsylvania, *concerning* Alexander Underwood.

HE was born in Maryland in the year 1688, and being convinced of the truth some time after he arrived to man's estate, was chosen an elder of the meeting where he then resided; afterwards removing to this then remote part of the country, in the fifty-seventh year of his age he appeared in the ministry, and travelled twice on that service to North-Carolina, of which visits we receiv'd comfortable accounts from friends there; and when at home was enabled to minister suitably to the state of the church, to the comfort of the true mourners in Zion, and encouragement of the faithful travellers. Towards the latter part of his time, his bodily strength much failed, yet he visited some of the neighbouring meetings, and families of friends, to the comfort of the faithful, his ministry continuing to be sound and lively.

In

In his last sickness he seemed much resigned, and at one time said, 'He had the 'company of his good master to comfort 'him in his affliction.' At another said, 'That he could say with the Psalmist, that 'the good hand that was with him in his 'young years, had not forsook him now in 'his old age.' And divers times signified, 'He still felt the comforter with him;' saying, 'His day's work was done.' A little before his departure, he sang praises and hallelujahs, to his great Lord and master. Then prayed for the little handful; and taking leave of all present, continued in a sweet frame of mind, singing praises until he could not be understood, and quietly departed this life, the 31st of the tenth month 1767, and was interr'd the 2d of the eleventh month, in the seventy-ninth year of his age. May we who are left behind, be engaged to follow his example, that so our end may be like unto his.

A Testimony from Bradford *Monthly-Meeting in* Pennsylvania, *concerning* ABRAHAM MARSHALL.

WE understand he was born at Gratton, in Derbyshire Old England, and educated in the profession of the church of England; in his youth he was favour'd with a visitation of divine love, but not

keeping

keeping clofe thereunto, when amongft his companions he fuffered lofs. When about fifteen or fixteen years of age, our worthy friend John Gratton being abroad in truth's fervice, was concern'd to have a meeting at a town called Alnwick, where this our friend then refided, who fo powerfully declared the truth, that he amongft divers others was convinced; and carefully abiding under the difcipline of the crofs, he in time received a part in the miniftry. About the year 1697, he came over to Pennfylvania, and for fome time refided near Derby, where he enter'd into a married ftate, and in a few years afterwards removed to the forks of Brandywine, then a new fettled part of the country, the neareft meeting being about eleven miles, which he feldom miffed attending when of ability of body; he was alfo inftrumental in fettling this called Bradford meeting, within the compafs of which he refided the remainder of his days. He was an example of plainnefs and felf denial, and concern'd for the fupport of the difcipline. He travelled into New-Jerfey and the fouthern provinces where his fervice in the miniftry was acceptable, his doctrine being found, and his life, converfation and deportment adorning the fame. When far advanced in age, his hearing and memory failing, render'd his ufefulnefs not fo extenfive as in his younger years. For fome time before his deceafe, he feemed very defirous of his change, often expreffing,
'That

' That people should so live in this world as to fit them for another.' About twenty-four hours before he died, he said to those with him, ' Let me go, let me go. People should live in love:' Then said, ' Farewell, farewell;' after three or four weeks illness or rather growing weaker with age, he departed in a composed frame of mind, on the 17*th* of the twelfth month 1767, and on the 20*th* was interr'd in friends burying-ground at Bradford. By the general account, in the ninety-seventh year of his age, but we have some reason to believe he was one hundred and three.

Mary Marshall, his widow was born in Kent in Old England, and came to America with her father when about two years and an half old. She survived her husband about fifteen months, and departed this life, after about four days illness, quiet and easy, in the eighty-seventh year of her age, leaving a good favour in our remembrance.

A Testimony from the Monthly-Meeting of Friends in Philadelphia, *concerning* BENJAMIN TROTTER, *who was born in this city, in the ninth month of the year* 1699.

HE was early visited, and reached unto by the reproofs of divine light and grace, for those youthful vanities and corrupt conversation, which by nature he was prone

prone to and purſued, to the grief of his pious mother, who was religiouſly concerned to reſtrain him; but as he became obedient to the renewed viſitations of the heavenly call, denying himſelf of thoſe things he was reproved for, he not only learned to ceaſe from doing evil, but to live in the practice of doing well; and continuing faithful, became an example of plainneſs and ſelf-denial, for which he ſuffered much ſcoffing and mocking of thoſe who had been his companions in folly; yet he neither fainted nor was turned aſide by the reproaches of the ungodly, which thus fell to his lot, for his plain teſtimony againſt their evil conduct.

In the twenty-ſixth year of his age, he appeared in the work of the miniſtry, and laboured therein in much plainneſs and godly ſincerity, adorning the doctrine he preached, by a humble circumſpect life and converſation, being exemplary in his diligence and induſtry to labour honeſtly for a livelihood, though often in much bodily infirmity and weakneſs, deſiring, as he ſometimes expreſſed, that he might owe no man any thing but love. His inoffenſive openneſs and affability, drawing many of different denominations to converſe with him, he had ſome ſeaſonable opportunities of admoniſhing and rebuking the evil doer and evil ſpeaker, which he did, in the plainneſs of an upright zeal for the promotion of piety and virtue, tempered with true brotherly kindneſs

kindness and charity; respecting not the person of the proud nor of the rich, because of his riches, but with christian freedom, declaring the truth to his neighbour, and was thus in private as well as public, a preacher of righteousness.

In his public ministry he was zealous against errors both in principle and practice, and constantly concerned to press the necessity of obedience to the principle of divine grace; a manifestation of which is given to every man; knowing, from his own experience, that it bringeth salvation to all them that obey and follow its teachings, and was frequently enabled with energy and power to bear testimony to the outward coming of our Lord Jesus Christ, his miraculous birth, his holy example in his life and precepts, and his death and sufferings at Jerusalem, by which he hath obtained eternal redemption for us.

In his public testimony a little before his last sickness, he expressed his apprehensions, that his time among us would be short, and fervently exhorted to watchfulness and care, to keep our lamps trimmed, and our lights burning, and urged the necessity of being prepared to meet the bridegroom, as not knowing at what hour he will come.

He travelled several times, and visited most of the meetings of friends in this province and New-Jersey, and some in the adjacent provinces, but was not much from home; being upwards of forty years a diligent

gent attender of our religious meetings in this city, zealously concerned for the maintaining our christian discipline in meekness and true charity, careful in the exercise of that part of pure religion, visiting the widow and fatherless in their afflictions, and often qualified to administer relief and consolation to their dejected minds.

Afflictions of divers kinds, and some very deep and exercising, fell to his lot through the course of his life, which he was enabled to bear with exemplary patience and resignation, and particularly through his last illness, in which, for upwards of six weeks, he underwent great difficulty and pain, being afflicted with the asthma and dropsy, so that he suffered much, yet was never heard to utter a murmur or complaint, but frequently expressed his thankfulness, that he had not more pain, and often engaged in prayer, that he might be preserved in patience to the end, which was graciously granted him; so that he was capable of speaking to the comfort and edification of those who visited him; and from the fervent love of the brethren, which evidently appeared thro' his life, and most conspicuously during his last illness, and even in the hour of his death, we have a well-grounded assurance that he is passed unto life, and hath received the reward of the righteous.

His body was attended by a great number of friends and others, his fellow-citizens of divers religious denominations, to our meeting-house ing-houfe in High-Street, on the 24*th* of the third month, 1768, and after a folemn meeting, was interr'd in our burial-ground in this city.

A Teftimony from Richland *Monthly-Meeting in* Pennfylvania, *concerning* EDWARD ROBERTS.

HE was born in Merionethfhire, in the principality of Wales, in the third month 1687, and came into Pennfylvania about the twelfth year of his age; was early convinced of the principle of truth as held forth by friends, with whom he joined in communion, and by his godly life and converfation through the courfe of his time, was nearly united to them. His miniftry was attended with divine fweetnefs and energy, labouring faithfully therein to the comfort and edification of the living whilft health and bodily ability continued; being a lively example of humility, plainnefs, temperance, meeknefs and charity, and of juftice and uprightnefs in his dealings amongft men, which gained him the love and efteem of people of all denominations. He was a tender affectionate hufband and father, earneftly concern'd to train up his children and family in the fear of God, and example and inftruct them in the paths of virtue, and alfo manifefted a true zeal for promoting and
preferving

preserving peace and good order in society, wherein he was often singularly serviceable. His bodily strength gradually diminishing, he was reduced even to a child's state, in which he quietly departed this life, without much sickness, on the 25th of the eleventh month 1768, in the eighty-second year of his age; a minister above 40 years.

A Testimony from Abington *Monthly-meeting in* Pennsylvania, *concerning* MARY KNIGHT.

SHE was the daughter of John and Mary Carver, who came from England in the year 1682, and was born in or near Philadelphia soon after her parents arrived, being one of the first children born of English parents in Pennsylvania. Her parents settled at Byberry in Philadelphia county, and educated her in our religious profession. When about eighteen years old, she married Isaac Knight and became a member of Abington particular meeting: Some time after she appear'd in meetings in a few words in simplicity and innocency, and in the exercise of her gift tho' small, visited divers meetings in some of the adjacent provinces, from whence she generally produced accounts of friends acceptance of her services: And continuing in a steady perseverance, according to her talent, as she advanced to old age, her zeal for the cause of truth and good

good of souls manifestly increased; frequently recommending faithfulness, and a daily watchfulness against the enemy of souls, whom she often said, 'Was unwearied, and had followed her all her life long, being yet as busy as ever, to draw her mind from off her watch;' she would frequently express, that she had great cause of thankfulness to the God and father of all our mercies, who had supported her through many besetments, with his gracious promise, that if she would be faithful according to the measure of grace bestowed, he would be with her to the end.

Towards the close of her days, bodily weakness increased, yet she was remarkably diligent in attending meetings, and with ardency exhorted all, ' To come taste and ' see for themselves that the Lord is good, ' for he had been good indeed to her soul,' with other expressions tending to encourage well-doing. She seemed so fill'd with love to God, love to her friends, and love to her fellow creatures in general, that we have reason to believe God was with her, and that her last days were her best days. A good end crowns all.

She departed this life, the 4*th* of the third month 1769, and was buried at Abington the 6*th* of the same month, aged near eighty-seven years.

A Testimony

A Testimony from Abington *Monthly-Meeting in* Pennsylvania, *concerning* THOMAS WOOD.

OUR said friend was born in England, of parents not professing with us, who brought him over with them when very young, and resided in New-Jersey in the early settlement of that province. Soon after he became capable of religious consideration, he was convinced of the principle of truth as professed by us, on which account he underwent the displeasure of, and some severities from his father, but being steady and prudent in conduct, and faithful to his convincement, he at length so gained on his father's affections, that after some time he became reconciled and friendly to him.

He became a member of this monthly, and of Abington particular meeting, on or about the thirtieth year of his age, and so continued to the end of his life, being always, when at home and in health, a constant attender of those meetings, tho' living at a considerable distance therefrom.

When about forty-eight years of age, he appeared in the ministry, and became a faithful labourer therein according to ability. He had little or no school-learning, yet delighted much in hearing the scriptures read, and often promoted the reading of them in his family; by means whereof and a retentive memory, he sometimes, thro' the assistance of divine grace, quoted texts from

from them in his miniftry, which was not in the enticing words of man's wifdom, but in the demonftration of the fpirit, often adminiftring comfort to, and true fympathy with, the afflicted and mourners in Zion.

He divers times vifited moft of the diftant meetings of friends on this continent, and on his return produced fatisfactory accounts of his fervices in thofe vifits. He often communicated good and wholefome advice to his neighbours of other religious denominations, amongft whom he was generally refpected, as a good neighbour, and an honeft, innocent, inoffenfive man.

Altho' he did not appear to be much gifted for the exercife of the difcipline, yet being a conftant attender of meetings appointed for that purpofe, and a diligent waiter therein, there was a language intelligible in his folid filence, which communicated inftruction to his friends, who were always well pleafed with his company.

He was a promoter of that weighty fervice of vifiting friends families, wherein he was ufefully engaged, even when thro' old age and bodily weaknefs, it appear'd to human probability too hard and arduous an undertaking; but having difcovered a willingnefs to make trial, he joined with fome other friends, and was fupported with inward and outward ftrength to go through the fervice, to his own and his friends great fatisfaction. After which his ftrength and faculties declining, he was moftly confined
at

at home. On being visited by his friends, he appear'd much in the innocent and child-like state, retaining his wonted mark of discipleship, viz. love to his brethren, in which he continued to the last, and departed this life, the 7th of the third month 1769; from the clearest information we could obtain, he was in or about the ninety-fourth year of his age; having been a member of our meeting about 64 and a minister upwards of 45 years.

A Testimony from Abington *Monthly-Meeting in* Pennsylvania, *concerning* ISAAC CHILD.

THOSE who die in the Lord, cease from their labours and the troubles of this life, and ascend to the heavenly mansions, where they are forever blessed: And all that can be said on their behalf, cannot in any degree advance their happiness nor add to their worth; yet there is something due to the memory of the righteous, such whose lives have been conspicuously virtuous, who have laid down their heads in peace, are gone from works to rewards, and left a sweet favour.

Our dear and well esteemed friend Isaac Child, having departed this life, we find a freedom to give the following testimony concerning him while amongst us.

In the year 1764, he, with his wife and two children, came well recommended to us from Buckingham monthly-meeting; when he found a draught and freedom to come and settle amongst us, and a favourable opportunity prefenting, he was not hafty in his determination, but, agreeable to the good and wholefome rule of our difcipline, laid the matter before the monthly-meeting he then belonged to, for their advice.

This worthy friend approved himfelf to be one who had fubmitted to the yoke and crofs of Chrift in his youth, and by the influence and operation of truth upon him, was made fenfible of the neceffity of living a circumfpect and felf-denying-life; and as he yielded obedience to the dictates of grace, being thereby fubjected to the divine will and requirings, the Lord was pleafed to employ him in his vineyard, and to qualify him for fervice therein, both in the exercife of the difcipline of the church, and as a minifter of the gofpel.

He was exemplary in life and converfation, his deportment being meek, humble and innocently cheerful, yet guarding againft any thing that would tend to lightnefs in behaviour, his company was pleafant, and his words favoury and edifying: A tender affectionate hufband and parent, a kind friend and neighbour; not of a murmuring difpofition when he met with difappointments and afflictions, but freely fubmitted to what was permitted to come upon him.

He

He was zealous for the cause of God, and the support of christian discipline in its various branches, not hasty in giving his sentiments on matters relative thereto; but after deliberately waiting for a proper qualification, he mostly spake close and pertinent, with clearness and soundness of judgment. He was concern'd for the close and due exercise of the discipline against offenders, not willing that any part of it should be dispensed with, through partial favour or affection, but that true judgment, according to their transgressions, should be placed upon them, the church cleansed from defilements and reproaches, and that the libertine professor and the circumspect walker might be truly distinguished. Yet he was at times, led into sympathy and travel of soul for such who through inadvertency had missed their way, and were in some measure sensible of their error; to those he some times extended private admonition and counsel, in love to their souls, and with desires for their restoration. It may truly be said, he was endowed with a large share of natural understanding, which being sanctified by divine grace, he became well qualified for service in the church.

As a minister, he approved himself one rightly called to the work, having experienced a growth from a good beginning to a large advancement, and at times, thro' divine aid was enabled to deliver much excellent doctrine to the comfort and edification

tion of such whose minds were gathered into a true inward worship of God in spirit: And the negligent were exhorted to more attention in the great work of religion and their souls salvation.

He often sounded an alarm to the rebellious and gainsayers, with a warning to repent and amend their ways, that their souls might be saved in the day of trouble. He had a clear delivery and ready utterance, his stile being familiar to the lowest capacities, his matter well connected, his doctrine sound, his powerful ministry having a great reach upon the people. He frequently attended burials, both within the compass of our own meeting, and some more distant, saying, ‘ It was better for him to go to the ‘ house of mourning than the house of ‘ mirth ;’ at which times there was often large gatherings of divers sorts of christian professors, where he frequently appeared in testimony, much to their satisfaction; being favour'd with a clear sight of the states of the people, and enabled faithfully to speak what was given him, in a close searching manner, without affectation, and in that universal love which wishes well to all men.

He travelled abroad but little, except to some neighbouring yearly-meetings and some other meetings adjacent. In his last public testimony, which was in our monthly-meeting, he was led to speak of the vallies that were to be raised and the hills brought down; that when the Lord was
pleased

pleased to raise some as out of the low vallies and adorn them with his jewels, it made them appear above their brethren; but when those jewels were taken off, they were then on a level; this was agreeable to his own experience, he having at times witnessed a being baptised into lowliness of mind and nothingness of self; under which he appeared much resigned to the divine will, often sitting in silence, as one who had neither call nor commission to speak; for he never discovered a desire to be heard in words, until he had received a renewed qualification, in pure love, to speak to the people, and, as upon the walls of Zion, to proclaim the everlasting gospel of peace, and the means of salvation through Christ our Saviour.

In the time of his last sickness (which was about nine days) he was preserved in patience and resignation of mind; and near the morning before his departure, being clear in his understanding, and sensible of death approaching, he was drawn forth in fervent supplication to the Almighty: After which laying still for some time, he departed like a lamb, without sigh or groan, on the 5*th* of the fourth month 1769, aged thirty-five years, having been a minister about 11 years, and a member of our meeting near 5 years. A large number of friends and others paid their last office of love towards him, in attending his interment at friends buryingground at Abington, on the 8*th* of the said month, at which time a solid meeting was held.

An

An additional Teſtimony concerning ISAAC CHILD, *from* Buckingham *Monthly-Meeting in* Pennſylvania.

NOTWITHSTANDING our much eſteemed friend Iſaac Child, removed himſelf and family from within the compaſs of our monthly-meeting near five years before his deceaſe, yet we find freedom to give this ſhort teſtimony concerning him, having been favoured to ſit under many living and powerful teſtimonies deliver'd by him whilſt among us.

We are fully ſatisfied he was one whom the Lord in his wiſdom ſaw meet to make uſe of for the work of the goſpel, having fitted, qualified and called him forth when but young, to publiſh the glad tidings thereof; to which divine call and holy requiring, he gave up in obedience, and ſuffered not the things of this world to take up his mind, but in true fervency of zeal and love for the cauſe of truth, he ſpent much time in its ſervice. His teſtimony was living, ſound and delivered with divine authority; for he handled not the word deceitfully, nor endeavoured to pleaſe itching ears; but as a true ſervant of Jeſus, waited to be renewedly endowed with power from on high, whereby he was directed to divide the word aright, and ſpeak home to the ſtates and conditions of the people: He was alſo zealouſly concerned for the promotion of diſcipline and good order in the church; and for the management of the affairs thereof, he appeared remarkably well qualified; his weighty admonitions being enforced by a pious life and converſation. May we, under the conſideration of the great loſs the church has ſuſtained by his and ſome others deceaſe, be excited ſo to follow their footſteps, that with them we may be partakers of that incorruptible inheritance which is reſerved for the righteous, when time here ſhall be no more.

A Teſtimony from Buckingham *Monthly-Meeting in* Pennſylvania, *concerning* JOHN SCARBOROUGH.

HE was born of honeſt parents, and educated within the compaſs of this meeting; in his youth was ſomewhat airy, but when arrived to riper years he embraced the truth and appeared cloſely to follow the dictates thereof to the end of his life.

About the year 1740 he appeared in the miniſtry and experiencing a growth therein, he at different times viſited moſt of the northern colonies, in which ſervices he always had our concurrence, and at his return produced certificates of friends unity with his miniſtry and labours of love; the remembrance whereof yet lives as a memorial in the minds of many.

He earneftly laboured for the good and falvation of men, and tho' not learned, fpoke with great propriety, yet plain and familiar, his doctrine being found, lively and edifying, which being adorned by a pious life and innocent converfation, feafoned with true charity, made him juftly efteemed by people of all denominations.

He was fteadily concern'd to promote good order and difcipline, and therein to act uprightly for truth's caufe without partiality. With great cheerfulnefs giving up much of his time, and labouring for the reftoration of fuch who had mifs'd their way; and altho' he ufed great plainnefs in admonifhing tranfgreffors, feldom gave offence; being a man of remarkable felf-denial and endued with much mildnefs, made him very ferviceable in the affairs of the church in general, and tended to fupport the authority of truth.

In his declining years he was affected with bodily weaknefs, yet his zeal for the caufe of truth did not abate, but the life and power ufually attending his miniftry rather increafed. In his laft teftimony at our meeting, he was highly favoured, the power of truth rifing into dominion; with much falutary counfel and fatherly admonition he feemed to take a final farewell of his brethren, and fervently prayed for our prefervation. As his departure drew nigh, he often exprefs'd his willingnefs to leave this world, faying, ' He did not know any ' thing

'thing that remained undone to compleat
'his days-work, and that no cloud nor any
'thing appeared in his way.' He departed
this life, the 5th of the fifth month 1769,
in the sixty-sixth year of his age; and as a
good and faithful servant, we doubt not, is
entered into everlasting joy and happiness.
The fresh remembrance of his loving and
kind deportment and many faithful services,
impress our minds with a deep sense of his
worth and our great loss.

A Testimony from Gwynedd *Monthly-Meeting in* Pennsylvania, *concerning* Mary Evans.

SHE was born in Philadelphia, in or about the year 1695, her father dying when she was young, she was educated by her mother in the principle of truth as professed among us; in her young years she was sober and grave in her behaviour and deportment; and about the time she came forth in the ministry, she went through close trials and deep conflicts, as we have frequently heard her relate, in which the divine arm was her support, brought her through, and qualified her for religious service.

In the year 1736, she was married to our worthy friend Owen Evans, and thereby became a member of this meeting. Her public appearances were not very frequent, but
when

when she spoke, her testimony was fervent, sound and edifying, her conduct and conversation being agreeable to her religious profession. She was several times drawn forth in the love of the gospel, to visit friends in most of the provinces on this continent, also the Island of Tortola, which she undertook with the unity of her friends at home, and returned with clear and satisfactory accounts of her labours amongst those whom she visited. She was a lover and promoter of peace and good order in the church and amongst her neighbours, and was frequently engaged in that weighty service of visiting friends families, to good satisfaction. In the year 1757, she met with a close exercise, in the loss of her husband, who was removed from her by death, which she bore with becoming resignation. After which, she lived some years with her daughter, who was married and settled in Philadelphia; but returned back again within the compass of this meeting, frequently saying, ' She apprehended it to be her duty, ' to spend the remainder of her days a- ' mongst us;' labouring faithfully, as one that foresaw her time was short. Her last illness was lingering, which she bore with becoming resignation; a few days before her death, some friends had a sitting with her in her chamber, when notwithstanding she was weak in body, she was enabled to speak for a considerable time, in a lively and instructive manner, much to their satisfaction.

faction. She departed this life, the 20*th* of the fifth month 1769, and was interr'd in friends burying-ground at Gwynedd, the 22*d* of the same.

A Testimony from Middletown *Monthly-Meeting in* Pennsylvania, *concerning* GRACE CROASDALE.

AS memorials of the virtuous lives and acts of the righteous when deceased, may afford matter of help and encouragement to survivors to follow their pious examples; we are therefore engaged to give this short testimony concerning our esteemed friend Grace Croasdale.

She was born the 6*th* of the eighth month 1703, of reputable parents, members of this meeting, who brought her up to industry and plainness in speech and habit; being married young, she early entered into the cares of a family; and being religiously inclined, and of a cheerful active disposition, approved herself well qualified for such a charge; instructing her children and family both by precept and example, in piety and plainness, as well as the necessary cares of life. As she advanced in years, she grew in religion, and became very serviceable in divers stations in the church. About the year 1745 she first appear'd in the ministry, in the exercise whereof she was acceptable and edifying,

fying, exhortimg all to the true love and fear of God, and a humble attention to the divine principle of truth in themselves; adorning her doctrine by a life and conversation answerable thereto. The latter part of her time, when more disengaged from the cares of a family, she was much devoted to the service of truth, and occasionally visited many of the meetings of friends in our own and several of the neighbouring provinces.

She was a peaceable kind neighbour, a visitor and sympathizer with the sick and afflicted whether in body or mind; and appear'd eminently qualified for that weighty service of visiting families, in which she was often engaged, not only within the compass of our own particular meeting, but of divers others, to general satisfaction.

Having lived in much love and unity with friends, she had to reflect thereon with great peace and satisfaction of mind in her last illness, during which she was signally favoured with the incomes of divine love and heavenly consolation; in the aboundings whereof, she was frequently drawn forth in thanksgivings and living high praises to the Lord.

She departed this life, the 23d of the tenth month 1769, and was buried the 24th of the same, in friends burying-ground at Middletown.

A Testimony

A Testimony from Evesham Monthly-Meeting in New-Jersey, concerning Josiah Foster.

HE was born in Rhode-Island, of honest parents, who died whilst he was young, from which time until he came to man's estate, we have no account of him, only that some of us have heard him say, he was much delighted with mirth and vanity. Soon after his arrival at manhood, he came into New-Jersey, where he married, and settled at Evesham; not long afterwards he was convinced, and effectually reached with the power of truth, through the living ministry of that eminent minister of Christ Jesus, Thomas Wilson; and by the operation of divine grace in his heart, he gradually experienced a growth therein. Thus advancing in true obedience, he witnessed an overcoming of his own strong will (as some of us have heard him relate with awful gratitude to the divine hand) and in due time he became a father and elder in the church; being tenderly concerned for the promotion of the truth, which had in measure set him free from the body of sin and death, communicating suitable advice and counsel to such as were tender, and a sharp reprover of obstinate sinners; his advice being much enforced by his upright uniform conduct.

In conversation he was free and open, and easy of access: In meetings for worship and discipline

discipline (which he diligently attended whilst of ability) his deportment was awful, reverent and unaffectedly grave, waiting for the arising of life, which qualified him to be of great service in the society. He was of a benevolent disposition, his heart and house being open to entertain strangers, especially travelling friends; nor was his benevolence confined to those of our own society; for, being blessed with affluence, many widows and fatherless received his hearty assistance. He was well beloved by most or all who were acquainted with him; his conversation and conduct truly demonstrated, that he had learn'd to do to others, as he would be done unto; which is truly worthy the imitation of all. Being desirous to retire from the cares of the world, he removed to Mount-Holly, where he resided until he was taken with a paralytick disorder, which much impaired his natural faculties, after which he return'd to his former settlement at Evesham under the care of his son. Altho' his disorder render'd him incapable of much conversation, yet he gave evident signs of a lively sense of divine goodness accompanying him to the last; and quietly departed this life, the 9*th* of the first month 1770, in the eighty-eighth year of his age, and was buried the 11*th* of the same month at Evesham.

A Testimony

A Testimony from the Monthly-Meeting of Friends in Philadelphia, *concerning* DANIEL STANTON.

WHEN John the Divine was in exile in the isle of Patmos, " He heard " a voice from Heaven, saying, write,— " blessed are the dead, who die in the Lord, " from henceforth, yea saith the spirit, that " they may rest from their labours, and " their works do follow them;" which we believe now is the portion of our worthy friend, concerning whose faithful services we are engaged from the united motives of love and duty, to give this testimony; desiring, that all who read it, and more especially the youth, may be excited, by his example, to seek an early acquaintance with the Lord, and to take up their daily cross in the prime of their days. Thus, they also, may become shining lights and instruments of good to others.

He was born in this city, in the year 1708, and his father dying before his birth, and his mother a few years after, he suffered great trials and hardships when very young: Being early concerned to seek the knowledge of God, he had a fervent desire to attend religious meetings, though subjected to many difficulties and discouragements, before that privilege was allowed him; yet, being earnest in his desires to obtain divine favour, he was eminently supported

ported under great conflicts and probations, and, continuing faithful to the degrees of light and grace communicated, a difpenfati- of the gofpel miniftry was committed to him, fometime before the term of his apprenticefhip was expired; and abiding under the fanctifying power of truth, he grew in his gift, and became a zealous faithful minifter.

He was very exemplary in his induftry and diligence, in labouring faithfully at his trade, to provide for his own fupport, and after he married, and had children, for their maintenance; and was often concerned to advife others to the fame neceffary care; yet he continued fervent in fpirit for the promotion of truth and righteoufnefs, fo that he was foon engaged to leave home, and the neareft connections of nature, to publifh the glad tidings of the gofpel, and frequently vifited moft of the meetings of friends in this and the adjacent provinces, and feveral times as far as the eaftern parts of New-England. Having thus honeftly difcharged his duty among us above twenty years, and feeling his mind conftrained in the love of the gofpel, to vifit the few friends who remained in fome of the Weft-India iflands, and from thence the meetings of friends in general through Great-Britain and Ireland, he communicated his concern to a few of his moft intimate friends, who having unity therewith, he was encouraged to lay it before our monthly-meeting. Before he entered

entered on this weighty service, he passed through a near trial and affliction in the death of his beloved wife; under which exercise he was graciously supported by the arm of divine strength, which had often been revealed for his help, in times of inward conflicts and outward distresses.

His concern to travel in the service of truth continuing, and the meeting having full unity with him therein, he embarked in the fifth month 1748, accompanied by our dear friend, Samuel Nottingham, in a vessel bound for Barbados, and having visited the few meetings in that island, they went by way of Antigua to Tortola, where they continued sometime, having some difficulty to get a passage to Europe; and their voyage thither was attended with some singular hazards and dangers, which occasioned their landing in Ireland; where our friend Daniel continued some months, visiting the meetings of friends in that kingdom; and after he apprehended himself clear, went over to England, and visited the meetings generally in that nation, and in Wales and Scotland, where his meek circumspect conduct and conversation, and lively edifying ministry, rendered his visit very acceptable, and his memory precious.

In his return home, and for sometime after, he was in a low afflicted state of mind; being apprehensive, that through diffidence, and the want of perfect resignation to the divine will, he had omitted fully performing

ing the service required of him, by not visiting the few friends in Holland: Yet he was mercifully preserved, and after a time of deep exercise, raised again to sing of the mercies and loving-kindness of God on the banks of deliverance.

He several times, with other friends appointed to that service, visited the families of friends in this city, and between the years 1757 and 1760, being accompanied by our friend John Pemberton, he visited the families of friends generally within the limits of our meeting; which weighty exercising service, he was enabled to perform to our edification and satisfaction. After which, he was frequently engaged to excite friends to this useful and edifying practice.

In the twelfth month 1760, he set out on a visit to the meetings in the western parts of this province, and from thence in Maryland, Virginia, and North and South-Carolina, and returned in the sixth month following; since which he frequently visited many of the meetings near home, and some as far as Long-Island, and other parts of the province of New-York. Within the last two years, he visited the families of friends of some of the meetings in West-Jersey, in the city of New-York, and part of Long-Island; and after his return from this service, with great peace and satisfaction, he expressed his apprehension that he was now clear of all places, and that his stay here was near over; having

an

an evidence, that he had been faithfully concerned from his youth to fear and serve God.

His chief labour and religious exercises were in this city, where he was a diligent attender of all our meetings, and often on committees appointed on the services of the church; in which he was solid and weighty in spirit, waiting for the springing up of life, being steadily concerned both in and out of meetings, to live near the divine fountain: Thus he was very frequently qualified, and enabled to stir up the pure mind, and to recount the gracious dealings of God to mankind, and as a faithful embassador to warn the negligent to flee from the wrath to come, and to excite the people to bring forth fruits answerable to the great mercies graciously bestowed on us; and was sometimes constrained to declare in a prophetic manner, a day of trial, in divers instances, very shortly before such a season came to pass.

He was of late deeply exercised in consideration of the evils of the horse races, stage plays, drunkenness, and other gross enormities encouraged and increasing in this city; closely exhorting our youth against those pernicious and destructive devices of the enemy of mankind; and under the awful sense that God will judge and punish the wicked and evil doers, he was often fervent in public supplications, that the Lord would lengthen out the day of his merciful visitation, on, and yet try the people longer; which seasons were solemn and humblingly affecting; manifesting, that although he was very close and sharp in reproof against evil, yet most tenderly concerned, that the transgressors of the righteous law of God might be prevailed with to repent, return, and live.

His love for the rising generation was very great; which he manifested by his affectionate notice of them, and especially of those who were religiously inclined, and his house was open to receive such, his conversation with them being seasoned with grace, and his counsel instructive and helpful to those who had seeking desires after the knowledge of truth, often lovingly inviting them to come, taste, and see, that the Lord is good; greatly desiring, that all who profess the truth, might walk agreeable to its dictates and be led thereby, as our worthy predecessors were, into that meekness, humility, and godly simplicity and plainness, which rendered them conspicuous and shining examples, and that none might rest short of the enjoyment of the life of religion, his zeal being great against such, who have the form of godliness, and by their actions manifest they have not the power thereof; and he often fervently advis'd and cautioned those who are eagerly pursuing the world, and by the surfeiting cares, and grasping after earthly treasures, frustrate the good purpose of the visitation of divine grace to them, and closely reminded those, who

in

in their small beginnings were low and humble, that now they were abundantly favoured, they should not set their affections on things below, but remember the rock from whence they were hewn; and his concern was great that those who had the glad tidings of the gospel to publish, might be true examples to the flock, and adorn the doctrine they had to deliver by a circumspect life and conversation, and where any by not steadily keeping to that which would have preserved them, had involved themselves in difficulties, either by letting their minds out to the gains and profits of this world, or otherwise, his travail was great for such that they might be brought through, and every cloud and mist removed.

He was much employed in visiting the sick and afflicted, to whom he administered his spiritual advice and experience, and often engaged in humble prayer for their support; and in the distributing to the necessitous according to his circumstances, he manifested his benevolent disposition.

As he had been many years under great exercise and suffering of spirit on account of the slavery of the poor Africans, and frequently bore testimony against that unrighteous gain of oppression, he was of late somewhat relieved, as he found the eyes of the people become more open to see the iniquity of the practice; and he died in faith, that the light of the gospel will so generally prevail, that the professors of christianity
will

will find it their duty to restore to these people their natural right to liberty, and to instruct them in the principles of the christian religion.

On the 5*th* day of the fifth month, he was violently seized with the bilious cholic, and continued in great pain several days; but afterwards being somewhat easier, he was at our morning and evening meetings on firstday, the 13*th* of the month, in which he was much favoured in his public ministry, and expressed that he thought his time would not be long with us. After this day's labour, he was again confined, yet being a little recovered he was at our meeting on fifthday, the 24*th* of the month, which being small, he expressed his sorrow for it, and encouraged friends to diligence in the attendance of week day meetings, the benefit of a faithful discharge of duty therein being great; the next day he was at our monthly-meeting, and to his own and our admiration was enabled to stay through both our sittings, though the last of them was longer than usual, and he afterwards expressed that he thought himself better in the meeting than when out; it was a season of divine favour, and some weighty matters being before the meeting, he with great openness spoke pertinently and clearly to them, encouraging friends to the supporting and maintaining our christian testimony, against all that is contrary to it: This was the last public meeting he was at, being the next morning early seized with a renewed attack of the same disorder, which increased on him several days, and was so fixed, that all the endeavours of several skilful physicians and tender nurses, were not effectual to remove it, tho' in some measure to mitigate the pain, that he suffered much, not being able to lie down in his bed several weeks, yet thro' all he was mercifully supported, in much resignation, and patience, rather inclining, if it was the Lord's will, to be released.

For two or three weeks before his sickness, he appeared very desirous of settling every thing he had to do respecting the affairs of this life, and desired a friend to review and transcribe the short memoirs he hath left of his travels and religious services, and to write his will, which he executed the day before he was first taken sick, and then appeared easy in his mind.

During the time of his sickness he often expressed his concern lest his friends should be too anxious for his recovery, saying, if he should live longer, and thro' any human frailty or infirmity occasion any reproach, it would be a cause of sorrow to them.

By the desire of his friends who attended him, he rode out several times, tho' not without much difficulty, and spent the two last days of his life at the houses of two of his intimate friends. As he drew near his end, the strength of his love to mankind in general, and his friends in particular, evidently

dently increased, much defiring the profperity of truth, and when a meeting time came had an earneft defire to be with friends, and particularly the day before his departure.

During his ficknefs, he frequently expreffed himfelf in a very feafonable, inftructive, and affecting manner; and the evening of the firftday before he died, feveral friends coming in to fee him, he fpoke a confiderable time to them, having before been defirous of fuch an opportunity of the company of his friends, to fit down and wait upon God, which was his great delight.

The laft day of his life he fpent at the houfe of his friend Ifrael Pemberton, at Germantown, and was unufually free and cheerful, even till ten o'clock at night, when he undreffed himfelf, and went into bed, remarking on lying down, that he had not before been able to do fo, for five weeks or upwards, and he foon after fell afleep, but in a fhort time was awakened by the return of pain and difficulty of breathing, which thro' his illnefs he had been much afflicted with, fo that he was oblig'd to fet up in bed, and thus continued, at intervals freely converfing with our faid friend, who fat up with him, and he expreffed his great thankfulnefs that his head was preferved free from pain and his underftanding clear, and that though it had been a time of clofe trial and deep probation, he could fay he felt the evidence of divine fupport ftill to attend him. After which, his pains increafing he got

got up and dressed himself, and walking about the room sometime, sat down in an easy chair, in which he fell into a sweet sleep, and in about three hours departed without sigh or groan.

Thus died this righteous man, who having fought the good fight and kept the faith, finished his course in full unity with us, and universally beloved by his fellow citizens, on the 28*th* day of the sixth month 1770, in the sixty-second year of his age and 43*d* of his ministry. His body was the next day attended by a large number of people of divers religious denominations to our meeting-house, and afterwards interr'd in friends burial-ground in this city.

A Testimony from Warrington *Monthly-Meeting in* Pennsylvania, *concerning* John Thomas.

HE was born in Chester county Pennsylvania, in the year 1716, of believing parents, and being religiously inclined from his youth, he received a part in the ministry, whereto being faithful, he experienced a growth therein. In the year 1766, he removed with his family, and settled in Warrington Township, York county, within the limits of our meeting: And tho' his time among us was short, yet we have this testimony to bear concerning him; that his labours

labours of love, accompanied with an exemplary conduct, were comfortable and instructing to us.

In his last illness (which was a consumption) he, at times in the beginning of it, complained to some of his intimate friends, of great poverty of spirit, and seemed deeply engaged to wrestle for strength, to bear with patience the present dispensation: And in due time it pleased the father of mercies who hears the secret cries of his depending children, to cause the mists to be dispelled, so that, in an opportunity which some friends had with him some little time before his departure, he was much favoured, and drawn forth to ' Declare of the tender deal-
' ings of the Lord with him, from his youth
' unto that time; earnestly exhorting friends
' to faithfulness, especially those on whom
' the Lord had bestowed a gift in the mini-
' stry;' saying, ' He had loved the Lord
' from his youth, that he had a small gift
' in the ministry bestowed upon him, in
' which he had been concerned to be faith-
' ful, and now he felt the comfort of it;
' feeling the ownings of the divine presence,
' whereby he was enabled to bear with pa-
' tience his bodily affliction; having an as-
' surance of immortal rest; and that tho'
' in the beginning of his illness, from the
' poverty of spirit that attended him, he
' was ready to conclude that the Lord had
' forsaken him, but now he answered him
' to the joy of his heart, and he had to
 ' magnify

'magnify his goodnefs, feeing his wifdom therein, in weaning his affections more thoroughly from all lower enjoyments, and placing them on things above.'

He advifed friends to humility, faying, 'The time draws near, that my body muft go down to the grave, wherein is no exaltation; and I have this teftimony to bear for the Lord, that as I have been engaged to love him and walk humbly before him, defiring he might give me ftrength, not having any dependance on my own wifdom, I have found him to ftrengthen me, and now find him to be near me in this pinching time, and comfort me with the joys of his prefence.' Many and comfortable were the expreffions which flowed from him, tho' weak in body, and fcarcely able to fpeak intelligibly, yet ftrong and lively in the inward man. In great fweetnefs of fpirit he departed this life, the 9*th* of the fifth month 1771, and on the 11*th* of the faid month, his corps, accompanied by a large number of friends and others, was interr'd in friends burying-ground at Warrington, a folemn meeting being held, and divers living teftimonies borne, to the efficacy of that divine power which gives victory over the world.

A Teftimony

A Testimony from Salem *Monthly-Meeting in* New-Jersey, *concerning* MARY LIPPINCOTT.

FROM a motive of love and esteem, to the memory of this our ancient worthy friend, and that survivors may be encouraged by such pious examples, to embrace the truth and persevere in the way to salvation, we give forth this testimony.

She was the daughter of Henry and Elizabeth Burr, by whom she was religiously educated, we believe to good effect; for in her very young years, she closed in with the love and mercy of God extended to her, and did not incline to vanity and lightness, but was a good example to other youths.

She married young, and with her husband Jacob Lippincott, settled among us. Her exemplary conduct, as a wife and when a widow, both in the church, in her family, and her neighbourhood gained our great esteem; being given to hospitality and liberal to the poor.

She was an earnest traveller in spirit for the cause of truth on earth, solid and weighty in her deportment, affable and instructive in conversation, frequently imparting seasonable admonition and counsel to her children and others, and tho' endowed with superior natural understanding, was not exalted therewith.

In the decline of life, she underwent much bodily infirmity, yet diligently attended meetings when of ability, where she was a humble waiter for the arising of the pure truth, travelling in the deeps for the exaltation thereof; well qualified for services in the church, a true mourner in Zion, being grieved for the corruptions, vain fashions, and customs of the times, and in observing the gaiety and lightness apparent in some, when they came to places for worship. It fell to her lot in the course of her time, to meet with a large share of exercises and trials, which she bore with great resignation; and was a true sympathizer with those under affliction in body or mind whom she often visited. Sometime before her last sickness, she signified her apprehension, that her day's work was near over; and departed this life, the 9th of the first month 1771, and on the 12th was interr'd in friends burying-ground at Pilesgrove; in the seventy-third year of her age, having been an elder many years.

A Testimony from New-Castle *Monthly-Meeting in* Great-Britain, *concerning* WILLIAM HUNT.

OUR dear friend William Hunt, of New-Garden, in Guilford county, North-Carolina, accompanied by his nephew

phew Thomas Thornborough, of the same place, being on a religious visit to friends of this nation, departed this life, at the house of a friend near New-Castle upon Tyne. The deep regard we bear to his memory and eminent services, engageth us to transmit the following testimony concerning him.

They arrived in London about a week after the yearly-meeting 1771, and attending several meetings in that city, proceeded northward, visiting friends in divers counties in England, and also in Scotland. The ensuing winter was spent in visiting Yorkshire, Lancashire and Ireland, returning to London in time to attend the yearly-meeting there in 1772; then attending the yearly-meetings in Essex, Suffolk and Norfolk, and proceeding through Lincolnshire to Hull, they took shipping for Holland, and after visiting the few friends there, they embarked for Scarborough, but by contrary winds landed at Shields, the 25*th* of the eighth month, and after being at their meeting on the 26*th* came that afternoon to the house of a friend near New-Castle upon Tyne.

From accounts received, and our own knowledge of his conduct and ministry, we have good cause to believe, that in all his travels in Europe, he behaved as a faithful minister of Christ, exemplary and uniform in conduct, of a weighty deportment and retired spirit, his conversation was grave and instructive, seasoned with love and sweetness,

sweetness, which rendered his company both profitable and desirable, his ministry was living and powerful, deep and searching, an excellent example in patiently waiting for the clear manifestation of the divine will, and careful to move accordingly, so that his appearances in meetings were mostly accompanied with great solemnity, in which he skilfully divided the word, being to the unfaithful as a two edged sword, but to the honest hearted travellers in Zion, and to such as were seeking the way to God's kingdom, his doctrine was truly refreshing. He was a man of sound judgment, quick of apprehension, and deep in religious experience; and altho' he was only in the thirty-ninth year of his age, yet such was his experience and stability, that he stood as an elder and a father in the church, worthy of double honour.

He attended the meeting at New-Castle, on the 27*th* of the eighth month 1772, in which he delivered a short and living testimony in the love of the gospel to his friends of that place; that afternoon he was cheerful, and expressed his satisfaction in being there, and upon being asked what place they intended for next, he replied, he saw no further at present than New-Castle. Next day he was taken ill, which was not apprehended to be the small pox 'till the fourth day of his illness; when the eruption appeared, he said to his companion, ' This sickness is nigh ' unto death if not quite;' his companion
signified

signified his hope that it might not be so, he replied, 'My coming hither seems to be 'providential, and when I wait I am in-'closed and see no further.' At another time he made the same remark to a friend, saying, 'It will be a sore trial to my compani-'on if I am now removed.' He also mentioned in an affectionate manner his dear wife and children to a friend who attended him, and requested some counsel and advice (which he then communicated) might be transmitted to them, if it should please the Lord to remove him, which was accordingly done.

On the third day of his illness, two friends from the country came to visit him, to whom he thus expressed himself, viz. 'I 'have longed to see you and be with you, 'but was put by,' one of them said, I hope we shall have thee with us yet; he answered, 'That must be left;' the friend said, that whatever affliction we are tried with, we may yet see cause of thankfulness; he replied, 'Great cause indeed, I never saw it 'clearer, O the wisdom! the wisdom and 'goodness, the mercy and kindness has ap-'peared to me wonderful, and the further 'and deeper we go, the more we wonder; 'I have admired since I was cast upon this 'bed, that all the world does not seek after 'the truth, it so far transcends all other 'things.' Two friends from Northumberland coming to visit him, he said, 'The 'Lord knows how I have loved you from
'our

"our first acquaintance, and longed for your
"growth and establishment in the blessed
"truth; and now I feel the same renewed
"afresh;' and said, 'He much desired they
"might fill up the places Providence intend-
"ed, and lay up treasure in Heaven,' adding,
"What would a thousand worlds avail me
"now?'

The disorder was very heavy upon him, having a load of eruption, under which he shewed great fortitude and patience even to the admiration of the physician and surgeon who attended him; his mind being mercifully preserved calm, and resigned to his master's will, whose presence he found to be near him in the needful time, saying, 'It
"is enough, my master is here;' and again,
"He that laid the foundation of the moun-
"tans knows this, if it pleases him he can
"remove it;' at another time he said with great composure, 'The Lord knows best, I
"am in his hands, let him do what he
"pleases.'

Perceiving a friend to be diligent and attentive to do what she could for him, he said,
"The Lord refresh thy spirit, for thou hast
"often refreshed this body, and whether I
"live or die, thou wilt get thy reward.'

After the second fever came on, finding himself worse, he said, 'My life hangs upon
"a thread.' The doctor being sent for, he said, 'They are all physicians of no value
"without the great Physician.' A friend said, I know thy dependance is on him, he answered,

swered, 'Entirely.' Understanding that two friends who had sat much by him, did not intend to leave him that night, he very sweetly said, 'And will you watch with me one night more?'

On being asked how he did, he said, 'I am here pent up and confined in a narrow compass, this is a trying time, but my mind is above it all;' which was evident to those about him, who were sensible of praises and sweet melody in his heart when few words were expressed.

A little before he died, he said triumphantly, 'Friends, truth is over all;' so in great peace departed this life, the 9th day of the ninth month 1772, and was interr'd in friends burying-ground in New-Castle upon Tyne, the 11th of the same month, accompanied by many friends; upon which occasion a solemn meeting was held, and divers testimonies borne to the truth, in the service of which he lived and died, an example to many brethren. A minister 24 years.

A Testimony from Burlington *Monthly-Meeting in* New-Jersey, *concerning* JOHN WOOLMAN.

HE was born in Northampton, in the county of Burlington, and province of West-New-Jersey, in the eighth month 1720, of religious parents, who inſtructed him very early in the principles of the chriſtian religion, as profeſſed by the people called Quakers, which he eſteemed a bleſſing to him, even in his young years, tending to preſerve him from the infection of wicked children; but through the workings of the enemy, and levity incident to youth, he frequently deviated from thoſe parental precepts, by which he laid a renewed foundation for repentance, that was finally ſucceeded by a godly ſorrow not to be repented of, and ſo became acquainted with that ſanctifying power which qualifies for true goſpel miniſtry, into which he was called about the twenty-ſecond year of his age, and by a faithful uſe of the talents committed to him, he experienced an increaſe, until he arrived at the ſtate of a father, capable of dividing the word aright to the different ſtates he miniſtered unto; diſpenſing milk to babes, and meat to thoſe of riper years. Thus he found the efficacy of that power to ariſe, which in his own expreſſions, ' Prepares the creature to ſtand ' like a trumpet through which the Lord ' ſpeaks to his people.' He was a loving huſband, a tender father, and very humane to every part of the creation under his care.

His concern for the poor and thoſe in affliction was evident by his viſits to them; whom he frequently relieved by his aſſiſtance and charity. He was for many years deeply exerciſed on account of the poor enſlaved Africans, whoſe cauſe, as he ſometimes mentioned,

tioned, lay almoſt continually upon him, and to obtain liberty to thoſe captives, he laboured both in public and private; and was favoured to ſee his endeavours crowned with conſiderable ſucceſs. He was particularly deſirous that friends ſhould not be inſtrumental to lay burthens on this oppreſſed people, but remember the days of ſuffering from which they had been providentially delivered, that if times of trouble ſhould return, no injuſtice dealt to thoſe in ſlavery might riſe in judgment againſt us, but, being clear, we might on ſuch occaſions addreſs the Almighty with a degree of confidence, for his interpoſition and relief, being particularly careful as to himſelf, not to countenance ſlavery even by the uſe of thoſe conveniencies of life which were furniſhed by their labour.

He was deſirous to have his own, and the minds of others, redeemed from the pleaſures and immoderate profits of this world, and to fix them on thoſe joys which fade not away; his principal care being after a life of purity, endeavouring to avoid not only the groſſer pollutions, but thoſe alſo which, appearing in a more refined dreſs, are not ſufficiently guarded againſt by ſome well diſpoſed people. In the latter part of his life he was remarkable for the plainneſs and ſimplicity of his dreſs, and as much as poſſible, avoided the uſe of plate, coſtly furniture and feaſting; thereby endeavouring to become an example of temperance and ſelf-denial, which, he believed himſelf called unto; and was favoured ed with peace therein, altho' it carried the appearance of great austerity in the view of some. He was very moderate in his charges in the way of business, and in his desires after gain; and tho' a man of industry, avoided, and strove much to lead others out of extreme labour, and anxiousness after perishable things; being desirous that the strength of our bodies might not be spent in procuring things unprofitable, and that we might use moderation and kindness to the brute animals under our care, to prize the use of them as a great favour, and by no means abuse them; that the gifts of Providence should be thankfully received and applied to the uses they were designed.

He several times opened a school at Mount-Holly, for the instruction of poor friends children and others, being concerned for their help and improvement therein: His love and care for the rising youth among us was truly great, recommending to parents and those who have the charge of them, to chuse conscientious and pious tutors, saying, ' It is a lovely sight to behold innocent chil- ' dren,' and that ' To labour for their help ' against that which would marr the beauty ' of their minds, is a debt we owe them.'

His ministry was found, very deep and penetrating, sometimes pointing out the dangerous situation which indulgence and custom leads into; frequently exhorting others, especially the youth, not to be discouraged at the difficulties which occur, but press after

ter purity. He often expressed an earnest engagement that pure wisdom should be attended to, which would lead into lowliness of mind and resignation to the divine will, in which state small possessions here would be sufficient.

In transacting the affairs of discipline, his judgment was sound and clear, and he was very useful in treating with those who had done amiss; he visited such in a private way in that plainness which truth dictates, shewing great tenderness and christian forbearance. He was a constant attender of our yearly-meeting, in which he was a good example, and particularly useful; assisting in the business thereof with great weight and attention. He several times visited most of the meetings of friends in this and the neighbouring provinces, with the concurrence of the monthly-meeting to which he belonged, and we have reason to believe had good service therein, generally or always expressing at his return how it had fared with him, and the evidence of peace in his mind for thus performing his duty. He was often concerned with other friends in the important service of visiting families, which he was enabled to go through to satisfaction.

In the minutes of the meeting of ministers and elders for this quarter, at the foot of a list of the members of that meeting, made about five years before his death, we find in his hand-writing the following observation and reflections. 'As looking over the mi-

'nutes

'nutes made by perfons who have put off this body, hath fometimes revived in me a thought how ages pafs away; fo this lift may probably revive a like thought in fome, when I and the reft of the perfons abovenamed, are centered in another ftate of being. The Lord, who was the guide of my youth, hath in tender mercies helped me hitherto; he hath healed me of wounds, he hath helped me out of grievous entanglements; he remains to be the ftrength of my life; to whom I defire to devote myfelf in time, and in eternity.'

Signed, John Woolman.

In the twelfth month 1771, he acquainted this meeting that he found his mind drawn towards a religious vifit to friends in fome parts of England, particularly in Yorkfhire. In the firft month 1772, he obtained our certificate, which was approved and endorfed by our quarterly-meeting, and by the half year's meeting of minifters and elders at Philadelphia. He embarked on his voyage in the fifth and arrived in London in the fixth month following, at the time of their annual meeting in that city. During his fhort vifit to friends in that kingdom, we are informed that his fervices were acceptable and edifying. In his laft illnefs he uttered many lively and comfortable expreffions, being 'Perfectly refigned, having no will either to live or die,' as appears by the teftimony of friends at York in Great-Britain, in the fuburbs whereof, at the houfe
of

of our friend Thomas Prieſtman, he died of the ſmall-pox, on the 7*th* day of the tenth month 1772, and was buried in friends burying-ground in that city, on the 9*th* of the ſame, after a large and ſolid meeting held on the occaſion, at their great meeting-houſe, aged near fifty-two years; a miniſter upwards of 30 years, during which time he belonged to Mount-Holly particular meeting, which he diligently attended when at home and in health of body, and his labours of love and pious care for the proſperity of friends in the bleſſed truth, we hope may not be forgotten, but that his good works may be remembered to edification.

A Teſtimony from the Quarterly-Meeting at York *in* Great-Britain, *concerning* JOHN WOOLMAN.

THIS our valuable friend having been under a religious engagement for ſome time, to viſit friends in this nation, and more eſpecially us in the northern parts, undertook the ſame in full concurrence and near ſympathy with his friends and brethren at home, as appeared by certificates from the monthly and quarterly-meetings to which he belonged, and from the ſpring-meeting of miniſters and elders, held at Philadelphia, for Pennſylvania and New-Jerſey.

He arrived in the city of London the beginning of the laſt yearly-meeting, and after attending that meeting travelled northward, viſiting the quarterly-meetings of Hertfordſhire, Buckinghamſhire, Northamptonſhire, Oxfordſhire and Worceſterſhire, and divers particular meetings in his way.

He viſited many meetings on the weſt-ſide of this county, alſo ſome in Lancaſhire and Weſtmoreland, from whence he came to our quarterly-meeting in the laſt ninth month, and though much out of health, yet was enabled to attend all the ſittings of that meeting except the laſt.

His diſorder then, which proved the ſmall-pox, increaſed ſpeedily upon him, and was very afflicting; under which he was ſupported in much meekneſs, patience, and chriſtian fortitude; to thoſe who attended him in his illneſs, his mind appeared to be centered in divine love; under the precious influence whereof, we believe he finiſhed his courſe, and entered into the manſions of everlaſting reſt.

In the early part of his illneſs he requeſted a friend to write and he broke forth thus.

' O Lord my God! the amazing horrors
' of darkneſs were gathered around me and
' covered me all over, and I ſaw no way to
' go forth; I felt the miſery of my fellow
' creatures ſeparated from the divine har-
' mony and it was heavier than I could
' bear, and I was cruſhed down under it; I
' lifted up my hand, and ſtretched out my
' arm,

'arm, but there was none to help me; I
'looked round about and was amazed: In
'the depths of mifery, O Lord! I remem-
'bred that thou art omnipotent, that I had
'called thee father, and I felt that I loved
'thee, and I was made quiet in thy will,
'and I waited for deliverance from thee;
'thou hadft pity upon me, when no man
'could help me; I faw that meeknefs under
'fuffering was fhewed to us in the moft af-
'fecting example of thy fon, and thou waft
'teaching me to follow him, and I faid, thy
'will O father, be done.'

Many more of his weighty expreffions might have been inferted here, but it was deemed unneceffary, they being already publifhed in print.

He was a man endued with a large natural capacity, and being obedient to the manifeftations of divine grace, having in patience and humility endured many deep baptifms, he became thereby fanctified and fitted for the Lord's work, and was truly ferviceable in his church; dwelling in awful fear and watchfulnefs, he was careful in his public appearances to feel the putting forth of the divine hand, fo that the fpring of the gofpel miniftry often flowed through him with great fweetnefs and purity, as a refrefhing ftream to the weary travellers towards the city of God: Skilful in dividing the word, he was furnifhed by him in whom are hid all the treafures of wifdom and knowledge, to communicate freely to the feveral

ftates

states of the people where his lot was cast. His conduct at other times was seasoned with the like watchful circumspection and attention to the guidance of divine wisdom, which rendered his whole conversation uniformly edifying.

He was fully persuaded that as the life of Christ comes to reign in the earth, all abuse and unnecessary oppression, both of the human and brute creation will come to an end; but under the sense of a deep revolt, and an overflowing stream of unrighteousness, his life has been often a life of mourning.

He was deeply concerned on account of that inhuman and iniquitous practice of making slaves of the people of Africa, or holding them in that state; and on that account we understand he hath not only wrote some books, but travelled much on the continent of America, in order to make the Negro masters (especially those in profession with us) sensible of the evil of such a practice; and though in this journey to England, he was far removed from the outward sight of their sufferings, yet his deep exercise of mind remained, as appears by a short treatise he wrote in this journey, and his frequent concern to open the miserable state of this deeply injured people: His testimony in the last meeting he attended was on this subject, wherein he remarked, that as we as a society, when under outward sufferings, had often found it our concern to lay them before those in authority, and thereby in the

the Lord's time, had obtained relief, so he recommended this oppressed part of the creation to our notice, that we may as way may open, represent their sufferings in an individual, if not a society, capacity to those in authority.

Deeply sensible that the desire to gratify people's inclinations in luxury and superfluities, is the principal ground of oppression, and the occasion of many unnecessary wants, he believed it to be his duty to be a pattern of great self-denial, with respect to the things of this life, and earnestly to labour with friends in the meekness of wisdom, to impress on their minds the great importance of our testimony in these things, recommending to the guidance of the blessed truth in this and all other concerns, and cautioning such as are experienced therein, against contenting themselves with acting up to the standard of others, but to be careful to make the standard of truth manifested to them, the measure of their obedience; for said he, 'That pu-
' rity of life which proceeds from faithful-
' ness in following the spirit of truth, that
' state where our minds are devoted to
' serve God, and all our wants are bounded
' by his wisdom; this habitation has often
' been opened before me as a place of re-
' tirement for the children of the light, where
' they may stand separated from that which
' disordereth and confuseth the affairs of
' society, and where we may have a testi-
' mony of our innocence in the hearts of
' those who behold us.'

We conclude with fervent defires, that we as a people may thus, by our example, promote the Lord's work in the earth; and our hearts being prepared, may unite in prayer to the great Lord of the harveſt, that as in his infinite wiſdom he hath greatly ſtripped the church, by removing of late divers faithful miniſters and elders, he may be pleaſed to ſend forth many more faithful labourers into his harveſt.

The following Minutes of ſome of his Expreſſions in the time of his ſickneſs, were preſerved by our friend Thomas Prieſtman *and others who attended him,* viz.

FOURTH-DAY morning, 30*th* of the ninth month 1772, being aſked how he felt himſelf, he meekly anſwered, I don't know that I have ſlept this night, I feel the diſorder making its progreſs, but my mind is mercifully preſerved in ſtillneſs and peace: Sometime after he ſaid he was ſenſible the pains of death muſt be hard to bear, but if he eſcaped them now, he muſt ſometime paſs thro' them, and he did not know that he could be better prepared, but had no will in it. He ſaid he had ſettled his outward affairs to his mind, had taken leave of his wife and family as never to return, leaving them to the divine protection; adding, and tho' I feel them near to me at this time, yet I freely give them up, having a hope that they will

will be provided for. And a little after said, This trial is made easier than I could have thought, my will being wholly taken away; for if I was anxious for the event it would have been harder, but I am not, and my mind enjoys a perfect calm.

In the night a young woman having given him something to drink, he said, My child thou seems very kind to me a poor creature, the Lord will reward thee for it. Awhile after he cried out with great earnestness of spirit, Oh my father! my father! and soon after he said, Oh my father! my father! how comfortable art thou to my soul in this trying season. Being asked if he could take a little nourishment; after some pause he replied, my child I cannot tell what to say to it; I seem nearly arrived where my soul shall have rest from all its troubles. After giving in something to be inserted in his journal, he said, I believe the Lord will now excuse me from exercises of this kind; and I see no work but one which is to be the last wrought by me in this world, the messenger will come that will release me from all these troubles; but it must be in the Lord's time, which I am waiting for. He said he had laboured to do whatever was required, according to the ability received, in the remembrance of which he had peace; and tho' the disorder was strong at times, and would like a whirlwind come over his mind; yet it had hitherto been kept steady and center'd in everlasting love; adding, and if that be mercifully
continued,

continued, I afk nor defire no more. Another time he faid, he had long had a view of vifiting this nation, and fometime before he came had a dream, in which he faw himfelf in the northern parts of it, and that the fpring of the gofpel was opened in him much as in the beginning of friends, fuch as George Fox and William Dewfbury, and he faw the different ftates of the people, as clear as he had ever feen flowers in a garden; but in his going along he was fuddenly ftopt, tho' he could not fee for what end; but looking towards home, fell into a flood of tears, which waked him.

At another time he faid, my draught feemed ftrongeft towards the north, and I mentioned in my own monthly-meeting, that attending the quarterly-meeting at York, and being there looked like home to me.

Fifth-day night, having repeatedly confented to take medicine with a view to fettle his ftomach, but without effect; the friend then waiting on him, faid thro' diftrefs, what fhall I do now? He anfwered with great compofure, Rejoice evermore, and in every thing give thanks; but added a little after, this is fometimes hard to come at.

Sixth-day morning he broke forth early in fupplication on this wife, O Lord it was thy power that enabled me to forfake fin in my youth, and I have felt thy bruifes for difobedience; but as I bowed under them thou healed me, continuing a father and a friend; I feel thy power now, and I beg that in the

approaching

approaching trying moment thou wilt keep my heart ftedfaft unto thee. Upon his giving directions to a friend concerning fome little things, fhe faid I will take care, but hope thou wilt live to order them thyfelf; he reply'd, my hope is in Chrift, and tho' I may feem a little better, a change in the diforder may foon happen, and my little ftrength be diffolved, and if it fo happens, I fhall be gathered to my everlafting reft. On her faying fhe did not doubt that, but could not help mourning to fee fo many faithful fervants removed at fo low a time; he faid all good cometh from the Lord, whofe power is the fame, and can work as he fees beft. The fame day he had given directions about wrapping his corpfe; perceiving a friend to weep, he faid I would rather thou wouldft guard againft weeping for me, my fifter, I forrow not, tho' I have had fome painful conflicts, but now they feem over and matters well fettled, and I look at the face of my dear redeemer, for fweet is his voice and his countenance is comely.

Firft-day, 4*th* of the tenth month, being very weak and in general difficult to be underftood, he uttered a few words in commemoration of the Lord's goodnefs; and added, how tenderly have I been waited on in this time of affliction, in which I may fay in Job's words, Tedious days and wearifome nights are appointed unto me, and how many are fpending their time and money in vanity and fuperfluities, while thoufands and

and tens of thousands want the necessaries of life, who might be relieved by them, and their distresses at such a time as this, in some degree softened by the administring suitable things.

Second-day morning the apothecary who appeared very anxious to assist him, being present, he queried about the probability of such a load of matter being thrown off his weak body, and the apothecary making some remarks implying he thought it might; he spoke with an audible voice on this wise, My dependance is on the Lord Jesus, who I trust will forgive my sins, which is all I hope for, and if it be his will to raise up this body again, I am content; and if to die, I am resigned; and if thou canst not be easy without trying to assist nature, I submit. After which his throat was so much affected, that it was very difficult for him to speak so as to be understood, and frequently wrote when he wanted any thing. About the second hour on fourth-day morning he asked for pen and ink, and at several times with much difficulty wrote thus, I believe my being here is in the wisdom of Christ, I know not as to life or death.

About a quarter before six the same morning he seemed to fall into an easy sleep, which continued about half an hour, when seeming to awake, he breathed a few times with more difficulty, and expired without sigh, groan, or struggle.

A Testimony

A Testimony from Derby *Monthly-Meeting in* Pennsylvania, *concerning* WILLIAM HORNE.

HE was born in the county of Sussex, Great-Britain, in the year 1714, and came with his parents to Philadelphia about the year 1724; in 1736 he came to reside in this township, where he continued the remainder of his life. He married in 1737, and in 1746 he appeared in public testimony in our religious meetings, and being obedient to the heavenly call, became an able minister of the gospel.

In the year 1752 he visited the meetings of friends in New-England; and in the fourth month 1763 embark'd for Great-Britain, where he visited the meetings generally in England and some part of Wales, returning home in the tenth month 1764, to the great satisfaction of his family and friends. He also, at several other times, visited most of the meetings in Pennsylvania and New-Jersey, and the back parts of Maryland and Virginia; it appearing, by certificates produced, that his labours of love were acceptable to friends.

His ministerial labours were frequent, lively and edifying, adorning the doctrine he preached by a circumspect life and conversation, being zealously concerned for the maintenance of good order in the church, a good example in his family, careful to bring up up his children in diligently attending religious meetings, and manifesting his care in divers respects for their present and future welfare. Kind and hospitable to friends, his house and heart being open for their reception.

He departed this life, at his own habitation, the 11th of the eleventh month 1772, in the fifty-ninth year of his age and the 26th of his ministry, and was interr'd in friends burying-ground at Derby aforesaid.

A Testimony from Little Egg-Harbour *Monthly-Meeting in* New-Jersey, *concerning* JOHN RIDGWAY.

HE was born in the county of Burlington, in West-New-Jersey, in the year 1705, and soon after came with his parents and settled within the compass of this meeting: He was religiously educated, which as he grew in years, had a good effect, by his yielding obedience to the heavenly vision of light and grace in his own mind, which weaned him from the vanities of the world. He was a steady and constant attender of meetings when at home and in health; and altho' his circumstances in life made him apprehend it necessary to follow the sea for a time, yet by attending to the divine principle of grace, he was preserved from that extravagance in his conduct and conversation on too prevalent in men in that bufinefs. He was early in life appointed to the ftation of an elder in the church, in which he conducted with reputation; being of a benevolent fpirit, his heart and houfe were open to entertain his friends and others, cheerfully and liberally affifting the poor in many refpects; and in an extenfive commerce and converfation amongft men of various ranks, he demeaned himfelf with a becoming gravity, which render'd him truly worthy of efteem. He was carefully concerned that his children and other youth, might partake of the benefits of a fober education; and in his declining years, was much afflicted with bodily indifpofition, which he was enabled to bear with patience and refignation; often expreffing a defire to be contented in the divine will.

He quietly departed this life, on the 21/t of the fifth month 1774, aged near feventy years, and was buried at Egg-Harbour.

A Teftimony from Plainfield *Monthly-Meeting in* New-Jerfey, *concerning* JOHN VAIL.

OUR worthy and much efteemed friend John Vail, was born at Weft-Chefter, in the province of New-York, and removed from thence while young to Woodbridge, where he fettled and married. He was when a youth, reached by the power of truth, and

and submitting to the cross, he became sober and religious; and continuing faithful and obedient to what he believed to be his duty, the Lord in infinite mercy, was pleased to bestow on him, a gift in the gospel ministry, and he proving faithful with the one talent, witnessed an increase and growth in the truth, and was enlarged in his public testimony, whereby the church was edified, and the faithful comforted. Having a regard to the putting forth of the divine hand, he waited in meetings for proper qualifications to minister in the ability that God gives, whereby he was often enabled, not only to reprove the unrighteousness of men, but to speak comfortably to those who mourned for the pride and abominations of the times. He often mentioned the plainness and simplicity which our forefathers appeared in, and was sorrowfully affected for many of the present generation, in that they slighted their good examples, and indulged themselves in many things which those worthy men bore a faithful testimony against. He was a diligent attender of meetings, and very exemplary in being early there, even to old age, when of ability of body; often exciting friends to that duty, not as formalists, but patiently to wait for qualification to perform acceptable worship to the Almighty. His outward circumstances being low, he was very industrious, labouring with his hands for the support of himself and family, to

an

an advanced age, being very loth to be burdenſome to friends.

He lived to a good old age, and on his death-bed, expreſſed his great ſatisfaction, and reſignation to the will of the Almighty, and ſaid he had often conſidered that paſſage of ſcripture, " If our hearts condemn " us not, God is greater," adding, ' But ' my heart condemns me not, for I have ' walked in innocency from my youth up:' He divers times ſignified his being ready and willing to leave the world. As our dear friend walked in righteouſneſs and humility, he increaſed in divine experience, and his lamp ſhone bright to the laſt. He departed this life, on the 27*th* of the eleventh month 1774, in the eighty-ninth year of his age, much beloved by his friends, neighbours, and acquaintance in general, a large number of whom attended his corpſe to the grave, where, after a ſolid meeting on the occaſion, it was interr'd in friends buryingground at Rahway.

A Teſtimony from Goſhen *Monthly-Meeting in* Pennſylvania, *concerning* THOMAS GOODWIN.

HE was born in the principality of Wales in the year 1694, and came over to Pennſylvania with his parents about the year 1708; and according to the beſt accounts

counts we can collect, he appeared in the miniftry near the fortieth year of his age; and became a faithful labourer in the Lord's vineyard. He fundry times vifited friends in the adjacent provinces, feveral of which vifits he performed even in old age; and about the fixty-ninth year of his age vifited friends in many parts of England and Wales; and fome years after, friends in Ireland; which vifits were acceptable, as appeared by feveral certificates given by friends amongft whom he laboured. He was zealous for the promotion of good order in the church, and often fervently engaged in our meetings for difcipline, to recommend friends to a humble waiting for the pointings of truth, as the alone fafe guide and qualifier for every good word and work.

He was exemplary himfelf, and careful to bring up his family in the practice of attending meetings on the firft and other days of the week; was zealous in promoting and faithful in performing that good work of vifiting friends families: His miniftry was found and edifying, being in the demonftration of the fpirit and power; and he may be faid to be of the number of them that through faith have obtained a good report.

The laft year of his life, he was prevented from travelling far abroad, by reafon of a lingering and painful diforder, but when able to attend his own meeting, he frequently appeared in the miniftry, tho' under much bodily infirmity. And altho' he was as a shock of corn fully ripe, gathered in its season, yet we are sensible of the loss the church has sustained by his removal; but we trust it is his everlasting gain, and that he now enjoys the fruits of his labours. His last expressions were, 'Lord Jesus receive 'my soul.'

He departed this life, the 16*th* of the fourth month 1775, and was buried in friends burying-ground at Goshen, on the 19*th* of the same, aged eighty-one years, and a minister about 41 years.

A Testimony from Nottingham *Monthly-Meeting in* Pennsylvania, *concerning* JOHN CHURCHMAN.

HE was born at Nottingham in Chester county, Pennsylvania, the 4*th* of the sixth month 1705, of religious parents, John and Hannah Churchman; and by his own account, was remarkably reached and made sensible of the inward appearance of grace and truth when very young; but through inattention thereto, suffered loss. About the twentieth year of his age, thro' the great loving kindness of a merciful God, the divine visitation was again renewed wherewith he closing in, became subject to the Lord's hand, who was about to prepare him as a chosen instrument for service. In his twenty-fifth year he married, and soon after was recommended

recommended to the station of an elder, wherein we find, he acted with great caution, humility and fear, and being qualified for the fervice of vifiting families, was employed therein.

His firft appearance in public miniftry, was in the year 1733, and by humble obedience to the giver, he improved in the gift, and became an able minifter of the gofpel; in which fervice he travelled much, having vifited the meetings of friends in this and feveral of the adjacent provinces, moftly feveral times; and in the fummer 1742, he perform'd a religious vifit to friends in New-England, and the year following to New-York and parts adjacent, which he repeated in 1774. In the year 1750 a concern ripened, which he expreffed had for fome years before, at times, refted with weight on his mind, to crofs the feas in the fervice of the gofpel, wherewith he had the free concurrence of his brethren at home (being always very careful in that refpect;) and fpent upwards of four years on a general vifit to the meetings of friends in England, Scotland, Wales, Ireland and Holland, and alfo to the particular families of friends within the compafs of divers meetings in different parts of Europe; and by feveral certificates produced to our meeting after his return, the unity and fatisfaction of friends in thofe European countries with his exemplary conduct and religious labours were fully expreffed.

Although

Although he was of a weakly conſtitution, and often infirm, eſpecially in the latter part of his life, yet he appeared to be much devoted to the ſervice of truth and the good of mankind, and gave up his time for that purpoſe, when he apprehended it was required of him, being favoured with a ſufficiency of outward things, and we believe he ſtood looſe from the world and its connections, not ſeeking, but refraining opportunities he might have had to get outward riches; he viſited neighbouring yearly, quarterly, and other meetings of friends at times to his laſt year, and was truly uſeful in the diſcipline of the church, being eminently qualified for that ſervice, and was a good example in a diligent care to attend all the meetings both for worſhip and diſcipline to which he belonged, cautious of being forward in his public appearances, and for the moſt part exampled us to ſilence in our meetings at home, eſpecially in the latter part of his time; yet when he did appear in teſtimony, we think it may be truly ſaid, his doctrine dropt as the dew, being lively and edifying to the honeſt hearted, tho' cloſe and ſearching to the careleſs profeſſors, as well as to the profane and hypocritical. The elders who have ruled well are to be accounted honorable, ſo the remembrance of the fatherly, diligent, humble, upright, honeſt, and ſelf-denying example of this our deceaſed friend, as alſo his various ſervices in our meetings and neighbourhood remain freſh, and of a pleaſant favour to many minds.

In

In his last illness, which held him upwards of three weeks, he appeared mostly sensible, and manifested much patience and resignation, uttering many lively expressions to those attending him, and to divers friends who came to see him; some of which being taken down in writing, are hereunto subjoined, viz.

Some Account of the last illness of our friend John Churchman, *and of divers of his weighty expressions, near the close of life.*

ON the 11*th* of the sixth month 1775, he return'd home, after performing his last journey, on a visit to most of the meetings on the Eastern-Shore of Maryland, and attending the yearly-meeting at Third-Haven in Talbot county. On the 14*th* of the same month, he went to the weekday meeting at London-Grove, to meet with a committee of our quarterly-meeting on particular business, and returned to our meeting at Nottingham the next day, on the first day of the week following was there also, in the same week he attended our preparative and monthly-meetings, but a fever daily increasing upon him, he was afterwards chiefly confined at home.

On the 4*th* of the seventh month he expressed himself thus, ' I am glad that I am at home, ' I have ever found it best when my service ' abroad was over, to get home as quick as
' might

' might be, and though I have felt great in-
' ward poverty and weakness since my last
' journey, so that I can neither see my be-
' ginning nor ending, but seem as if all
' were hidden, yet I hope if Providence shall
' see meet to remove me at this time, some
' light will appear again, and that it will
' be otherwise before I go.'

At another time he spake to this purpose,
' I have found myself much stripped as to a
' sense of good, and tried with poverty ma-
' ny days. I suppose I have been accounted
' by some, as one of the better sort of peo-
' ple, but have seen great occasion to beware
' of a disposition that would seek to feed up-
' on the praise or commendations of others;
' a carnal selfish spirit is very apt to present,
' and creep in here if possible, and I have
' seen it hurt many who have had right be-
' ginnings, it always introduceth dimness,
' and oppression, to the pure, precious, in-
' nocent life of truth, which only groweth
' up into dominion, through deep abase-
' ment of soul, and the entire death of self.'

At several other times he signified to this
effect, ' My present baptism of affliction
' hath tended to the further refinement of
' my nature, and to the bringing me more
' perfectly into the image of my master.'

He frequently expressed his full submission to the divine will either respecting life or
death, several times saying, ' I now expe-
' rience my life and my will to be slain, and
' I have no will left.'

'In

In the two last weeks of his time it appeared that his desire and hope, mentioned in the forepart of his illness, for light again to appear, was fully answered by the fresh influence thereof, so that altho' his pain was often great, he would many times in a day break forth into a kind of melody with his voice, without uttering words, which as he sometimes intimated, was an involuntary aspiration of his soul in praise to the Lord, who had again been pleased to shine forth in brightness after many days of poverty and deep baptism, which tho' painful, had proved beneficial to him, being a means of further purifying from the dregs of nature, saying he was at times afraid to discover that melody in the hearing of some that visited him, left they could not comprehend its meaning, and might therefore misconstrue it.

On second day morning the 17*th* of the seventh month, being asked by a friend how he was, he replied, ‘ I am here in the body ‘ yet, and when I go out of it I hope there ‘ is nothing but peace,’ and soon after further said, ‘ I have seen that all the bustles, ‘ and noises that are now in the world will ‘ end in confusion, and our young men that ‘ know not an establishment in the truth ‘ and the Lord's fear for a ballast, will be ‘ caught in a trying moment.’ At another time he said, ‘ I feel nothing but peace, hav- ‘ ing endeavoured honestly to discharge my-
‘ self

'self in public, and privately to individu-
'als as I apprehended was required, and if
'it be the Lord's will that I should go now,
'I shall be released from a great deal of
'trouble and exercise, which I believe friends
'who are left behind will have to pass
'through.'

On the 20*th* of the same month he thus expressed himself, 'I love friends who abide
'in the truth as much as ever I did, and I
'feel earnest breathings to the Lord, that
'there may be such raised up in the church
'who may go forth in humility, sweetness,
'and life, clear of all superfluity in expressi-
'ons and otherwise, standing for the testi-
'mony, that they may be useful to the
'church in these difficult times.'

About three days before his death, several friends being in his room, he spake as follows,
'Friends in the beginning, if they had
'health and liberty, were not easily divert-
'ed from paying their tribute of worship
'to the Almighty on week days as well as
'first-days, but after awhile when outward
'sufferings ceased, life and zeal decaying,
'ease and the spirit of the world took place
'with many, and thus it became customa-
'ry for one or two out of a family to attend
'meetings, and to leave their children much
'at home; parents also if worldly concerns
'were in the way could neglect their week
'day meetings sometimes, yet be willing to
'hold the name, and plead excuse because
'of a busy time, or the like, but I believe
'that

'that such a departure from primitive integrity ever did, and ever will, occasion a withering from the life of true religion.'

To a friend who came to visit him on the 21st of the seventh month he said, 'I feel that which lives beyond death and the grave, which is now an inexpressible comfort to me after a time of deep baptism that I have passed through, I believe my being continued here is in the will of Providence, and I am fully resigned.'

His illness increasing he said but little on seventh-day the 22d; in the afternoon he was very low, and speechless about twelve hours; early on first-day morning he recruited a little, and gave directions about his coffin to a friend who sat up with him, being a joiner; continuing rather easier the forepart of that day and appearing cheerful, he expressed divers weighty sentences like farewell exhortations to some who came to see him; on second-day morning he sat up a considerable time, in the afternoon he appeared lively and sensible, tho' very weak, thus expressing himself, 'I am much refreshed with my master's sweet air, I feel more life, more light, more love and sweetness than ever before,' and often mentioned the divine refreshment and comfort he felt flowing like a pure stream to his inward man, saying to those who were with him, 'I may tell you of it, but you cannot feel it as I do.'

In the evening a young person coming into the room, looking at her earnestly and affectionately,

fectionately, he said, 'Deborah arose a mo-
'ther in Israel,' and shortly after, 'The
'sweetness that I feel;' then his difficulty
of breathing increased, and being turned
once or twice, he requested to be helped up,
and was placed in his chair, in which he expired about the ninth hour on second-day
night the 24*th* of the seventh month 1775, being aged near seventy, and a minister about 42
years, and was buried on the 26*th* in friends
grave-yard at East-Nottingham, a large concourse of people attending, after which a solemn meeting was held.

A Testimony from New-Garden *Monthly-Meeting in* Pennsylvania, *concerning* SARAH MIL-
HOUSE.

SHE was religiously inclined from her
youth, and when married, was a good
example in her family as a wife and a parent,
of an inoffensive life and conversation, and
a diligent attender of religious meetings,
until prevented by age and bodily infirmity:
Her appearances as a minister were not frequent, but savoury and in few expressions.

In her last illness she seem'd resigned either to live or die, and by her sensible expressions and good advice to her children and
others, she appeared in a living humble
frame of mind, and signified, 'She did not
'see any thing in her way.'

She quietly departed this life, the 26th of the eighth month 1775, aged about seventy-four years; and on the 27th was interr'd in friends burying-ground at New-Garden.

After her decease, was found, wrote with her own hand, as follows, 'Oh! that my
'children would walk in the truth, the pure,
'inward, everlasting truth, which is Christ;
'seek unto him in secret and great humility,
'who alone can preserve you in every try-
'ing time which must be met with in this
'life, that we may be prepared for that life
'which is everlasting; seek it before any
'earthly treasure.'

A Testimony from Gwynedd *Monthly-Meeting in* Pennsylvania, *concerning* WILLIAM FOULKE.

HE was born of religious parents, early settlers of Gwynedd, from whom he received a pious education, to which, with the visitation of divine grace, he so far attended from early youth, that in the several characters of husband, father, master, and neighbour, with his hospitality and charitable disposition to the poor, he was much endeared to his family, friends and neighbours. Being a man of integrity and a lover of peace, he endeavoured to promote it in others, and was remarkably endued with a happy talent
for

for compofing differences and reclaiming offenders, in which fervices he was much exercifed.

In the ftations of an elder and overfeer which he filled for a number of years, he was exemplary and ferviceable. His health gradually declined for feveral months; and though his diforder proved lingering, he was enabled to bear it with refignation and patience, expreffing the expectation of his change with calmnefs.

The day before his deceafe, a friend who vifited him, mentioned, what a comfortable reflection it muft be to him, when drawing near to the clofe of life, that he had filled up the ftation alloted him in a good degree of faithfulnefs; he replied, ' I have no fight
' when my change may be, I endeavour to
' be refigned, I have not any thing to boaft
' of, I have not any thing to expect from a-
' ny works I have done, it was but little;
' but I have experienced that the Lord is
' merciful, in whom I truft, having redeem-
' ed my foul from deftruction. I much de-
' fire to be within the pale of happinefs,
' fomewhere within the door where I may
' find a quiet habitation.'

He continued fenfible to the laft, and departed this life, on the 30*th* of the eighth month 1775, in the fixty-feventh year of his age, and on the 1*ft* of the ninth month, was interr'd in friends burying-ground at Gwynedd.

A Teftimony

A Testimony from the Monthly-Meeting of Philadelphia, *concerning* SARAH MORRIS.

SHE was born in this city, being the daughter of our ancient friends Anthony and Elizabeth Morris, who were careful to instruct her in the fear of the Lord, a diligent attendance of our religious meetings, and an early acquaintance with the holy scriptures; the advantage whereof she at times expressed to be a great comfort to herself, and of benefit to others. Her father died when she was about seventeen years of age, and near his end gave this testimony respecting her, 'That she had never disobeyed him, and was his comfort;' which we insert with desires it may so impress the minds of youth, that by duly regarding the divine command of obedience to parents, they may be their comfort, merit the like testimony, and secure peace to their own minds. She was endued with understanding superior to many, which, with her sociable, agreeable disposition, occasioned her conversation in the younger part of her life to be sought and acceptable to such who were accounted wise in the estimation of the world; but from her religious inclination prefering the company of those who exceeded her in age and experience, she was mercifully preserved from the snares and temptations to levity and vanity by which many of the youth are too readily captivated.

The state of mind and religious exercise she was brought under, through the early visitations of divine grace, being sensibly expressed in a short account written by herself, we think worthy to be preserved, directed as follows,

'To all to whose hands this may come, be
'it known,

'That, I having been one who was born
'of religious parents, was by that means fa-
'voured with a sober and virtuous educa-
'tion, but what was far beyond all outward
'blessings, the Lord in his mercy was pleas-
'ed to make very early impressions of reli-
'gion on my soul, by his immediate grace
'and good spirit, and made me sensible of
'the touches of divine love when very
'young, and at times these merciful visita-
'tions were continued from my very infan-
'cy (and through every part of life) by
'which I was in a good degree preserved
'from the evils and vanities of the world,
'and not only so, but comforted and sup-
'ported in every time of trouble and diffi-
'culty, as there was a secret regard to that
'good hand which is, and ever will be the
'help of all those who put their trust in it.
'But tho' the Lord had so favoured me that
'I was made capable of being in some re-
'spects serviceable amongst my acquaintance
'and friends, from a propensity in my na-
'tural disposition (which is likewise a bless-
'ing from Heaven) to assist or oblige those
'with whom I conversed; yet after it pleas-
'ed

'ed God, by the death of a sister whom I
' entirely loved, to give me a fresh instance
' of the uncertainty and unsatisfactoriness
' of all temporal blessings, he was pleased
' to strengthen my desires after the enjoy-
' ment of that which is eternal and fadeth
' not away; and strong cries were raised in
' my soul that I might be brought to a near-
' er acquaintance, and a more constant a-
' biding with him who is the beloved of
' souls, and who, by the secret touches of
' divine goodness, had raised such a hunger
' and thirst after righteousness, that my soul
' could not be satisfied short of it: I say, af-
' ter it had pleased God thus to incline my
' mind to seek after a more full enjoyment
' of that inward life and virtue which is
' communicated and conveyed to the soul
' through the illumination of the holy spi-
' rit, I was visited with sickness, in which
' I had so a near a prospect of eternity, that
' I seemed just entering into it; O! then,
' the emptiness and vanity of all the world;
' the pleasures and friendships of it appear-
' ed in a clear and strong light; nothing
' then but the hope of an entrance into the
' kingdom of Heaven seemed of any value;
' and that hope the Lord was at that time
' pleased in some degree to afford me; but
' yet I thought I saw a great deficiency, and
' was made to desire of the Lord, that if it
' was his will to restore me, he might ena-
' ble me to live more close to his teachings,
' and follow him more fully than I had hi-
'   therto

'therto done; but in order to this, a work
'of greater mortification than ever had
'been experienced by me, was necessary.
'Great distress of soul and affliction of bo-
'dy was I brought into, insomuch that I
'knew not where, or what I was; such
'temptations and buffetings of Satan that
'I had till now been a stranger to, were
'suffered to beset me, in the absence of spi-
'ritual comfort and refreshment, yet in all
'this the Lord was very merciful, and let
'me see that his dealings with my soul were
'in order to qualify and fit for some fur-
'ther service; O! then the solemn engage-
'ments my soul was willing to enter into at
'this Bethel! If thou O Lord! will be with
'me in the way that I go, and give me
'bread to eat and raiment to put on, in a
'spiritual sense, and bring me to my hea-
'venly father's house in peace, thou shalt
'be my God, and I will serve thee! And
'the Lord, who knew the tenderness of my
'heart (at that time, for it was his own
'work) was pleased graciously to shower
'down of the heavenly rain of his king-
'dom, by which my soul was greatly com-
'forted and refreshed in his presence; and
'in a true sight and sense of my own no-
'thingness and inability to do any thing
'that was acceptable in the sight of G d
'without his assistance, was my spirit great-
'ly humbled before him, and a resignation
'wrought in my will to be given up in all
'things to him, who had thus enabled my
'soul

'soul to praise his name upon the banks of
' deliverance from great and sore conflicts
' and troubles, which were unknown to
' any in that day, for then was the Lord my
' refuge and sure hiding place, and under
' the shadow of his wing was I kept, and
' in the sweet enjoyment of divine love,
' light and life, at times was made to say,
' surely nothing shall ever be able to make
' a separation from the love of God in Christ
' Jesus: But alas! this lasted not long, for
' when it was clearly shewn me what was
' required of my hands, which was to bear
' a public testimony for God, and to declare
' unto others what he had done for my soul,
' then consultations with flesh and blood
' began, tho' the merciful visitations of love
' were long continued unto me; yet doubts,
' fears and reasonings increased, so that
' great darkness and distress came upon me,
' nor could I now apply with that confi-
' dence and trust as formerly, to him a-
' lone who can help, but began to disclose
' something of my condition to others,
' from which time I was sensible that my
' strength decreased; yet all this while I
' was willing to hope that a fresh visitation
' might be sometime afforded, for without
' it, I saw my state very dangerous; what
' would I not then have done to have reco-
' vered my former condition? I went un-
' der great distress and perplexity day and
' night for some months, the comfortable
' refreshments and divine openings with
' which

'which I had been so plentifully favoured, were withdrawn, and I left in unspeakable anguish and distress; under this sense of terror I cried to the Lord to shew me his will and enable me to perform it, but the sense of his love was so far withdrawn, and fears and doubts had so prevailed, that I began to question every thing, and by degrees the unwearied adversary hath so prevailed, or it is so suffered for ends I know not, that I am at this time, according to my weak apprehension, left very much to myself without the sensation of divine love upon my soul, or the ability to seek after it, or rightly to wait for it, or to stir or move any way as to my soul, but, in a stupidity not to be described, stript of all inward comfort, and not able to take pleasure in any thing this world can afford.'

Being, through the mercy of the Lord, preserved under this close probation, and, in his time, graciously relieved by the quickening virtue of his divine presence and power, she, in great abasement and humiliation, became resigned to his holy requirings, and appeared in public testimony in one of our religious meetings; being thus brought forth in the ministry, through great mortification of her own will, her appearance was much to the comfort and satisfaction of friends, it being evident to the sensible and judicious members of the church, that she was rightly called to this weighty work; and divers nearly sympathizing with her, were spiritual helpers, watching over her in much love and tenderness; and through faithfulness to her gift, she increased in knowledge and experience, and became an able gospel minister, being found in doctrine, pertinent in exhortation, clear and audible in utterance, and careful to adorn the doctrine she preached by a pious exemplary life and conversation.

Her first journey in the service of truth was to some adjacent meetings as companion to our valuable friend Margaret Ellis; being afterwards, through the efficacy of divine love, drawn forth to visit many of the meetings in this province, New-Jersey and the yearly-meetings in Maryland and Long-Island; and in the year 1764, in company with our friends Joyce Benezet and Elizabeth Smith, attended that at Rhode-Island; though her religious labours were chiefly in this city, manifesting among us a steady uniform concern for the cause of truth, and preservation of true christian fellowship, not only in the exercise of her gift in the public ministry, wherein she was eminently favoured, but also of our christian discipline among friends of her own sex, for which she was well qualified and of real use.

After the decease of her ancient mother, who, in the ninety-fourth year of her age, departed in a calm and peaceful state of mind, toward whom she had manifested a filial affection and care, an exercise which she had many years been under to visit friends in

in Great-Britain now reviving, the weight of the service, and her apprehension of being disqualified therefor, affected her so deeply, that she was reduced to such a low state of mind and body, her recovery appeared doubtful; but after a distressing season of conflict, she was favoured with strength to communicate her concern to this meeting, and obtaining a certificate of the near sympathy and concurrence of friends, she was left to proceed, with their free approbation, as the Lord might be pleased to furnish ability; and her affectionate niece Deborah Morris's offer to accompany her, being also concurred with, they embarked for London, in the third month 1772, where being arrived, tho' continuing in a weak state of health, she was enabled to perform her visit to friends in most of the principal counties and towns from Exeter in the west as far north as Cumberland, and those called the Eastern-Counties; attending two yearly-meetings in London, and divers general meetings in other parts of the nation; and being favoured with strength beyond expectation, and with that wisdom which truth gives to those who faithfully resign to its holy requirings, discharged her religious duty to the edification of the churches and her own peace; returning home in the ninth month 1773, accompanied by her said niece, who had been truly helpful to her, and three friends from Great-Britain on a religious visit; her having been thus mercifully sustained

ed through this weighty service, and under such apparent infirmity, advanced to the seventieth year of her age, was both matter of comfort, and occasion of grateful admiration to friends.

Having, soon after her return, attended the general meeting at Shrewsbury, the quarterly-meeting of Bucks and some other meetings, she united that winter with our valuable friends, M. Leaver and E. Robinson, from Great-Britain, in visiting many of the families of friends in this city, being eminently favoured with divine help therein, as she had been at times before in the like service.

In the fifth month 1774, she visited friends at New-York and Long-Island, attending the yearly-meeting there, and divers others; and in the same summer and fall, visited some meetings in New-Jersey and this province, besides diligently attending those in this city as she was enabled, being favoured in most of them with a lively edifying testimony.

For about six months before her departure, a dropsical disorder subjected her to great bodily weakness; yet her love to God, his truth and people, was so prevalent, that when unable to walk to a meeting, she was divers times carried to her seat; one of the last she attended in public, was on the *4th* of the sixth month 1775, to which she was with great difficulty brought, and was enabled to bear a lively testimony; affectionately expressing her great concern for the welfare

welfare of the people, that they might be gathered to God, and mentioning the paſſage of our bleſſed Saviour weeping over Jeruſalem, tenderly exhorted the riſing youth to embrace the call of the Lord, ſubmit to his teaching, and thereby experience preſervation.

During her illneſs, ſhe had to endure great bodily pain, and at times, depreſſion of ſpirit; yet was at ſeaſons much favoured, and uttered many comfortable and edifying expreſſions, ſome of which being noted down, are as follows, viz. ſixth month 1775. On hearing the ſound of a drum paſſing, it being a time of great commotion, ſhe ſaid, 'Oh, it is the ſpirit of Chriſt that is the 'chriſtians glory and ſtrength! It makes us 'humble, meek and wiſe, it is this teacher 'that cannot be removed; a guide into that 'righteous way, which if but lived in, 'would have kept off this impending ſtorm. 'O! that they would even now but humbly 'ſeek to learn the chriſtian warfare, and be 'earneſtly engaged to fight under the ban- 'ner of Chriſt, to know their own hearts 'luſts totally ſubdued.' At another time being in great pain, ſhe cried out, ' O ſweet 'Lord Jeſus, that thou wouldſt be pleaſed to 'give me a little eaſe, who am an unwor- 'thy creature, undeſerving thy ſweet pre- 'ſence; but thou art merciful, and thou, 'O Lord! knoweſt that nothing leſs can 'eaſe and comfort me; thy living preſence 'is all I want.' And after the favour was

granted

granted, which for an hour she enjoyed, she said, 'Oh! how good is my God, thus to hear my feeble cry; O how sweet is this ease! All my pains are eased by one secret look from thee; O! that I could be thankful enough for this favour; this sweet tho' short quiet, which we cannot get at but when thou, O father! pleases. O! that the people would but believe, that in thy peace their strength consists; and that they would more generally seek to know it before it is too late; but too many are contented without witnessing the frequent renewings of divine love, in which only there is life, if they are but preserved from gross evils and go on in prosperity, they sit down easy and think all is well; but O! that they may not too late find their mistake, and that they have pleased themselves with favours which they have unthankfully received, and so stopt short of greater, by not desiring them, and more frequently than the day, waiting to know the renewings of that life, without which there is no life to the truly begotten children, and which would shew them, not only what they ought to do, but would give them strength to do it.'

Seventh month 2d; in a quiet sitting of some friends in her room, she said in substance, 'If I may take the freedom to express my experiences of the Lord's gracious dealings with me, when in a land of darkness and drought, where no water is, a land

'a land of pitts and deferts, befet as with
' noxious creatures, and amongft ferpents
' and fcorpions, from whence none could
' deliver but him who can open and none
' can fhut; I have feen the neceffity, after
' having done the will of God, to wait
' with patience to receive the promife of
' him who is the fame to-day as yefterday,
' and will fo continue forever. Many are
' the comfortable affurances in holy writ to
' thofe who keep the word of his patience;
" I will keep fuch in the hour of temptation,
" which fhall come upon all the earth, to try
" them that dwell therein;" I have many
' times, my dear, may I not fay my beloved
' friends, for fo at feafons you have been
' to me, tho' at other times I hardly dare
' fay fo; I have many times been glad to
' feel a little opening of ftrength with my
' friends, and may fay, I am thankful for
' this quiet folemn opportunity, for great
' have been and ftill are my trials, and clofe
' may be your provings; I don't fpeak it to
' difcourage any, but I find without the re-
' newings of divine love and life, we are
' incapable of keeping the word of his pa-
' tience, being fo frequently befet and fur-
' rounded with weaknefs and infirmities;
' O! may you, my dear friends, who have
' been called and anointed for fervices, wit-
' nefs a renewed fupply of holy oil, where-
' by your lamps may be kept burning, and
' your lights fhining; and experience the
' law to go forth from Zion, and the word

of

' of the Lord from Jerusalem, and remem-
' ber your covenants made in the day of
' deep distress; may you be supported thro'
' every future difficulty and trial, and I
' thro' the present conflict; that when eve-
' ry pool and channel of comfort shall be
' dried up, and all human help found un-
' availing, we may witness him to be near,
' who hath promised, for the cry of the
' poor and for the sighing of the needy he
' would arise; therefore, cry mightily to him,
' that we may know him to do so for us;
' for I find, without sensibly feeling the
' drawing cords of his love, which opens
' and enlarges the heart, we cannot apply
' those gracious promises to our comfort;
' and when he draws, let not the cares of
' this life, nor slavish and unnecessary fears,
' prevent your following him faithfully,
' whatever afflictions may attend; O! may
' we be so preserved in his holy hand, as
' that nothing may be suffered to pluck us
' out of it, and so assisted to conduct, as to
' be found among that happy number who
' have come through many tribulations,
' where all sorrows and sighing will be done
' away and all tears wiped from our eyes,
' to join those who can acceptably sing the
' song of praise, having had their robes
' washed in the blood of the lamb and made
' white.' And on the 3d, tho' with some
difficulty of utterance, said, ' Though the
' floods beat high at times, and the waves
' roared, she was then sensible of the divine
                                    ' love

'love being present, and in that love saluted
'her friends, as she hoped each one there
'had in a greater or lesser degree, known
'the sanctifying power of religion on their
'minds; she very earnestly and affection-
'ately urged them to a more close and so-
'lemn attention to this important work,
'not to rest satisfied short of witnessing
'daily advancing forward on the way; that
'when this earthly tabernacle was dissolved,
'we might have a well grounded hope of a
'house eternal in the Heavens, whose maker
'and builder was God. That our blessed
'Saviour had told his immediate followers,
'in his father's house were many mansions,
'and that he went to prepare a place for
'them, that where he was they might be
'also; and that tho' the sensible enjoyment
'of divine love was much withdrawn from
'many who had formerly been eminently
'favoured with its living influence; yet not
'to be discouraged, as living faith in Christ
'Jesus (tho' but in a small degree) was
'abundantly sufficient for our strength and
'safety; and as his divine love still continu-
'ed with those who are far advanced and
'as on the verge of time, it would also be
'the guide and blessed guardian of the
'younger in years, as they humbly and
'steadily kept upon their watch, and paid
'a due obedience to the divine instructions
'of his holy spirit.'

The last night of her life, being in bodily pain, and under some discouragement of mind,

mind, she was reminded of some late favours of divine love extended to her; after laying sometime in awful silence, she replied, 'Now I see it to my comfort, that the Lord 'hath been with me through all this illness, 'and I, at times, knew it not, such was my 'distressed situation, it was hard for me to 'believe it.' Afterwards falling into a sweet sleep, she in about two hours awaked much refreshed, and remarked, she had not slept so sweetly in all her illness, for she had been in company with her father's God, mother's God and her God; asked her niece (Deborah Morris) who had with abundant care attended on her, if she thought life would hold all night, who answering, she thought it might, as the night was far spent, she desired her said niece would sit by her until the Lord came, (meaning to close her life) then slumbered again, and awakening, admired, saying, 'It is strange I should 'sleep at such a time as this.' Being told her work was done, and it was a favour to her she could sleep, she replied, 'I believe 'it is, and am thankful;' inquiring what time it was, on being told it was after three o'clock, she lifted up her hands as engaged in mental prayer; soon after uttered some words but not intelligibly, and seeming again to drop into a sweet sleep, neither stirred or spoke more, but continuing till between eight and nine o'clock, passed easily away, on the 24*th* of the tenth month 1775, in the seventy-second year of her age, and 31*st* of

her

her ministry, fitted, no doubt, for the enjoyment of that rest, which is prepared for the righteous, having accomplished her warfare in the church militant.

Her burial on the 26*th*, after a solemn meeting, was respectfully attended by many friends and others of her fellow-citizens, to our grave-yard in this city.

A Testimony from Wrights-Town *Monthly-Meeting in* Pennsylvania, *concerning* ZEBULON HESTON.

HE appeared early in the ministry, continued faithful, and died in good unity with the church. His ministry was lively and edifying, in the exercise whereof, he several times travelled through this and the neighbouring colonies: And at the age of near seventy-years, performed a religious visit to the Delaware Indians, residing to the westward of Pennsylvania, which visit was cordially received, as appears from a copy of a speech made by one of their chiefs (captain White Eyes) and the delivery of a belt at the same time in token of friendship, at a meeting for worship in their town on the river Muskingum, which were produced to our meeting at his return.

In his last illness, he expressed his satisfaction with the dutiful deportment of his children towards him as a parent, and gave them

them salutary advice; exhorting them, 'Not to give their minds too much to temporal things, nor seek after worldly enjoyments, but learn to get wisdom and understanding, which would make them shine as stars in the firmament; and to remember their several duties, and be ready at the cock-crow, or at midnight; praying his God and father to be with them and bless them.' After a time of silence, he said, 'I am at peace with all men. Lord thou hast been with me in times past, be with me in my last moments, and I pray my God and father, that he will bear me up as in the hollow of his hand, to my everlasting home.'

In regard to outward affairs, he expressed himself in the following manner, 'If the world would have lived in love and unity one with another, it appears to me, that no good thing would have been withholden from us, but it seems to be dark times, and things lay very wide. But it looketh to me, there will be a gathering home from off the barren mountains and desert hills, of them that are little thought of at this time. Lord, let thy will be done and not mine. If it be thy will that I must depart from my brethren in the time of their trouble, I willingly yield in obedience. If it be thy will that I should be spared a while longer, I willingly bear my part of the burdens whatsoever thou pleasest to lay upon me.' Many more
similar

similar expressions, he frequently uttered during his last illness, under which he was supported in a truly pious and resigned state of mind.

He departed this life, the 12th of the third month 1776, in the seventy-fourth year of his age.

A Testimony from Kingwood *Monthly-Meeting in* New-Jersey, *concerning* MARY HORNER.

SHE was born at Mansfield, in the county of Burlington, New-Jersey, in the year 1736, of parents in membership with friends, and was educated in the profession of the truth as held by us. Her tender mind while in her minority, was sensibly reached with a divine visitation of the love of God, and as she grew to riper years, she was preserved in a good degree of circumspect walking in the fear of the Lord; her conversation being serious, sensible and guarded, and oftentimes her grave deportment was useful as a check to her companions. In the year 1757 she was married to Isaac Horner, and filled the station of a faithful and prudent wife and mother. In the beginning of the year 1768, she appeared in public as a minister, her testimony being short and lively. In the year 1770, she removed with her husband and family, to settle within the compass of this meeting,

and

and has fince refided among us. She was remarkable for her unreferved charitable opennefs and innocent freedom of deportment towards all; and through the influence of the love of God fhed abroad in her heart, by a life of unaffected piety, and a godly circumfpection of conduct and deportment, fhe obtained a good report. She was divers times, with the concurrence of her friends, engaged in gofpel love, in vifiting meetings abroad, and had good fervice in vifiting families, not only within the compafs of this monthly-meeting, but others.

Having taken a cold, it brought on a decay, under which fhe languifhed upwards of eight months, near half of which time fhe neverthelefs attended meetings. During her indifpofition, her quiet compofure of fpirit, and cheerful refignation to the will of her heavenly mafter was truly edifying. She told a friend who vifited her not long before her departure, that 'Though death appear-
' ed a dark paffage, yet all was light beyond
' it.' And to another, who at parting, bid her farewell, fhe faid, ' I fhall fare well
' when I am rid of this body.' She was remarkably clear in her underftanding, and faid, ' Though bodily weaknefs prevail-
' ed, yet her fpirit felt no diminution of
' ftrength;' and exhorted thofe about her, to place their reliance on the Lord alone,
' A confidence,' faid fhe, ' In which I have
' never been difappointed.'

One

One evening near her close, she broke forth into expressions of praise to the Almighty, and humble acknowledgments, 'That he 'had to her, performed all his promises, 'had prepared and sanctified her, and 'brought her to that hour; and that she 'should praise him as long as she continued 'in the body, and at the conclusion, cheer- 'fully surrender husband and children, and 'all that he had given her, into his hands.'

In or near her last hour, she beckoned her husband, to come and take his leave of her, and then composedly said, 'Thou art a 'welcome messenger, thou art welcome, 'take me quickly.'

She died the 31*st* of the fifth month 1776, in the fortieth year of her age, having been engaged in the ministry upwards of 8 years.

A Testimony from Salem *Monthly-Meeting in* New-Jersey, *concerning* JAMES DANIEL.

HE was born of pious parents, and thereby knew the advantage of a religious education, which he frequently expressed by way of encouragement to parents and youth, as a means by which he had in a good degree been guarded in the time of his youth, from the vanities of the world. Yet as he grew in years he clearly saw he wanted the experimental part of the christian religion, without which he could not at-tain to that which his soul exceedingly longed for; and under a sense of this want, was brought at times very low, and for some years had to pass through a state of mourning and deep exercise, being baptized as under the cloud and in the sea in a spiritual sense; which brought him to a passive submission to the divine will, so that it pleased the Lord, in the returns of his favour, to visit him with the day spring from on high; and having learned obedience through the things that he suffered, he gave up to the heavenly vision, and came forth in the ministry in a few words, mostly in scripture language, in great simplicity; and altho' not eloquent, yet being faithful in the little, he became much enlarged in his gift, having clear openings in the scriptures, and at times much favoured with clear prospects of the states of meetings and individuals, that he had to speak to secret and hidden things, in the demonstration of the spirit and with power, which reached the witness in many hearts. He was a father to the young in experience, and zealous to reprove lightness and vanity where he saw occasion.

He travelled in the work of the ministry, in several of the American provinces, and once to England, of which services we had comfortable accounts. He was zealous for the support of our christian discipline, was favoured with a good understanding, exemplary in his life and conversation, and lived much in the simplicity of the truth, which
made

made him near to his friends, and a useful member in society. Being weak in body, a considerable time before his decease, he said, ' It seemed as if his day's work was ' done, and nothing lay upon him;' observing that some worthy friends had of late been removed without much foresight of their latter end, and had not much to communicate, he said, ' If it should be his case, ' he would not have it looked upon as in ' displeasure, for he was clear and easy in ' his mind, and that he believed his stay ' would not be long;' which proved according to his prospect; for being taken with something of a quinsy followed by an ague, he said, ' He thought that would be his last ' illness,' adding, ' I have never been de-' sirous to know when my time was near at ' an end, but have long been desirous to ' live so as to be ready, and I think I am ' ready. I have endeavoured to be faithful ' in the discharge of my duty in every re-' spect, and have nothing lies against me, ' but seem at quiet. I have in other illnesses ' been pretty much resigned, yet there seem-' ed something of a choice to live, but in ' this I have not that choice, but I am rea-' dy.' He quietly passed away, after a short illness of about fifteen hours, on the 18*th* of the twelfth month 1776; aged seventy-two years. Having been a minister about 40 years.

A Testimony from Evesham *Monthly-Meeting in* New-Jersey, *concerning* HANNAH FOSTER.

SHE was the daughter of Enoch and Sarah Core, of Evesham aforesaid, and was born the 17th day of the tenth month 1710; her father dying while she was very young, left her and three other children under the care of their mother, whose religious concern for them was very great; as some of us have heard our said friend often express both in public and private.

She was naturally of a cheerful disposition, and at times when young in years, she suffered an airy spirit to prevail so far as to lead her into lightness, yet, thro' divine favour, the solid instruction and example of her mother, had such influence on her mind, as to preserve her from gross evils; which we have often heard her express with awful reverence.

In the year 1729, she was married to our friend William Foster, and entered into the care of a family, at which time, the cares of this world had great effect on her mind, as some of her last expressions herein after mentioned will more clearly evince.

Some time after her marriage, it pleased the Lord to renew his visitation of love to her soul, and to shew her the vanity of all temporal enjoyments without his love; and she yielding obedience to the heavenly vision, and being given up to serve the Lord, had
a gift

a gift in the miniftry committed to her, in which we have reafon to believe, fhe was in a good degree faithful to improve, and through divine aid, became a lively minifter.

She vifited moft of the meetings on the continent of America, except fome part of Virginia and Carolina; and the accounts received of her religious labour in the miniftry, were comfortable and fatisfactory. Her humble awful waiting in religious meetings was edifying; fhe was much concerned that good order might be preferved, and careful to example and admonifh her offspring in the fear of the Lord, more than to influence their minds to feek after the treafures that are tranfitory and perifhing. A near fympathizer with the afflicted, either in body or mind, often vifiting fuch and adminiftring to their relief.

Towards the latter part of her time, her health was much impaired, yet fhe grew more lively in the miniftry, and in fome of the laft meetings fhe attended, was enabled in a folemn manner, to invite the youth to join the heavenly call of God, and to be faithful in their gifts, and then they would be raifed like an army in his power, to fubdue the works of darknefs, which fhe faw much prevailed amongft them; remarking fome parts of the epiftle from our laft yearly-meeting, refpecting fome hopeful youths who attended that folemn fervice.

In her last sickness, which tho' short, was sharp, she was preserved in much patience and stillness; and when it was apprehended she was near expiring, a friend who came to visit her, taking leave of those attending her, she held out her hand to the said friend and desired to be raised up, when with considerable difficulty she said, 'That there was
'a time when her heart and mind was
'much set on the world and the things of
'it, and it prospered with her according to
'her desire; but she blessed the name of
'the Lord, who soon let her see the vanity
'and emptiness of all worldly treasure, and
'that she was thankful he had enabled her
'to yield obedience to the heavenly visitati-
'on, and in some degree to answer his re-
'quirings, for it now yielded her more
'peace, than if she had possession of the
'whole world, if it was of tenfold more
'value than it is; and that her prayers had
'often been to the Lord, that he might yet
'favour the rising generation with the like
'visitation of his love,' with some other words which could not be understood. She appeared in a sweet frame of mind, and after a short pause, took her solemn leave of the said friend; after which she lay still, and in a few hours quietly departed this life, on the 14*th* of the first month 1777, and was buried in friends burying-ground at Evesham the 17*th* of the same, where a solemn meeting was held; aged sixty-six and a minister upwards of 40 years.

A Testimony

A Testimony from the Falls *Monthly-Meeting in* Bucks *county, concerning* Joseph White.

AS the memory of the just is pronounced blessed, we think it expedient to give forth a testimony concerning this our esteemed friend.

He was born at the Falls the 28*th* of the eleventh month 1712-13; being young when his father died, he was brought up under the care of his relations and friends: And through the early extendings of heavenly regard whilst young, and attending to the teachings of divine grace, he was led and preserved from many of the follies and extravagances incident to unthinking youth. About the twentieth year of his age he appeared in public testimony in our religious meetings, and continuing in a good degree faithful to the measure of light and grace communicated, he grew in his gift, and became a lively and able minister.

He was naturally of an open cheerful disposition, and honestly concerned for the promotion of piety and virtue, and for the support and maintenance of good order in the church; for which service he was eminently gifted, and truly serviceable amongst us, being often concerned that the authority of truth might be kept up in all our meetings of discipline, and that true judgment might be placed upon the disorderly and irreclaimable. He was exemplary in his life

life and converfation, a diligent and timely attender of our religious meetings when health of body permitted; and was often favoured therein in public teftimony and fupplication, much to the comfort and edification of the truly humble waiters. And altho' he had a large gift in the miniftry, he many times fat meetings in filence, waiting upon the Lord, not being hafty or forward in the exercife of his gift; but careful not to minifter without the heavenly life and power that firft raifed him up in the miniftry, whereby his public fervice was greatly to the confolation and refrefhment of many.

He feveral times had a concern to vifit the churches abroad, and with the concurrence of this meeting, vifited many of the meetings of friends in this and feveral of the adjacent provinces, and once through fome parts of Maryland, Virginia and North-Carolina: And having for fome confiderable time been under a weighty concern to pay a religious vifit to friends in feveral parts of Europe, he with the concurrence and unity of his friends took fhipping for that purpofe in the year 1758, and after a fhort paffage landed in England, and having pretty generally vifited friends meetings in England and Ireland, and fome parts of Wales, he returned to his family and friends, having been from home in truth's fervice near three years: And at his return from thefe these visits produced certificates of friends unity and good satisfaction with him, and his public service amongst them.

He was divers times appointed and engaged in the service of visiting families, being well qualified for that weighty service.

He much loved the company and conversation of his friends; was a loving and affectionate husband, a tender parent and a good neighbour, generally beloved by his friends and others that knew him, being in several respects useful and serviceable in the neighbourhood where he lived.

He was attended from his youth at times, with a pain at his breast, with intermissions of health, sometimes for years, and at other times but short; but as he advanced further in age, intermissions of health grew short and pain increased, which brought on other bodily infirmities, which he bore with patience and resignation, often craving he might not be off his watch when his pains were exquisite, nor his faith fail in the time of trial, believing it to be the goodness of God, through his thus dealing with him, more and more to wean him from all outward connections and nearest ties of nature, that being as the pure gold, refined through the furnace, he might with triumph join the redeemed that were gone before, which he at times had a foretaste and evidence of; but the time when, as he himself sometimes expressed, he did not then see, believing it to be consistent with divine wisdom to keep it hid from him.

The latter part of his time for several months, he slept but litte in the night season, being at times engaged in reverent intercessions and divine contemplation, and appeared to be waiting for the solemn moment.

He lived in the compass of the Falls particular meeting until a few years before his death, and then removed to Makefield, (a branch of the same monthly-meeting,) and having for some months felt strong desires (if favoured with health) to go to the Falls meeting, and on a monthly-meeting day set out to go there; but the weather being cold and he in a weak state of health, soon found himself unable to perform the journey, and returned home. But sometime after feeling his bodily strength somewhat restored, and love renewed, he set out, in company with his wife, one first-day morning, and got to the meeting where he was favoured with an open time in public testimony, much to the satisfaction of those present. After the meeting was over and friends gone out, a friend being desirous of speaking to him, not seeing him out of doors, returned into the house, and found him sitting on a seat, unable to move without help; the friend assisted him, and took him to his house, where he was taken care of: The fit being of the paralytick kind, was much more favourable than at some other times, tho' it continued ebbing and flowing for several hours; in which time

time he expressed several things, some of which being then taken down, are nearly as follows.

Being asked by his son Samuel how it was with him; he answered, 'I dont know but
' that I am near my end. My desire at this
' time for thee is, that thou seek unto the
' Lord for assistance, to govern thee in thy
' conduct in this fluctuating life, for I have
' found him to be a sure help and counsellor
' to me; and if thou follow after him in
' truth and sincerity, as I have endeavoured
' to do, he will be unto thee a sufficient
' director, a teacher that cannot be removed
' into a corner: I have not been anxious to
' gather a portion of this world, nor make
' to myself mammon of unrighteousness,
' for I think I have seen a snare that has attended many young people on these accounts. I have ever from my youth had
' a desire to be more in substance than in
' shew: Let me appear as I might in the
' sight of men, their praise I sought not
' for; but I have sought the honour of God,
' therefore there is a place where no trouble
' shall annoy, prepared for me as a reward
' for obedience: You that stay, be more
' humble, and when trouble awaits you,
' look not upon nor trust to the arm of flesh
' for assistance, but stay yourselves upon
' him who suffered for you, for me, and
' for all mankind; for I have for sometime
' believed, and lived in the hopes thereof,
' and am now in measure confirmed, of
' more

'more glorious things yet to be revealed to
'the church of Chrift, and that further and
'greater difcoveries will yet be made, with
'refpect to the chriftian religion than ever
'yet has been fince the apoftafy.'

And after a fhort paufe he broke forth in thefe expreffions, 'The door is open, I fee
'an innumerable company of faints, of an-
'gels, and of the fpirits of juft men, which
'I long to be unbodied to be with, but not
'my will, but thy will be done O Lord! I
'cannot utter nor my tongue exprefs, what
'I feel of that light, life and love that at-
'tends me, which the world cannot give,
'neither can it take away from me. My
'fins are wafhed away by the blood of the
'Lamb that was flain from the foundation
'of the world: All rags and filthinefs are
'taken away, and in room thereof love and
'good will for all mankind: O that we may
'become more united in the church mili-
'tant, and nearer refemble the church
'triumphant! O that we all might make
'fuch an end as I have in profpect, for its
'all light, all life, all love and all peace,
'the light that I fee is more glorious than
'the fun in the firmament; come Lord Je-
'fus Chrift, come when thou pleafes, thy
'fervant is ready and willing; into thy
'hands I commit my fpirit, not my will,
'but thy will be done O Lord! Let this
'mortal body be committed to the duft, be
'with me, with my children and my grand-
'children; be with all them that love thee,
'that

'that love thy appearance. O the pains that I feel, that attend this mortal body, they are more comely to me than jewels! I rejoice in my sighs and groans, for to me they are most melodious; I am near to enter that harmony with Moses and the Lamb, where they cry holy, holy, holy, I cannot express the joy I feel. My heart (if it were possible) would break for joy: If any inquire after me, after my end, let them know all is well with me.'

Many more weighty expressions he spoke, which not being taken down, cannot be recollected.

The next day his pain abating, and finding himself somewhat relieved from his disorder, he was taken to his own house, where he remained in a weak state of health for sometime, being unable to go much abroad. And one night some short time before his death, his pain had been sharp the forepart of the night, but the latter part it abating, his wife lay down by him, and fell asleep, but he as usual slept not, but after sometime called to his wife in these words: 'My dear, I believe I must take my leave of thee. I have never seen my end till now, and now I see it is near, and the holy angels enclose me around, waiting to receive me;' his wife asked him if she should call up the children, he said, he did not see any thing further he had to say to them, except to his son Joseph, who being called, and he having exprest what he had on his mind, was much spent, and appeared as tho' he was near his desired port; but after sometime he revived, with these words, 'Life is yet strong in me and will not yield;' thus he continued the few concluding days, waiting in resignation and retiredness of mind, until the repeated returns of the paralytick complaint reduced his faculties and senses so, that he knew not what was done for some days, and departed in much stillness as in a sleep, the 10*th* day of the third month 1777, and was decently interr'd in friends burying-ground at the Falls meeting-house, the 12*th* of the same; his body being attended to the grave by a number of friends and neighbours.

May we under the consideration of our great loss of him, and many other faithful labourers in the Lord's vineyard, now removed from us, be excited so to follow their footsteps, that with them, we may be partakers of that incorruptible inheritance, which is reserved for the righteous, when time here shall be no more.

Aged sixty-four, and a minister about 44 years.

A Testimony

A Testimony from Haddonfield *Monthly-Meeting in* New-Jersey, *concerning* JOSEPH GIBSON.

PRECIOUS is the memory of the righteous, those who have been bright examples of holiness in their day, and therein preachers to others in life and conversation: It lives in our hearts to give this short testimony, that such was our ancient and beloved friend Joseph Gibson, an elder of this meeting. He was born at Woodbury in the year 1690, and became early acquainted with the seasoning virtue of truth, which preserved him in a good degree, from the vanities of youth, and made him in love with plainness and sobriety while young; by a watchful attention to this divine principle, he attained a pious and innocent stability of conduct through life, not often equalled; that it may be justly said, he was "An Israelite indeed in whom there was no guile." A diligent attender of meetings, and a lively example there, in awful humble labour for that bread which strengthens and nourishes the soul; wherein he continued steadfast to his concluding period. We could enlarge, but conclude with the words of the Psalmist, "Mark the perfect man, and behold the upright, for the end of that man is peace;" which we believe was in an eminent degree the case of this our friend, who "Being dead, yet speaketh."

He departed this life, after a short illness, on the 9th of the fourth month 1777, and was buried the 11th, in friends burying-ground at Woodbury aforesaid; aged about eighty-seven years.

A Testimony from Pipe-Creek *Monthly-Meeting in* Maryland, *concerning* Rachel Farquhar, *late wife of* William Farquhar junr.

SHE was born at Castleshane, in Ireland, in the year 1737, and removed to Pennsylvania with her parents, John and Elizabeth Wright, who, after some years, settled in York county, within the compass of Warrington monthly-meeting, of which she was a member, till her marriage and removal with her husband to Pipe-Creek.

She was religiously inclined when young; and about the fifteenth year of her age, by a fresh visitation of divine love, was engaged to seek after divine wisdom; so that she became an early example of piety and virtue; an encourager and promoter of virtuous inclinations in her companions and acquaintance; her steady conduct, and kind and exemplary conversation, gained the love and esteem of her friends and neighbours.

After her marriage, which was near the beginning of the twenty-third year of her age, she continued a diligent attender of meetings

meetings for worship and discipline when ability of body would admit; and when there, was of an exemplary solid deportment, so that she was favoured to become a useful member of society, of sound judgment.

She first appeared in the ministry in the second month 1771, and tho' not large was pertinent in testimony; often admonishing such as were forgetful of their known duties, and sharply reproving where a wrong spirit prevailed: Yet frequently speaking comfortably to the bowed down mourners in Zion, with whom she often travelled in spirit, endeavouring according to her ability, to lend a hand of help to such.

The last meeting she was at, was on a first-day, about a week before she died, in which she was much favoured, and spake concerning Israel's journey from Egypt to Canaan, advising not to settle short of a possession in the promised land. As she was walking home with her husband in a solid frame of mind, she said, ' In my father's ' house are many mansions;' signifying, ' If she might be favoured with one of the ' least of them, she would be content.'

She departed this life, the 19*th* of the fourth month 1777, and was interr'd in the family burying-ground on the 21*st* of the same month; in the fortieth year of her age and 7*th* of her ministry.

A Testimony from the Monthly-Meeting of Philadelphia, *concerning* Mary Emlen.

THIS our beloved friend arrived in Pennsylvania, with her parents Robert and Susannah Heath, from Great-Britain, about the year 1701, in the ninth of her age; and in 1716, was married to George Emlen and settled in this city.

About the year 1728, a remarkable visitation being extended to friends in this city, the hearts of divers were humbled, and, in the efficacy of divine love, several were constrained to open their mouths in our religious assemblies, in public testimony, and acknowledgments of the Lord's goodness and gracious dealings with their souls.

Our worthy friend Daniel Stanton, in his journal, mentions this as a memorable time, and names the several friends who then came forth in the ministry, of which number this friend was one; who being faithful, grew in her gift, and not only laboured in this city, but divers times was drawn forth in the love of the gospel, to visit the meetings in other parts of Pennsylvania and New-Jersey. And in the year 1744, in company with our dear friend Mary Evans, visited the meetings of friends in New-England; and was several times engaged with others in the weighty and profitable work of visiting the familes of friends in this city, and through divers meetings in the country;
in

in which fervices, her labours were acceptable, being qualified in a peculiar manner for that work.

Her miniftry was lively, and delivered in much innocency and brokennefs of fpirit. Being a woman of integrity, fhe loved chriftian candor and plain dealing, and was preferved clear in her underftanding, and in her love to truth. During her illnefs, which was fhort, fhe was favoured with an earneft of that divine peace and reft which is prepared for the righteous.

She departed this life, in this city, on the 1ft of the fixth month 1777, and was interr'd in friends burial-ground the 3d following, attended by many friends and others; aged eighty-four years.

A Teftimony from Wilmington *Monthly-Meeting in the county of* New-Caftle *on* Delaware, *concerning* ELIZABETH SHIPLEY.

OUR beloved friend Elizabeth Shipley, daughter of Samuel Levis, was born in the Townfhip of Springfield, and county of Chefter in Pennfylvania, on the 26*th* day of the tenth month 1690. She was led in the prime of youth to deny herfelf, take up her crofs, and follow Chrift; and being found walking in a good degree, in obedience to the meafure of grace received, about the twenty-fourth year of her age fhe appeared in the miniftry; and being faithful in the improvement of her talent, it pleafed the Lord to make her an able and fkilful minifter of the gofpel. She travelled in the fervice thereof in this land, both fouthward and northward in the early part of her time, and vifited Barbados in company with Jane Fenn, in the year 1725; but as fhe kept few minutes, we have little account of her labours abroad.

In the year 1728, fhe was married to William Shipley, near Springfield aforefaid, where they lived until the year 1736, about which time they removed with their family to this place; and we believe fhe was an inftrument in the Lord's hand, to fettle a meeting here, and gather many to it. In 1743, fhe embark'd for England with our friend Efther White, and the veffel going by way of North-Carolina, while there, they vifited fome meetings in that province; after which they failed again, and arrived at Liverpool on the 26th of the feventh month, and in gofpel love, vifited generally the meetings of friends in England, Scotland and Ireland, to their own fatisfaction; and, as appears by accounts from friends there, to the comfort of many. She alfo made feveral fhort vifits to the neighbouring provinces; and in the feventieth year of her age, in company with our friend Hannah Fofter, vifited feveral of the northern provinces. She was feveral times exercifed in
that

that important service of visiting families, in which her company and labour was very acceptable.

Her deportment in meetings was grave and solid, her gift in the ministry lively and edifying, in prayer awful and weighty, not being forward in appearing.

Although her natural strength was much abated in the latter part of her time, yet her faculties remained bright, and her ministry accompanied with life and power.

In the time of her last illness, as several friends who came to visit her were sitting by her, she appeared filled with divine power, and spoke in a lively manner, of the drawings of the father's love to bring her to settle in this place, and said, that his promises had been fulfilled to her; advising to faithfulness in doing the work of their day; that for her own part, she was as a shock of corn fully ripe, and should shortly be gathered to the haven of rest.

In a little time after this, she was removed to West-Marlborough; at which place she finished her course, on the 10th day of the tenth month 1777, in the eighty-seventh year of her age, a minister about 63 years. She was interr'd in friends burying-ground on the 12th of the same month, where a solemn meeting was held on the occasion.

A Testimony

A Testimony from Wilmington *Monthly-Meeting in the county of* New-Castle *on* Delaware, *concerning* Esther White.

OUR beloved friend Esther White, daughter of Thomas Canby, of the county of Bucks in Pennsylvania, was born in the second month 1700. In her young years she loved to attend religious meetings, and to see friends behave solid therein, being herself an example of piety. She married John Stapler, of the county aforesaid; and being called to the work of the ministry, she became a faithful labourer. About the thirty-fourth year of her age, her husband was removed by death; after which she married John White, and in the year 1739 removed with their family to this place.

In the spring of the year 1743, she, in company with our friend Elizabeth Shipley, sailed for England by way of North-Carolina, and while there, visited some meetings in that province, then embarked, and arrived at Liverpool in the seventh month following, and in gospel love, visited the meetings of friends generally through England, Ireland and Scotland, to their own satisfaction, and, as appears by accounts received, to the comfort and edification of many; and returned home in the latter part of the year 1745, to the joy of her friends and family.

In the year 1750, she visited most of the meetings of friends in Maryland, Virginia and

and the Carolinas; and in 1756, in company with Grace Fisher, those in New-Jersey, and New-York Government: And in 1760, in company with Hannah Foster junr. those on the Eastern-Shore of Maryland, and the counties on Delaware: She also often visited the neighbouring meetings; and in 1776, and the seventy-seventh year of her age, after a long time of sickness, she, in great bodily weakness, attended the quarterly-meeting at Fairfax in Virginia, much to her own peace and friends satisfaction.

She was an useful member of society, and a woman of uncommon cheerfulness of spirit, although largely experienced in afflictions; through which she was mercifully supported by divine sufficiency; and being instructed in sorrow, had a sympathizing heart with the afflictions of others, and was ready to communicate to their relief both in spirituals and temporals. Her deportment was grave and solid, her ministry lively and edifying, even to old age. She was frequent in exhorting and encouraging friends to faithfulness in these times of great trial and outward commotion; that they might, with the wise builder, dig deep, and experience their foundation to be laid sure, that neither winds nor floods might move them. She was careful to maintain brotherly love, sometimes saying, that 'Love was her life, 'that she could not live without it;' and being livingly sensible of the preciousness thereof, was desirous to promote it in others.

After

After a life in which she had to endure several long and trying seasons of sickness, and to pass through many deep baptisms of sorrow, through which she was supported with becoming cheerfulness, patience and resignation; she departed this life, on the 5th day of the twelfth month 1777, in the seventy-eighth year of her age, having been a minister upwards of 50 years; and on the 7th of the same month and 1st of the week, was interr'd in friends burying-ground in Wilmington; being much beloved by her neighbours, her funeral was accompanied by many friends and others, and was a solemn opportunity.

May the great Lord of the harvest, who is removing many eminent ministers from his churches, be pleased to raise up others to stand faithful witnesses for his name and truth in the earth.

A Testimony from Deer-Creek *Monthly-Meeting in* Maryland, *concerning* JOSEPH JONES.

HE was born in the city of Worcester, in Old-England, in the year 1686. His parents being of the church of England, educated him in that way during his abode with them, which was until he was about fourteen years of age. In the year 1700 he arrived

arrived at Philadelphia, and going into New-Jerſey, there reſided until twenty-one years of age.

He was convinced of the truth about the year 1708, and in 1712 appeared in the miniſtry, being then in the twenty-ſixth year of his age: Having, ſince his convincement, undergone many ſore conflicts, by reaſon of a backwardneſs to comply with the Lord's requirings whereunto he had divers times been diſobedient through diffidence and weakneſs, but at length he gave up, and therein found peace.

After his marriage, he reſided about twelve years at Nottingham, in Cheſter county Pennſylvania, and then removed to Deer-Creek where he continued. He was of an innocent life and harmleſs converſation; and in him were blended thoſe truly chriſtian virtues which render religion lovely and deſirable; even the irreligious eſteemed him an ornament to the chriſtian profeſſion. Being very converſant in the holy ſcriptures, and favoured with a retentive memory, he was enabled to quote them with propriety, and very often ſuitably apply them to inſtruction and edification.

Divine love, as witneſſed by the believers in Chriſt, was a ſubject upon which he frequently expreſſed himſelf, in engaging and perſuaſive terms; inviting others to come and be made partakers of ſo glorious a treaſure; adding, ' It had been the crown and
' joy

' joy of his life, the comfort and support of
' his old age, and was presuaded would not
' forsake him in death.'

Of earthly treasure he possessed little, but he appeared to be one of those poor of this world, whom the apostle James mentions, as "Chosen by God, rich in faith, and heirs of the kingdom, which he hath promised to them that love him." In this happy situation he was supported with christian fortitude, through times of adversity and deep affliction.

His wife dying in the ninth month 1777, to whom he had been an affectionate companion upwards of sixty years, he did not long survive her, but, about four months afterwards, was visited with his last illness, in which he suffered much pain, but was composed; some days before his departure he grew easy, and in his latter moments, when exhausted nature scarcely left him strength to utter himself intelligibly, he lamented the state of the careless and unconcerned, who did not duly and timely consider their latter end.

He seemed very desirous to be dissolved and be with Christ; and on the 8*th* of the first month 1778, as a shock of corn fully ripe, he was removed from works to rewards, in the ninety-third year of his age; leaving behind him the favour of a good name, being generally beloved by people of all ranks and denominations who knew him. On the 11*th* of the same month, he was interr'd in friends burying-ground at Deer-Creek.

A Testimony

A Testimony from Uwchlan *Monthly-Meeting in* Pennsylvania, *concerning* GRIFFITH JOHN.

HE was born (by his own account) in Pembrokeshire, in the principality of Wales, in the year 1683, and was in his youth an earnest seeker after righteousness among divers forms of religion, until he became measurably convinced of the principle of truth as held by friends, by perusing William Penn's key to christian knowledge, before he had much if any outward acquaintance with them: And coming over to this country when a young man, he soon after joined with friends in religious fellowship; and being faithful to the manifestations of divine grace in his heart, he had a gift in the ministry bestowed upon him; and tho' not large, was savoury and edifying; which, together with his exemplary life and conversation, manifested him to be an heavenly minded man, much redeemed from the love and spirit of this world.

He was not anxious about the increase of outward riches, but easy and content with a small share thereof; so much as served for bodily support in great simplicity and plainness, he thankfully received; having a testimony against all superfluity, and every thing tending to exalt the mind of man, or promote

promote worldly greatness in any degree; seeking above all, the kingdom of Heaven and the righteousness thereof.

He was a lover of peace amongst brethren and in his neighbourhood; and by precept and example, laboured to promote it; being at times concerned to travel about on foot, even in advanced age, to his friends houses, and pay short visits in true christian love, and drop weighty and edifying hints, tending to stir up the pure mind; and scarcely any thing was said by him at any time but what had a tendency that way.

He was a remarkable and worthy example, in constantly and early attending our religious meetings, until upwards of ninety years of age; when through weakness and infirmity, he was confined at home, and underwent great bodily affliction with true christian fortitude and resignation to the divine will, patiently waiting his change; which was on the 29*th* of the sixth month 1778; aged about ninety-five, and a minister near 70 years.

A Testimony from the Monthly-Meeting of Friends of Philadelphia *for the* Southern-District, *concerning* JOHN HALLOWELL.

HE was exemplary in a diligent attendance of our religious meetings and solid patient waiting therein, and serviceable among

among us according to ability, in the support of the difcipline; of a meek and quiet fpirit, careful not to give juft occafion of offence to any. He was appointed an elder in the year 1772, in which ftation he conducted to good fatisfaction.

In the early part of the eighth month 1777, he was taken unwell, and being under great bodily pain, often begged for patience, faying, he was afraid to afk for any thing elfe. After he had been confined about two weeks, his pain fomewhat abating, he called his children together, and fpoke to them as follows: ‘ It looks as if I may
‘ fhortly be taken from you, and I think I
‘ have nothing to charge myfelf with, in
‘ regard to bringing you up; I have with
‘ great care watched over your morals, and
‘ anxioufly endeavoured by example, to
‘ teach you to walk in the fear of the Lord;
‘ but a backward difpofition prevailing,
‘ which I fear, has fometimes kept me from
‘ doing the good I might have done in the
‘ world, has at times, when my heart has
‘ been earneftly engaged for you, caufed me
‘ to keep filence, when it might have been
‘ profitable to have thus addreffed you:
‘ Look to the Lord my children, and afk of
‘ him to direct your ways. He muft be the
‘ fupport of youth as well as of old age. It is
‘ him, and him alone you muft cleave to,
‘ if ever you expect to find peace that will
‘ be lafting. It is not moral rectitude, go-
‘ ing to meeting, or any outward acts of
‘ devotion

'devotion only, that will do for you. Religion is an inward work, and true worship must be performed in the heart, by quietly waiting on him who is the rock of ages. I know by experience what I say, therefore earnestly desire you to look to the Lord, live near him, and let his fear direct you in all you undertake. Keep out of the noises and confusions that are in the world, 'tis all delusion. To be blest with the presence of the Lord in a dungeon, is preferable to liberty enjoyed in palaces without it. And if it should please the Lord to take me from you, tho' we may part for a season, yet if we walk in his ways, we shall hereafter meet in eternal bliss.'

His disorder increasing, his pain at times was very great, which he was enabled to bear with a good degree of christian resignation; often desiring he might be endued with patience to hold out to the end. And altho' his outward tabernacle gradually decayed, yet the seasonable and lively expressions which he at times uttered, evidenced that his inward man was frequently renewed.

A few weeks before his departure, several friends coming to visit him, after a seasonable time of silence, he spoke as follows.

'I have often of late been led to examine myself, to see what it is that keeps me back, sometimes I think I see death advancing swift, and at other times quite
'gone;

'gone; at this time in particular, I have
' been led to confider whether there remains
' any thing for me to do, and if I have any
' thing in my heart againſt any perſon, that
' my love is not yet perfect; and upon a
' ſtrict examination, I find nothing but love
' to mankind univerſally. I have been great-
' ly tried with pain of body, and poverty
' and barrenneſs of ſpirit, but through mer-
' cy have been preſerved from murmuring;
' and I have a hope, that when I put off
' this body, I ſhall be at reſt; and that hope
' is an anchor to the ſoul.'

A day or two before his departure, his pain much abated, and tho' he was reduced very low, yet was preſerved in much calmneſs and ſerenity of mind, ſaying, ' He
' thought his diſſolution was near; that he
' had done with every thing below, and ex-
' pected the change to him would be a hap-
' py one, believing a place of reſt was pre-
' pared for him.'

He quietly departed this life, the 26th of the ſeventh month 1778, in the ſixty-fourth year of his age, and his body was interr'd the day following in friends burying-ground in this city.

A Teſtimony

A Testimony from Pipe-Creek *Monthly-Meeting in* Maryland, *concerning* WILLIAM FARQUHAR.

HE was born in Ireland the 29th of the seventh month 1705, and came to America about the sixteenth year of his age, and settled in Pennsylvania, where he was convinced of the truth, and married among friends. In the year 1735, he removed and settled at Pipe-Creek, when there were very few inhabitants in those parts. Some years afterwards he was concerned that a meeting might be settled, which was allowed to be held at his house at times for several years; when the number of friends increasing, they concluded to build a meeting house, which our said friend zealously promoted. His house was much resorted to by travelling friends and others, both in that early period and since, to whom he was courteous and kind.

Some years after the settlement of a monthly-meeting at Fairfax, of which he was a member, he was appointed to the station of an elder, which he filled with propriety and reputation; being an example of plainness, and anxiously careful for the education of his children. He was, at times, concern'd in meetings, to exhort friends to keep to the testimony of truth, and particularly the youth, for whom he seemed zealously concerned, that as they grew in years they might grow in grace.

For some months before his decease, he was in a weak state of body, yet frequently attended meetings, and the last time of his being there was about four days before he died; the night following being in much pain, he several times cried out, 'O Father! mitigate my pain if it be thy will;' and was favoured to keep in the patience and resignation, waiting for his change. The day before he died, his wife leaning over him mourning; he said to her, 'Weep not for me, but for thyself and others. The Lord is near.'

He departed this life, the 21st of the ninth month 1778, and was buried in the family burying-ground on the 23d of the same month; aged near seventy-three years.

P. S. I am willing to communicate a few hints of what has often passed through my mind concerning my dear husband, whose memory, to me, remains precious. He was much concerned for the welfare of the young and rising generation, often cautioning and exhorting friends in their several stations, strictly to examine the great duty and charge committed to their trust; and in a particular manner, his offspring, that they would mutually live in love with each other, and that they might be careful to bring up their children in the nurture and admonition of the Lord.

ANN FARQUHAR.

A Testimony

A Testimony from the Monthly-Meeting of Philadelphia, *concerning* MARY PEMBERTON.

SHE was the daughter of Nathan and Mary Stanbury, of this city, who were removed by death in her tender age, after which she was put under the care of our friends Richard and Hannah Hill, by whom she was religiously educated: She was endued with good natural understanding, and being obedient to the discoveries of divine grace in her own mind, she experienced a growth and advancement in the life of religion, and through its gradual work, became a useful and active member in the church, being many years in the station of an elder and overseer. Her conversation was lively and instructive, her deportment solid and exemplary, and in our religious meetings, it was often apparent she was favoured with the preparation of a broken heart and contrite spirit for the solemn performance of divine worship. She felt the affliction of others with tender sympathy, and was enabled through divine help to bear her own, which were various and proving, with great resignation and christian fortitude. She was first joined in marriage to Richard Hill; and sometime after his decease, to our worthy friend Robert Jordan; and lastly, in the year 1747, to our valued friend Israel Pemberton lately deceased; and
through

through the several vicissitudes of life, she was favoured to persevere with great stability and prudence.

The following was found among her papers after her decease, by the date whereof it is supposed to have been wrote on an occasion of very deep and uncommon affliction.

'Fourth month 16*th* 1761. This being
'a day of great salvation, wherein the di-
'vine power hath manifestly appeared in
'bringing relief and succour to my distress-
'ed soul, and working deliverance for me
'which no human means could have effect-
'ed; I earnestly desire, in the depth of hu-
'mility and awful reverence, that it may
'be a day never forgotten by me, but that
'thanksgivings and living-praises may fill
'my heart to the Lord Jehovah, in whom
'is everlasting strength, whose arm alone
'hath brought salvation, blessed be his
'name, his faithfulness faileth not those
'whose trust and confidence is in him.'

The removal of her dear husband, into a state of exile in the ninth month 1777, was a renewed affliction to her, which she apprehended, as she expressed to a friend, might tend to shorten her stay in this world.

She fell into a gradual decline and weakness of body during his absence, which, though it increased upon her, she did not keep her bed but about four or five weeks, in which time she often expressed herself in a lively manner. On the 23*d* of the ninth month

month in the morning, her husband sitting with her, she said, 'It is now evident to me, my dear, we must soon part, we have passed through many deep trials; there is nothing between us but true love and great affection, I hope thou wilt be kept in true resignation; I had some hope of continuing sometime longer, both on thy account and for the sake of our dear grand-daughter, but I am not solicitous about it, not very solicitous.'

The afternoon of the same day, being in a sweet frame of mind, she said, 'They who live near the spring of life, are sensible their change will be for the better, a happy change from a state of deep affliction;' and sometime after said, 'The spring of life is often opened for the refreshment of the weary travellers.'

Tenth month 17th. Being low in body and mind, one of her daughters present, she said, 'Whenever my mind is turned to think of getting better, I am engaged to desire to be kept under the Lord's notice, who hath been good to me; the wonderful counsellor, the everlasting father, the prince of peace; few women, have had such scenes to pass through as I have had, but I have been favoured beyond what I expected.' About an hour before her departure, she said, 'Blessed father, look down upon me if it be thy holy will.' And shortly after said, 'Dearest Lord, take me to thyself; there is joy in Heaven, there 'is 'is joy in Heaven.' After which she fell into a sweet sleep, and peacefully breathed her last, on the 25th of the tenth month 1778, aged seventy-four years. And on the 27th was interr'd in friends burying-ground in this city.

A Testimony from Mount-Holly *Monthly-Meeting in* New-Jersey, *concerning* RACHEL LIPPINCOT.

A FEW years before she died, she removed from Haddonfield to live within the limits of this meeting. She was an exemplary sympathizing friend; her testimony in public meetings was short, yet savoury and seasonable. She was afflicted with a cancer in her breast, and in her illness expressed herself on this wise, 'Oh! if it be 'thy will, dear father, remove me before I 'be offensive to my friends, and grant me 'patience to bear all that thou in thy wis- 'dom may see meet to afflict me with.' To a friend present, she said, 'Oh! that love 'may increase and abound in this day of 'outward trials, and faithfulness be kept 'to, is my sincere desire; my trials through 'life have been many, but blessed be the 'Lord's holy name, when he has appeared, 'all darkness has vanished.'

She departed this life, the 29th of the ninth month 1779, and was interr'd in friends

friends burying-ground in Mount-Holly; aged eighty years.

A Testimony from Wilmington *Monthly-Meeting in the county of* New-Castle *on* Delaware, *concerning* DAVID FERRIS.

HE was the son of Zachariah and Sarah Ferris, and was born in Stratford, in Connecticut government, New-England, the 10*th* of the third month 1707. His parents being presbyterians, brought him up in that way, his mother being religiously disposed, and much concerned for her offspring, frequently gave them good advice and admonition, which had some good effect with this our friend, as he hath often been heard to express.

We find by some remarks he left, that about the twelfth year of his age, he was frequently visited and called unto by the divine monitor in his heart, to forsake evil and youthful vanities which he delighted in, and by being in a good degree faithful thereto, was for a time, preserved from them; but for want of attending to that which would have continued to preserve him, the pleasures and vanities of this world got hold of his mind, so that he took much delight in airy and vain company, musick and dancing, and such like amusements, until about the twentieth year of his age; when it it pleased the Lord to visit him with a sore fit of sickness, which proved of lasting advantage to him, as it occasioned him to take up a fresh resolution, to forsake the evil of his ways, and turn to the Lord with full purpose of heart, which he was, thro' mercy, favoured with ability in measure to perform.

He still continued in profession with the presbyterians, not having any knowledge of friends; although by attending to the teachings of divine grace, he became convinced of the principle we profess; and hearing of a yearly-meeting of friends to be held on Long-Island, went to it, with desires to discover whether they were a living people or not, for such he desired to find; where he met with what he often longed for, (a people that worshipped God in spirit and in truth) which was a great strength and confirmation to him, in forsaking the errors of his youth, and by yielding obedience to these inward motions, he gained strength, and was more and more enabled to bear a faithful testimony to the truth as it was made known to him.

In the sixth month 1733, he removed to Philadelphia, where he joined in religious fellowship with friends; in 1735 he married Mary the daughter of Samuel and Sarah Massey; and in 1737 removed to Wilmington in New-Castle county, where he resided the remainder of his days.

He

He made some appearance in the ministry about the year 1734, but through unfaithfulness to the divine call, he from time to time put it off, and remained in a neglect of duty therein upwards of twenty years; altho' he was often warned both immediately and instrumentally in a remarkable manner, which at length produced a submission to the divine will, so that in the year 1755, he was made willing to give up thereto, and therein found great peace.

He travelled thro' divers parts of this continent in the work of the ministry, and by certificates produced on his return home, it appeared, that his conduct, conversation, and labours abroad were exemplary and edifying, tending to the advancement of truth and righteousness. His doctrine was sound, and acceptable to the honest hearted, tho' sharp against the hypocrite and rebellious, yet tender to the mourners and disconsolate.

He was very serviceable in our meetings for discipline, which, with other meetings, he diligently attended, not suffering his outward affairs to hinder him from what he believed to be his religious duty. And altho' he followed shop-keeping for a living, it was his practice to shut up his shop and take his family with him to week day meetings, often expressing for the encouragement of others, that he believed it was attended with a blessing. He was free and open hearted to entertain friends, and concerned to bring
up

up his children in plainness, and instruct them in the fear of the Lord, believing that to be the best portion they could inherit; remarkably charitable to the poor, and often administred to their necessities.

Bodily weakness attended him during the last three years of his life, and near the close of his days, he was much afflicted with sickness, which he bore with patience, often expressing his prospect of his approaching end, and his resignation therein; saying, 'All is well.' Several friends being present, after a time of silence, he in a lively manner repeated the expressions of the apostle, "To me, to live is Christ and to die is gain."

He departed this life, the 5th of the twelfth month 1779, aged upwards of seventy-two, a minister about 24 years; on the 7th of the same month, his corps was interr'd in our burying-ground in Wilmington.

A Testimony from Chester *Monthly-Meeting in* Pennsylvania, *concerning* NATHAN YARNALL.

HE was born in the Township of Edgemont, in Chester county Pennsylvania, the 27th of the twelfth month 1707-8, and continued a member of this monthly-meeting to his end. In the days of his youth he had a strong bias to the diversions of the times,

times, which when given way to, he felt the secret reproofs of divine grace accompanied with great fervency of spirit, to witness forgiveness through Christ Jesus, by the operation of whose spirit, he obtained so great a victory, that he was (after a season of probation) entrusted with a dispensation of the gospel ministry, in the exercise of which, his doctrine was sharp against a state of lukewarmness about religion as well as open profaneness, seasonably instructive to the sincere seekers, exhorting them not to be satisfied short of witnessing a state of regeneration. He was often led to sympathize with the afflicted in spirit, unto whom his doctrine dropt as the dew, and was by many esteemed a nursing father in the meeting to which he belonged. He several times, with the concurrence of his friends, visited the churches in this and the adjacent governments; was zealously concerned that meetings for discipline might be maintained in the same authority wherein they were first established; and divers times was engaged in visiting families, for which weighty service he was well qualified. His concern for his children was great, which at times he expressed under the power of divine love, adopting the language of David, viz. " My children, know ye the God of " your fathers, and serve him with a per- " fect heart and willing mind; if ye seek " him, he will be found of you, but if ye " forsake him, he will cast you off forever."

For

For several years of the latter part of his life, he was afflicted with weakness of body, but not so as wholly to prevent his attending meetings, in which he was at times, powerfully drawn forth in testimony, and publicly expressed at Middletown a few weeks before his confinement, an apprehension that his work was nearly over. He was confined at home near three months, in which time he was visited by many friends, often had refreshing opportunities in his room; in one of which, (being about a week after his confinement) he was led to speak of the precious effects of unity; at another time, divers friends being present, after some silence, he expressed himself on this wise, 'How many opportunities of this sort I 'may yet have is unknown to me; this 'morning as I lay in bed, meditating on 'the things of God, it appeared to me as 'tho' my time in this world would be but 'short;' earnestly exhorting those present, to labour that they and their children might be prepared to meet with death. At several times he signified, ' He was like one that ' was waiting for his change,' expressing his resignation, and said, ' Whenever he turn- ' ed his mind inward he felt great peace, ' and that the thoughts of the grave was ' no terror to him.' He gradually weakened without much pain, till about two days before his departure, and continued sensible to the last, which was on the 10*th* day of the first month 1780, and on the 13*th* his
body

body was interr'd in friends burial-ground at Middletown, attended by a large number of friends and neighbours; aged near seventy-two, a minister about 35 years.

A Testimony from Nottingham *Monthly-Meeting in* Pennsylvania, *concerning* RACHEL BROWN.

SHE was the wife of Thomas Brown, of West-Nottingham, in Chester county Pennsylvania, and daughter of Ralph and Phebe Needham, of Kent county on Delaware, educated amongst friends, shewing in her younger years an inclination towards piety, and after her marriage was concerned at times to speak in testimony in our religious meetings, and tho' not large, yet frequently, especially in the latter part of her time, her appearances were attended with a lively favour, which, with her exemplary conduct, and zeal for the attendance of our meetings for public worship and maintaining good order in the church, rendered her services useful and acceptable among us; and towards the conclusion of her life, she appeared to be favoured with an increase of solidity and weight.

In her last illness which continued about three weeks, we believe she was much blessed with the incomes of divine love, uttering many weighty expressions, some of which being

being wrote down, are in fubftance as follows; 'Oh! that I had but power to exprefs the love I feel to flow towards the church, and thofe who are really joined thereto. Oh! the wonderful love of the father which I feel to flow even to the outcafts of the houfe of Ifrael.' At another time, 'Oh! the ftraitnefs and refinednefs of the path that leads to life and happinefs,' repeating her fenfe of the wonderful love of our Lord Jefus Chrift to his church, which feemed then remarkably opened to her, in an explanation of thofe expreffions in the eighth verfe of the fourth chapter of Solomon's Song, "Come with me from Lebanon, my fpoufe, with me from Lebanon; look from the top of Amana, from the top of Shenir and Hermon, from the Lions dens, from the mountains of the Leopards;" the myftery of which invitation, we underftand fhe fpoke of at divers times in her ficknefs in a lively manner, as it appeared to her applicable to the divine call of our Saviour to his followers, to come out of all high things, and for his fake who was plain, meek and lowly, to leave or forfake the loftinefs and grandeur of this world, things defirable to the proud flefhly part in us, to ceafe alfo from fpotted things, and thofe of a fierce devouring nature: And, as her laft teftimony againft the fuperfluity crept in among friends in relation to coffins and dreffing the bodies of the dead, fhe earneftly earnestly desired that her coffin might be quite plain, and that no needless things might be put on or about her.

She desired her love to her friends, saying, 'I have frequently desired your prayers for me, that I might have an easy passage, and now I am resigned, and desire to have no will of my own, but to wait with patience the Lord's time, and also for his salvation.' Remaining sensible after her speech failed, she quietly departed this life, the 11*th* of the fifth month 1780, in the fifty-third year of her age, and was interr'd in friends burying-ground at East-Nottingham on the 13*th* of the same month.

A Testimony from Haddonfield *Monthly-Meeting in* New-Jersey, *concerning* EPHRAIM TOMLINSON.

OUR said friend was born the 29*th* day of the eighth month 1695, and his parents settling somewhat remote from the then settlement of white inhabitants, it appears by a manuscript account he has left, that he used to walk on foot about ten miles to meeting, and being faithful to the manifestations of truth in his young years, was enabled to encourage his brothers to go with him to wait upon the Lord.

He makes mention of divers besetments and exercises he met with in his spiritual journey,

journey, but by waiting in ſtillneſs upon the Lord, he was pleaſed to appear for his help; and he was often drawn to retire in the woods and ſolitary places, when his mind was at times enlarged in prayer for himſelf and mankind univerſally.

He was a diligent attender of religious meetings whilſt of ability of body, ſeldom ſuffering the extremity of weather or his temporal concerns to prevent him from the diſcharge of his duty in this reſpect, altho' he lived at a conſiderable diſtance from the particular meeting to which he belonged, and was an exemplary humble waiter therein, for the ariſing of that life which is the crown of our aſſemblies.

He was an appointed elder for the meeting at Haddonfield, and conducted uprightly in his ſtation, which rendered him acceptable to his friends, being often employed in the affairs of truth; and was ſeveral times engaged in that weighty ſervice of viſiting families, in the performance whereof, he was ſometimes fervently and awfully drawn forth in ſupplication to the father of mercies.

He was juſt in his dealings among men, remarkably cautious in expreſſion, which, joined with a meek and pious life, rendered him a pattern among his fellow-believers worthy of imitation; and his light ſo ſhined forth before men, that others ſeeing his good works, were made to acknowledge he had attained the marks of a true diſciple and believer in Chriſt.

He

He departed this life, on the 2d of the eighth month 1780, having left a good favour, and we doubt not is made an inheritor of that incorruptible crown of righteousness, which is laid up for all those who keep the faith, and love the appearance of our Lord Jesus Christ.

He was buried in friends burial-ground at Haddonfield, attended by a considerable number of friends and others, on the 4*th* day of the same month; being in the eighty-fifth year of his age.

A Testimony from Uwchlan *Monthly-Meeting in* Pennsylvania, *concerning* SUSANNA LIGHTFOOT.

BY accounts we have had, she was born at Grange, in the county of Antrim, in the North of Ireland, the 10*th* of the first month (old stile) 1719-20, descended of religious parents professing the truth (John and Margaret Hudson.) Her father dying in low circumstances when she was young, she was placed out by her mother to earn her living by her own labour; who nevertheless sought a portion in the truth for her daughter, esteeming it the best riches; and lived to see the desire of her heart in that respect in a degree accomplished; for the tendering visitations of divine love being mercifully extended to this our dear friend
early

early in life, she happily closed in therewith, and witnessed an advancement in piety and godliness; such was her love to the truth and zeal for the attendance of meetings when young, she would go many miles on foot to them, and being an honest servant, laboured hard to make up the time to her employer. In these times, her cup was often made to overflow with the goodness of the Lord to her soul, which she has frequently been heard to speak of with tenderness of spirit, for the encouragement of servants and others in low circumstances; and that the rich and full who have horses to ride on, and are blessed both with the necessaries and conveniencies of life, might prize their time and privileges, and bring forth fruits adequate to the favours conferred on them.

A dispensation of the gospel was committed to her to preach, to which she gave up in the seventeenth year of her age; and we have reason to think, she grew therein as a willow by the water course; for in the exercise thereof, with the unity of her friends at home, she came over to this country with Ruth Courtny, in the latter part of the year 1737, and paid a religious visit to friends generally on this continent, we believe to good satisfaction; some of us having cause to remember her, and the sweetness of her spirit at that time. With the same friend she also travelled in England and Wales, in

1740, spending upwards of fifteen months there in the service of truth.

On the 25th of the ninth month 1742, she was married to Jesse Hatton; in which state, she for many years, underwent great outward difficulties, as well as inward exercises and trials on account of the cause and testimony of truth which she had espoused, and was favoured with firmness to hold her integrity thereto; which she has been heard to commemorate with thankfulness to the Lord her deliverer, rendering the praise to him alone, who, even during that trying dispensation, opened her way to labour considerably in his cause in many places, as in Ireland, Scotland, and again in England.

About the year 1754, she removed with her husband and family, and settled in Waterford, where she was made truly near to friends and useful in the Lord's hand.

In the year 1759 her husband died; and in 1760, being constrained by the love of truth, and having the concurrence of her friends at home and of the meeting of ministers and elders in London, she entered on a second visit to America, which for many years had rested weightily on her mind. In the ninth month of the same year she arrived here, and visited friends meetings gegenerally throughout this continent, as far southward as Charleston, in South-Carolina, and to the eastern parts of New-England, to the comfort and satisfaction of friends, leaving seals of her ministry in many

many places; and after a labour of upwards of two years, embarked for England. In the summer following she visited Munster province in Ireland. And on the 25th of the ninth month 1763, she was married to our friend Thomas Lightfoot; and continuing fervent in spirit for the discharge of her religious duties, finished her visit to that nation by midsummer following.

In the beginning of the eighth month 1764, she embarked at Cork with her husband and family in order to settle here, and arrived in the ninth month following, from which time she belonged to our monthly-meeting, whereof she was a serviceable member; likewise was engaged in the love of the gospel, to visit many of the meetings of friends in this and the adjacent governments, also the neighbouring yearly-meetings, and in the year 1774, went into New-England, with our friend Elizabeth Robinson from Great-Britain; in which visits her company and services were weighty, strengthening and establishing to friends.

At divers meetings previous to the breaking forth of the present calamity, she had, in an awful manner, to proclaim the approach of a stormy day, which would shake the sandy foundations of men; and many of the formal professors in our society should be blown away.

The last journey she took, was to the yearly-meeting at Third-Haven, in Maryland, held in the sixth month 1779, wherein deep wading and wasting exercise, with feebleness of body was her lot. Soon after her return home, a fit of illness contributed much to the breaking of her constitution; but the balm of sweet peace of mind was still her comfort and support. She recovered so as to get abroad again to her own and many other meetings about the country, and to our last yearly-meeting in Philadelphia, tho' in a weak state of health; the last she attended was our select meeting at Uwchlan, the 27th of the first month 1781, under an increasing weakness of body, but to the comfort of friends then assembled.

She was an excellent example of steady waiting upon the Lord in silence, and out of meetings solid and grave in her deportment, instructive and weighty in conversation, watchful over her own family for their good, bearing her testimony against wrong things in them as well as others; of a discerning spirit; and when her lot was cast in families as well as meetings, was often led to feel for and sympathize with the hidden suffering seed. Having passed through the deep waters of affliction herself, her eye was not unused to drop a tear for, and with others in distress either in body or mind, and she rejoiced in comforting and doing them good.

She was a living and powerful minister of the word, careful not to break silence in meetings, until favoured with a fresh anointing from the holy one, whereby she was

preserved

preserved clear in her openings, awful and weighty in prayer, her voice being solemn and awakening under the baptizing power of truth.

Many were the heavenly seasons with which she was favoured during a lingering illness, in some of which she was led to express herself in a lively edifying manner, and often, with divine pertinence to the states of those who were present; as also her belief that she should join the spirits of the just made perfect, in that city whose walls are salvation, and her gates praise.

One evening, after a solemn silence, she broke forth in a sweet melody, saying, ' I ' have had a prospect this evening, of join- ' ing the heavenly host, in singing praises ' to Zions king, for which favour my soul ' and all that is sensible within me, magni- ' fies that arm which hath been with me ' from my infant days, and cast up a way ' where there was no way, both by sea and ' land.' She then signified what an exercise she had laboured under for the good of souls, and how it wounded her very life, to behold the professors of christianity acting inconsistent with the example of a crucified Saviour.

She frequently supplicated the Lord for the continuance of his help, and that she might be endued with patience, adding, ' Oh! what would become of me now, if ' I had a wounded conscience? The work ' with me is not now to do: This winnow-
' ing

'ing day muſt come cloſer to the dwellings
'of ſome than ever it has done, even to the
'ſhaking of them from the gods of ſilver
'and of gold, hay or ſtubble.'

The quarterly-meeting being nigh, ſhe urged her huſband to leave her, ſaying, 'There is nothing yields ſuch comfort on 'a languiſhing bed as an evidence of hav- 'ing performed our religious duties to the 'beſt of our underſtanding, I can ſpeak it 'at this time by experience.' She ſpoke of the neceſſity there was for friends to guard againſt keeping in their families perſons of corrupt morals and evil communication, which hath a tendency to poiſon the tender minds of their children; and ſignified her apprehenſion, that ſome parents were ſtained with the blood of their offspring thereby. At another time, ſhe encouraged ſome that were preſent, to be faithful to the Lord, and to keep to their gifts, adding, 'Oh! 'what a fine thing it is to ſit lively in meet- 'ings, and to witneſs the holy oil to run as 'from veſſel to veſſel.' Feeling herſelf grow worſe, ſhe gave directions about the laying-out her body, that it ſhould be with exemplary plainneſs.

One morning, in the hearing of a few friends, ſhe cautioned againſt a light chaffy ſpirit getting up in a ſhew of religion, and was led in a remarkable manner, to utter reproofs againſt the ungodly Quaker, ſignifying a terrible day would ſooner or later overtake ſuch.

She

She expressed herself one day nearly as follows, 'When I have sat down in our 'meetings, and cast my eye over the peo-'ple, how have I been grieved to see the 'haughtiness of the young men, and the 'folly of the young women, looking one 'upon another, as if there was nothing to 'do; coming to meetings just to see and be 'seen: Oh! will not the Lord visit for these 'things? Yea, surely he will, and call to 'an account those haughty sons and for-'getful daughters; I have been grieved 'with it when I have sat as with my lips 'sealed; and yet there is a remnant that are 'near to my life among the youth.

At another time, being raised by divine aid from great weakness, she thus expressed herself, " The Lord will search Jerusalem, " he will blow away the chaff; but the " wheat, Oh! the weighty wheat he will " gather into his holy garner. It seems to 'me, that many of the better sort are hast-'ening to their graves. I do not repine at 'my afflictions, for how small are they, 'compared with his who suffered for us all, 'when he said, " My God, my God, why 'hast thou forsaken me?" Oh the professors 'of truth! How often have I thought of 'their great privileges! How often have 'they been called unto and watered! And 'yet remain unredeemed; there is much 'impurity about the skirts of some; if they 'refuse they will be rejected and others 'called in; he will have his table filled, he
'will

'will have a people that will stand for his name.' After sometime, asking for a friend, she said, ' I have something to say to thee about the city; the folly, I would not willingly call it iniquity, but upon a strict examination I believe it may be so called, of laying out their dead, has been a burden to me many times of late when I have been there, I have wondered at the pomp and vanity, and the cost, how much for no good purpose at all, but to be buried with the mouldering body. How much better it would be, to spare this expence for the benefit of some poor families? I did not know but I should have mentioned it at the yearly-meeting, but I got enfeebled, and I prayed it might rest on some others, that it might be done then or at some other time.'

In the afternoon of the same day, she mentioned some of the words of Amos, "I was no prophet, nor a prophet's son, but I was a gatherer of sycamore fruit;" 'low employments, said she, "But the Lord raiseth the poor out of the dust, and lifteth up the beggar from the dunghill to set them among princes. I have been one of sorrows, and much acquainted with grief. It is true, this has been a pleasant spot to live in, and with an agreeable companion, and it was nothing short of the good hand that thus provided for me, but I have never forgot the wormwood and the gall.'

She

She continued quiet and sensible the remainder of her time, saying, 'Oh dearest Lord! take me to thyself, even into thy heavenly kingdom; take me into Paradise, for I long to be with thee there.' After expressing the desire of her soul respecting one of her sons, she took leave of her husband and others present with a look of endearing love, and expired about the fourth hour in the morning, like one falling into an easy slumber, on the 8th of the fifth month 1781, and was interr'd the 11th at Uwchlan, attended by a very great concourse of people; on which occasion a meeting was held, and was indeed a good meeting, agreeable to a prospect she had in the early part of her illness; aged sixty-one, and a minister 44 years.

A Testimony from Evesham *Monthly-Meeting in* New-Jersey, *concerning* Thomas Evans.

HE was born the 12th day of the second month 1693, and descended from parents professing the truth, whose religious care over him, co-operating with the principle of divine grace implanted in his mind, was the happy means of fixing his attention, not on a corruptible inheritance, but on that which is incorruptible, eternal in the heavens, and fadeth not away. And as he was in a good degree faithful to the manifestation on of light afforded him, about the twenty-fifth year of his age, he entered on the work of the miniftry, in which he diligently laboured, vifiting, with the concurrence of his friends, divers parts of this continent. He was often led fenfibly to declare of the love and goodnefs of the Lord to thofe who diligently wait upon and feek him; and is worthy of remembrance for his fteady example in the attendance of meetings.

In his advanced years, he had divers painful times of illnefs, but was admirably preferved through them without the help of medicine. He was temperate in his living; and that innocency of life, meeknefs and love which attended him in his early years, fhined clear in his latter days, being often favoured (when his underftanding in worldly matters appeared to fail him) in a lively manner to fpeak to the ftates of the people when religioufly affembled, which made him near to many friends. He was a peace-maker amongft his neighbours and friends, and earneftly engaged for the univerfal advancement of true peace amongft mankind; bearing a faithful teftimony againft war, and againft the unneceffary diftillation and ufe of fpirituous liquors, and the prevailing and foolifh cuftoms and fafhions of the world.

In his laft illnefs, he was preferved in great patience and refignation through much bodily pain, fignifying his 'Satisfaction in
' having difcharged his religious duty; and
'that

'that all looked pleasant before him, and
'nothing remained for him to do, unless
'the Lord should again please to raise him,
'which was hid from his sight, but that
'he was quite resigned to his will in all
'things.'

In these trying hours, wherein he was enabled to drop many comfortable and edifying sentences to those who visited him, he appeared to be favoured with a foretaste of that true peace which is laid up in store for all them who hold out to the end in well-doing.

He departed this life, the 21*st* of the first month 1783, and was interr'd at Evesham on the 24*th*, aged near ninety, and a minister about 65 years.

A Testimony from the Monthly-Meeting of Philadelphia, *concerning* ANTHONY BENEZET, *an elder, deceased.*

ON this occasion, we may pertinently adopt the lamenting address of the disciples at Joppa, to the apostle Peter, on the death of Dorcas their sister, who had been " Full of good works, and alms deeds " which she had done. And all the widows " stood by him weeping, and shewing the " coats and garments which Dorcas had " made while she was with them." Acts ix. 37. 39.

He was born in France, at a town named St. Quintin, in the province of Picardy, on the 31*st* of that now called the first month, 1713. At which time romish bigotry and superstition subjected the protestants in that kingdom to very rigorous persecutions, which occasioned many thousands of them to leave it, among whom were the parents of our deceased friend, who removed from thence on the 3*d* of the second month called February, 1715, and after spending a few months in Holland, proceeded to London, where they resided about sixteen years, and in the month called November, 1731, they arrived in this city, being well recommended by divers friends.

In the fifth month, 1736, he was married to our friend Joyce Marriott, of this city, in whom he experienced a truly religious helpmeet, almost to the end of forty-eight years. Being dissatisfied with following mercantile business, to which he was brought up, he declined that occupation and sought other employments for the maintenance of his family, and they also engaging more of his time and attention than he found consistent with his peace of mind, he willingly embraced an opportunity which offered favourable to his inclination and concern for the instruction of youth in useful learning, by supplying a vacancy which happened in the year 1742 in the English-school under the direction of friends in this city; which by their encouragement he undertook, and continued

tinued in this employment through the remaining part of his life, except a small intermission of less than two years which he spent at Burlington, where he sought for greater retirement, and more leisure to attend to his religious concern for the general good of mankind: But did not find his mind at the ease he desired, until he returned to resume his employment of schoolkeeping in this city; where he experienced greater opportunity of extensive usefulness, in which he was assiduously diligent, suffering a small portion of natural rest to satisfy him; employing his pen day and night in the compilation of books and other writings for profitable instruction on religious subjects, chiefly extracted from various authors of eminence, particularly to inculcate the peaceable temper and doctrines of the gospel, in opposition to the spirit of war and bloodshed, as also to expose the flagrant injustice of slavery and the abomination of the African-trade; lamenting the sorrowful defection of professed christians in these respects, which deeply grieved his tender heart. The distribution of his labours have been found productive of much good, to render which more extensive, he held a correspondence with such persons in various parts of Europe and America, as united with him in the like concern, or were so circumstanced as to be likely to promote his pious well-meant views.

On

On the late ceffation of war between Great-Britain and America, apprehending the revival of commerce would be likely to renew the ignominious trade to Africa for flaves, which had been in fome meafure obftructed, among other endeavours to difuade from this cruel traffic, and having entertained a favourable opinion of the difpofition and fentiments of the queen of Great-Britain, hoping her influence might be ufeful to difcourage it, he was religioufly induced to tranfmit her a letter in 1783 on the fubject, with a prefent of a few books of a pious tendency, which he committed to the care of two of his friends in London, to deliver in fuch manner as they fhould judge to be moft fuitable; this fervice being performed foon after his deceafe; one of them, by a letter received within a few days paft, informs his friend here, that the letter from him with the books, had been delivered to the queen, who on her reading it, expreffed her perfuafion, ' That the writer ' was truly a good man, and that fhe kind- ' ly accepted his prefent,' engaging alfo to read the books.

(A copy of the letter is hereunto annexed.)

He was employed the two laft years of his life, as teacher in the fchool for the inftruction of the black-people and their offfpring, eftablifhed and fupported by the voluntary contributions of friends in this city, which by the indifpofition of the former
er

er teacher, had lain fometime vacant, undertaking this employment from an apprehenfion of religious duty, and an earneft folicitude that they might be better qualified rightly to enjoy the freedom to which great numbers of them had been of late reftored; for which purpofe he furrendered, with the confent of his friends, his other fchool, though to the manifeft difadvantage of his worldly intereft.

His confinement by his laft illnefs was not of long continuance, although he had not been in perfect health for more than a year before, but being of a lively difpofition, and remarkably temperate in his food, which was principally vegetables, he attended his fchool and other affairs until the increafe of his diforder difabled him.

He endured the bodily pains he fuffered with much patience, and was favoured with great calmnefs and compofure, being fenfible of his approaching diffolution, receiving his numerous vifitors with much kindnefs, but expreffed little to any of them concerning himfelf, abiding under that humble diffidence which was confpicuous in his conduct through life, confidering himfelf but as an unprofitable fervant. A fhort time before his confinement, in a familiar converfation, he took occafion to remark, that had he attended with due care to the profpects of duty given him in his younger years, he thought it was probable he might have

have been made inftrumental for more extenfive ufefulnefs to mankind.

On the day preceeding his death he took an affecting farewell of his wife, who was then alfo in a weak infirm ftate, when he reminded her of the affection and concord which had been maintained between them through the courfe of their union; and having fometime before reviewed and executed his will, in which he had devifed his whole eftate to her during her natural life, (excepting his fmall library and other books) and on her deceafe to certain truftees, the income thereof to be applied to the ufe and fupport of the Negro-fchool. He had in the time of his illnefs added a codicil, confirming the fame, with a refervation of fome fmall legacies to a few of his relations, indigent widows, and other poor perfons; and having copies tranfcribed, with inftructions for the diftribution of the books he had on hand, and for binding divers tracts on religious fubjects which remained in fheets, he delivered them to fome of his executors for their government; the laft of which he put into the hands of one of them not more than three hours before he departed, which was about fun-fet on the 3*d* day of the fifth month 1784, being the day of our quarterly-meeting; and on the 5*th* day of the fame he was buried in our grave-yard in this city; on which folemn occafion, a great concourfe of inhabitants of all ranks and profeffions attended, manifefting the univerfal versal esteem in which he was held, among whom also several hundred black-people in like manner testified the grateful sense they had of the benefits derived to them, through his acts of friendship and pious labours on their behalf.

Unwearied in his endeavours to promote the essential interest and well-being of men, it seemed as his 'Meat and drink' to tread the path of his divine master, in 'Going 'about, doing good.' His labours for the relief of the afflicted and oppressed, particularly that much injured people, the enslaved Africans and their descendants, having been unabated and succesful, beyond almost any advocate they have had in his time, devoting no small portion of his life and worldly substance, in vindication of their violated rights as men, and their instruction in things relating to their temporal and everlasting interest.

By an innocent unreserved affability, he gained esteem and acceptance among all classes of men; that love of his neighbour which was conspicuous throughout his communication, having a softening effect, even on rough untractable spirits, and so generally did his useful life and inoffensive demeanour engage the affections and regard of all ranks of the people among whom he dwelt, that at his decease, they seemed to unite in one common sentiment and declaration, of " Blessed are the dead which die " in the Lord."

He wanted neither abilities nor opportunity for using endeavours in the acquirement of wealth; but his moderation in this as in other respects, was uniformly manifest to all observers; being with little more than a bare competency, rich and liberal beyond most of those who are encumbered with the superabundant goods of this life.

This is a summary narrative of the useful life of our valuable friend, and as we mean not to extol the instrument, but to render to the Lord our creator the praise of his own works; let this account suffice, and excite in each mind a due observance of that gospel monition, " Go and do thou like-" wise."

The following is a copy of his letter to the queen, mentioned in the foregoing testimony, viz.

To CHARLOTTE, *Queen of Great-Britain.*

IMPRESSED with a sense of religious duty, and encouraged by the opinion generally entertained of thy benevolent disposition to succour the distressed, I take the liberty, very respectfully, to offer to thy perusal some tracts which I believe faithfully describe the suffering condition of many hundred thousands of our fellow creatures of the African race, great numbers of whom, rent from every tender connection in life, are annually taken from their native land, to endure in the American islands and plantations,

tations, a most rigorous and cruel slavery, whereby many, very many of them, are brought to a melancholy and untimely end.

When it is considered, that the inhabitants of Britain, who are themselves so eminently blessed in the enjoyment of religious and civil liberty, have long been, and yet are, very deeply concerned in this flagrant violation of the common rights of mankind, and that even its national authority is exerted in support of the African slave-trade, there is much reason to apprehend, that this has been, and as long as the evil exists will continue to be, an occasion of drawing down the divine displeasure on the nation and its dependencies. May these considerations induce thee to interpose thy kind endeavours on behalf of this greatly oppressed people, whose abject situation gives them an additional claim to the pity and assistance of the generous mind; inasmuch as they are altogether deprived of the means of soliciting effectual relief for themselves. That so thou may not only be a blessed instrument in the hand of him " By whom kings reign, and " princes decree justice," to avert the awful judgments by which the empire has already been so remarkably shaken, but that the blessings of thousands ready to perish, may come upon thee, at a time when the superior advantages attendant on thy situation in this world, will no longer be of any avail to thy consolation and support.

To the tracts on the subject to which I have thus ventured to crave thy particular attention, I have added some others, which at different times, I have believed it my duty to publish, and which I trust will afford thee some satisfaction; their design being for the furtherance of that universal peace and good-will amongst men, which the gospel was intended to introduce.

I hope thou will kindly excuse the freedom used on this occasion, by an ancient man, whose mind for more than forty years past, has been much separated from the common course of the world, and long painfully exercised in the consideration of the miseries under which so large a part of mankind equally with us the objects of redeeming love, are suffering the most unjust and grievous oppression, and who sincerely desires the temporal and eternal felicity of the queen and her royal consort.

ANTHONY BENEZET.

Philadelphia the 25th of the eighth month 1783.

A Testimony from Concord *Monthly-Meeting in* Pennsylvania, *concerning* PHEBE TRIMBLE.

THE memory of the just is pronounced "Blessed;" which we wish to be verified in the following memorial of this our esteemed

esteemed friend, by affording an excitement to survivors to walk in her steps.

The days of her youth and early periods of maturer age, were attended with close trials, stripping seasons, and deep baptisms, through all which the Lord her gracious helper (whose tender regard is ever manifested towards his humble depending children) preserved her, and raised her up to be a vessel in his house. About the forty-second year of her age, being in 1759, she settled with her husband William Trimble within the limits of this meeting, to which she was recommended by certificate from Goshen monthly-meeting, as an approved minister, which character she justly retained during her stay in mutability.

Her public appearances, tho' generally in few words, were truly acceptable and edifying, being clear, pertinent, comprehensive and savoury, and accompanied with deep humility and gravity of deportment. She was not forward in the exercise of her gift, but appeared desirous to proceed therein under divine direction. At two different times she visited friends in Maryland and Virginia, and once in North and South-Carolina, in which visits her gospel labours were well received.

Her common deportment was instructive; evidencing lowliness, meekness and self-denial; that it may justly be said, her 'Adorn-
' ing was that of a meek and quiet spirit.'
Her conversation, tho' pleasant and cheerful, was accompanied with that sweetness and

and gravity which rendered it both agreeable and profitable. Her heart and house were open to the reception and entertainment of her friends; nor was her benevolence and humane feelings circumscribed to those in religious communion with her; but the poor, we believe, of all denominations in the neighbourhood where she lived, partook of her kindness, and by her removal have lost a sympathizing friend.

During the time of her last illness, she was much given to stillness and retiredness of mind, being sometimes uneasy with friends conversing on temporal subjects in her presence. Her hope and faith in her dear redeemer, we believe did not fail her in this her last and trying period; though she was very lowly and humble in her own estimation, and at times almost diffident of her being worthy of divine regard: Thus in her case may be applicably revived, the ancient interrogation, "If the righteous scarce-"ly be saved, where shall the ungodly and "sinner appear?" May this awaken profitable reflections in the minds of all, especially the careless and indifferent.

On the 14*th* of the sixth month 1784, she quietly departed this life, in the sixty-seventh year of her age; and on the 16*th* was buried at Concord, attended by many friends and others, at which time was held a large and solemn meeting. And we doubt not but she is gone from works to an happy reward.

A Testimony

A Teſtimony from the Monthly-Meeting of Friends of Philadelphia *for the* Southern-Diſtrict, *concerning* JOHN REYNELL.

THOUGH none of us were acquainted with him whilſt he reſided in Great-Britain, the land of his nativity, yet we have cauſe to believe, from what himſelf has expreſſed, that he was early viſited with the offers of divine love, and by wiſely cloſing in therewith, he came to experience preſervation from many temptations and allurements wherewith the minds of unwary youth are liable to be enſnared.

To ſeveral of his particular friends, he, at times, mentioned ſome tranſactions previous to his coming to this country, which containing matter of encouragement to faithfulneſs in others, we apprehend may not improperly be here inſerted, viz.

When about eighteen years of age, purpoſing to embark on a voyage to Jamaica, and being thoughtful leſt he might lay down the body at that place, as had been the caſe with many, he received, as he believed, a divine aſſurance that his life ſhould be preſerved. During his reſidence there, he had a ſight given him, of a grievous calamity by means of a violent hurricane, to befall the inhabitants of the Iſland as a chaſtiſement for their iniquities, which came to paſs according to his proſpect. Soon afterwards an occurrence happening which occaſioned

casioned his being called upon to give evidence in a court of judicature, he was required to take an oath, which he conscientiously refusing, it proved for a time, no small trial of his faithfulness; and although he had few or none outwardly to look to for strength and encouragement under that exercise, he was nevertheless favoured to experience divine support to be near, so that neither threatning nor persuasion could prevail on him to deviate from our christian testimony in that respect. Very few of the members of our religious society then resided on that Island, yet a meeting-house belonging to friends still remaining in Kingston, he was not easy to omit attending at the times appointed for meeting, though he sometimes sat alone therein.

About the twentieth year of his age he came to Pennsylvania, and after settling in this city, he became a serviceable member among us both in a religious and civil capacity, cheerfully employing his talents and much of his time to beneficial and laudable purposes, and was often engaged as a peacemaker in reconciling differences.

As an elder, he approved himself in faithfulness and uprightness in the discharge of that important trust, being well qualified for the station he filled. A good example in diligently attending our religious meetings as long as ability of body permitted, and very useful in the exercise of the discipline. A man of integrity and sound judgment.

Being

Being favoured with an affluence of temporal riches, he endeavoured to fulfil his duty as a good steward, by liberally communicating of his substance to such as stood in need. Besides his repeated acts of liberality throughout the course of his life, the many charitable legacies he bequeathed by his will, are further proofs of his benevolent disposition. So that we believe it may justly be said, he was one that "Feared "God and hated covetousness."

In the spring of the year 1784, his natural strength evidently impairing, he beheld the prospect of his approaching dissolution with the serenity and composure of a christian; and continued gradually declining for several months, during which time he did not impart much respecting his own spiritual state, being desirous to be more in substance than shew, yet found it needful to keep up a steady watch until his warfare should be accomplished. Two friends visiting him one evening, he mentioned, ' That on look-
' ing over his past life, he was sensible of
' many deficiencies,' yet expressed ' A hope
' that all would be well.' On the evening previous to his departure, he said, ' I am
' ready. I feel myself happy, and surround-
' ed with divine glory;' and expired the 3d of the ninth month 1784, aged seventy-six years. His corps being interr'd the day following in friends burying-ground in this city, a solemnity covered the minds of many at the grave which was truly consolatory.

A Testimony

A Testimony from New-Garden *Monthly-Meeting in* Pennsylvania, *concerning* WILLIAM *and* KATHARINE JACKSON.

THEY were born in Ireland, came into this country with their parents, and settled within the limits of New-Garden meeting. About the year 1733 they were joined in marriage, proving true help-meets to each other; and as they advanced in age, grew in grace, and a qualification for service in the church in the prime of life, being of a meek and inoffensive disposition, well beloved and truly useful members in the meeting to which they belonged; in dealing with offenders, endeavouring to convince and restore, yet careful that the testimony of truth might be preserved blameless.

Notwithstanding their beginning in the world was small, a blessing attending their industry and frugality, they got a comfortable subsistance for themselves, and to bring up their family; cheerfully and kindly entertaining many friends in those early days, and having a near sympathy with the messengers and servants of the Lord, who were tried and proved with humbling baptizing seasons, were often enabled to speak a word of comfort and encouragement to such; affectionate and helpful to those in affliction, charitable and considerate to the poor, many partaking of their bounty, they were nearly united with friends.

Their care over their family, and concern to bring up their children in plainnefs, fimplicity, induſtry, and the attendance of religious meetings, was great. Katharine thro' weaknefs and infirmity, particularly in old age, often endured much pain in riding to meetings, yet when there, her folid innocent countenance and deportment therein were edifying. When near her end, during feveral weeks painful ficknefs, fhe retained her innocent fweetnefs of difpofition, exprefling refignation to her allotment; often advifing her children and thofe about her to live in love. Some of her laſt expreffions that could be underſtood, were, ' There is reſt and ' peace prepared for me, where I fhall fing ' hallelujahs to the higheſt!' And after a little paufe, faid, ' Thy fweetnefs, O Lord! ' is great.' She quietly departed the 2*d* of the fourth month 1781, in the fixty-eighth year of her age, and on the 5*th* was interr'd in friends burying-ground at New-Garden.

William was fupported under the trial of this feparation, with becoming refignation to the divine will; having through life been an example of punctuality, juſtice, temperance and brotherly kindnefs.

On account of bodily infirmity, which at times made riding hard to bear, he often went on foot, when above feventy-five years of age, upwards of four miles to meeting; his faithfulnefs and example wherein, the becoming manner of his fitting there, evidencing a watchful folid frame of mind,

was very inftructive. On the 22*d* of the tenth month 1785 (having been for fometime much confined at home) he was taken ill, and tho' afflicted with much pain of body, his underftanding was preferved found, and faculties clear. In the morning of the 23*d* to two of his children he faid, ' There ' is always fomething comes to take us out ' of the world, and if we are but prepared it ' is the lefs matter;' one of them expreffing a hope that he did not feel any thing to the contrary; he replied ' No, no, I don't, I have ' a comfortable hope and belief that all will ' be well.' Remarking fome little time after, on the fettlement of his affairs, his fmall beginning, and how he had been favoured through life; he expreffed his concern and fympathy for divers friends in ftraitened circumftances, and that he had been much exercifed at times on account of many in fociety who appeared forward and zealous, but thro' neglect or mifmanagement of their outward affairs, had miniftered caufe of reproach; obferving that it was wifdom not to appear in fhew more than in fubftance, either in our religious or temporal concerns. The night of the 25*th* he communicated to fome of his children much feafonable and heart-tendering advice; recommending above all things to ftrive for an everlafting inheritance, whereinto they might enter when done with time; concluding in thefe words, ' Love truth, love one another, love ' friends and all good people, even all man-
'kind,

' kind, and be careful to hurt none, no not
' the very meaneſt, if ye can do them no
' good, ye ſhould do them no harm.' Then
mentioning the uncertainty of his continuance here, gave directions that his coffin
ſhould be plain, no poliſh or ſtain upon it.

Being very low on the 28*th* and apprehenſive of his end being near, he ſpoke to ſome
of his children, deſiring, when the change
came, all might keep ſtill and quiet; adding, it was an awful time, and ought to
be ſo to thoſe about him. Some hours after, ſaying, it would be a relief if he might
be favoured in his paſſage, his bodily diſtreſs being great; ' But I muſt not com-
' plain, it don't become us to complain, but
' we may tell each other of our afflictions
' without complaining or murmuring; for
' the Almighty has been good to me in my
' affliction, ſo that we have great cauſe to
' love him.' A few hours after ſaid, ' What
' manner of perſons ought we to be, to bear
' every diſpenſation of affliction and trial
' that comes upon us, as we ought to do?'
Saying at another time, ' Many tedious days
' and weariſome nights had been his lot
' theſe eighteen months paſt.' His ſon expreſſing his belief that reſt would be very
acceptable, he replied, ' Yes, an everlaſting
' reſt.' On the 13*th* of the eleventh month
he uttered the following ſupplication, ' O
' Lord God Almighty! if it be thy bleſſed
' will, mitigate my affliction, and relieve
' me in my diſtreſs; not my will but thine
' be

'be done.' And a little after said, 'The appointed time will come, and it must be waited for, he knows best the right time; his wisdom is very great, and care and providence over his poor creatures very great indeed.' To one of his children, taking leave of him, he said, in substance, 'There is great corruption in the world amongst mankind, and need there is of care in bringing up children, and young people, to restrain them; for many are running as the wild asses upon the mountains.' A few days before he departed he said, 'It is a comfort to me to have my children with me, and it may be a satisfaction to them to see me go; I feel easy in mind on looking backward and forward, I see nothing in my way, the Lord has been good to us, and especially to me in my affliction.' Much more he expressed at sundry times, continuing sensible, but gradually weakening, he departed this life, on the 24*th* of the eleventh month 1785, in the eighty-first year of his age, having been an elder upwards of 40 years, and having ruled well was worthy of double honour, his memory being of good savour. On the 27*th* he was interr'd in friends buryingground at New-Garden; attended by a large number of people, with whom a solid meeting was held.

Some expressions of JOSEPH HUSBAND, *before and in his last sickness, read and approved in the Monthly-Meeting of Friends at* Deer-Creek *in* Maryland, *and directed to be forwarded to the* Western *Quarterly-Meeting.*

A CONSIDERABLE time before his decease, when in health, he sometimes mentioned to his friends, and frequently to his wife, his prospect that his time would not be long here, and in or near his last sickness, told her that he felt easy, and believed he should soon be taken from her. Some days before his death he appeared exceeding low in mind attended with many doubts respecting his past and then situation, remaining several days in great distress; after which it pleased the Lord to manifest himself to him in so extraordinary a manner, that his wife perceiving a change, asked him how he was; he answered I am better than I expected ever to be, my mind is now relieved, and, as a morning without clouds, all appears sushine, mentioning to her and a friend present, many trials and temptations he had experienced; at another time saying, deep has been the baptism I have passed through, my soul hath been dipt into a feeling sense of the state of unbelievers, yea, I have passed through the valley of the shadow of death, which I am now convinced we must do before we can experience a glorious resurrection unto eternal

nal life. And frequently said, my dear I feel thy sympathy and love, and ah! how precious do I feel the unity of the church; often mentioning divers of his near friends, and continuing in a sweet frame of mind, not complaining of pain (tho' the nature of his disease must have occasioned much) his countenance remaining serene and pleasant to the last; a few minutes before his death he spoke to this purpose, ' Give my dear
' love to friends, and tell them I die in the
' faith which I lived in, and firmly believe
' I shall soon enter into the mansions of eter-
' nal happiness prepared for the true believ-
' ers in Christ; and altho' I never did much
' for the cause and testimony of truth, I
' shall be with the believers, and that is
' enough;' soon after which he quietly departed this life, on the 6*th* day of the fifth month 1786, about the fiftieth year of his age; being the next day interr'd in friends burying-ground at Deer-Creek.

To which the Quarterly-Meeting held at London-Grove, *the* 21*st of the eighth month* 1786, *add.*

THE foregoing account concerning our friend Joseph Husband, being communicated to us, was read here and approved; and from the knowledge and sense many of us had of him for a number of years, this meeting is free to add, that it appears he was born in Cecil county, Maryland, came into religious membership with friends after
he

he arrived to man's eftate, having been convinced of the principle of truth while young, more by inward conviction than inftrumental means, as he was educated in the way of the epifcopal church (fo called) and even when a lad, had to pafs through many trials under his father, for declining that way of worfhip; and (as he related to his wife and others) he frequently felt great tendernefs towards the negro children with whom he was brought up, from the profpect of their ftate of flavery, which much affected him at times before he was ten years of age. He conducted with reputation and ftability as a ufeful friend, manifefting a lively unfhaken concern for the maintenance of our difcipline, the furtherance of our teftimony againft an hireling-miniftry, and flave-holding, as well as for the doctrine of peace, efpecially thro' the difficulties which occurred in the late times of public requifitions for the purpofes of war; fhewing chriftian fortitude, humility and refignation under fufferings and clofe trials of different kinds which fell to his lot. Sometime before his deceafe he appeared in public teftimony, in which he was not forward, but moftly brief, pertinent and acceptable to friends; being remarkably open to receive counfel as well as to give; we find the remembrance of his difpofition and fervice is fatisfactory, both among the members of the monthly-meeting he belonged to, and this meeting.

Abftract

Abstract from the Testimony of Concord *Monthly-Meeting as read and approved by* Chester *Quarterly-Meeting, held at* Concord *the 14th of the fifth month* 1787, *concerning our dear friend* EDITH SHARPLES, *deceased.*

SHE was born the 13th day of the fifth month 1743; her parents Nathan and Rachel Yarnall, members of Middletown particular meeting, having been careful to educate her in plainness and a diligent attendance of religious meetings, she retaining a thankful remembrance of their care over her, has been often heard to bless the Lord on their account, as by their good counsel and wholesome restraint, they contributed to her preservation out of the vain fashions and customs of the world.

By her own account, her mind was early in life accompanied with earnest desires after the knowledge of truth, and that she might never do any thing to offend him whom she often found near to her comfort, or that might bring a reproach on the profession she made; but giving way to her natural vivacity, she frequently indulged herself in what with some is accounted innocent pastime, for which she was often brought under condemnation; and about the twenty-fourth year of her age was plunged into great distress, being closely beset with the wiles of an unwearied adversary; but the Lord, who will not suffer his people to be tempted

tempted beyond what they thro' his grace are enabled to bear, made way for her escape from under the power of temptation, for which she had, in that day, as on the banks of deliverance, to sing to the praise of his holy name; saying, 'It is in my heart to
' praise thee O my deliverer! for thy ma-
' nifold kindnesses unto me a poor un-
' worthy worm; for altho', for disobedi-
' ence, thou hast seen meet to hide thy
' face for a moment; yet my soul is hum-
' bly bowed before thee, rendering unto
' thee the praise of all thy works; having
' witnessed the fulfilling of thy promise.
" But with everlasting kindness will I have
" mercy on thee faith the Lord thy re-
" deemer."

In the twenty-sixth year of her age she was married to Joshua Sharples, settled within the compass of New-Garden monthly-meeting, of which she became a useful member, being qualified for service in the church, whereto she attended with much satisfaction to friends, filling the stations of overseer and elder with diffidence under a sense of the weight thereof.

In the thirty-first year of her age she appeared in the ministry, and being faithful, grew in her gift, was found in doctrine, accompanied with a degree of heart-tendering authority to the careless and indolent, yet edifying and consolatory to the refreshment of the mourners in Zion.

In

In her approaches to the throne of grace in public supplication, she was awfully attended with deep solemnity.

She was a great lover of the scriptures, and well qualified to apply them to edification and instruction, being concerned to invite friends and others to a more frequent reading of them. The doctrines of the principle of truth as held by friends she was skilful in explaining, and was often exercised therein in mixed auditories, endeavouring to lead out of forms to the substance of true religion. Much of her time was thus employed in the public service of her Lord and master, cheerfully giving up to his holy requirings, but carefully concerned to wait for his putting forth.

Having peculiar service in visiting families, she was often usefully engaged therein; and about the year 1778 with divers other friends under appointment from the Western quarterly-meeting, in a general visit to all the meetings belonging thereto, she was exercised under a deep concern to labour that a reformation in life and manners might be really effected amongst the professors of truth. Soon after, being removed within the compass of our meeting, she engaged in a like visit to the meetings in our quarter, wherein, as in other of her gospel labours, she manifested an ardent desire for the promotion of the cause of truth, and that she might be favoured to do her days work in the day-time. And since, with the concurrence

rence of friends, vifited moſt of the meetings in the Southern governments; being diligent in the improvement of her time for the ſervice of truth, often drawn into family vifits, and to the afflicted either in body or mind, who experienced the confoling fympathy of her tender fpirit, in which and other gofpel labours fhe reaped the reward of peace and comfort to her own mind. When at home fhe was not only diligent in attending meetings herfelf, but careful to encourage and affift her family in their duty therein; in herfelf an example of plainnefs, and mindful to promote a like fimplicity in thofe under her direction, manifefting much concern that her children might be brought up in the truth, frequently retiring with them for their improvement, her faithfulnefs againſt wrong things in them being confiftent with the tendernefs of an affectionate mother. Great was her exercife for the rifing generation, that their hearts might be early dedicated to the Lord, and they thereby preferved in a conduct confiftent with our holy profeffion. Open and hofpitable in her houſe, a true helpmeet and affectionate wife.

Shortly after her return from a vifit to friends on the Eaftern-Shore of Maryland, in the fixth month 1786, fhe was brought very low thro' bodily indifpofition, but favoured with inward confolation and true peace, expreffing that fhe felt her mind much weaned from the things of this world,

and

and if it should please the Lord to call her hence she found nothing in her way. On a first-day afternoon, divers friends being present, after a time of silence, she spoke to this effect, 'I am glad of this opportunity; 'as I lay on the bed this morning, my mind 'was carried away to meeting with friends, 'and I thought if I had wings I could have 'flown thither for the great love I feel for 'the members of that meeting. Indeed we 'have had many favoured opportunities to-'gether; and you see I am in a poor weak 'way, and whether I shall get out again I 'have not seen, but am resigned, and feel 'the reward of peace; but if some friends 'of that meeting are not more faithful to 'the many gracious visitations which have 'been in mercy to them extended, weak-'ness will overtake them, and they be in 'danger of missing the answer of well done.' She recovered and afterwards had many heart-tendering opportunities with friends there, and others not in membership with us, toward whom she was remarkably led in testimony, in order that they might be gathered to the fold of rest.

About two weeks before her decease she attended several of the neighbouring meetings, expressing her satisfaction therewith; and on the first-day before her departure, was at New-Garden meeting and had acceptable service, having also a favoured opportunity the same evening in a friends family where she lodged on her return home, at at which time she was concerned to revive these expressions of the Psalmist,. "Lord "make me to know mine end, and the mea- "sure of my days, what it is, that I may "know how frail I am: Behold thou hast "made my days as an hands breadth, and "mine age is as nothing before thee." Which she enlarged on to edification. Next day she got home somewhat indisposed, but held up till the day following in the evening of the 16*th* of the first month 1787, when she was confined to her bed, and lay in a sensible resigned frame of mind, being, as we believe, well prepared for her awful change, appearing to have nothing to do but to die. Some of the last words she was heard to say were, ' I believe I am going,' and in about fifteen minutes after, quietly breathed her last on the 18*th*, and on the 20*th* was interr'd at Birmingham, aged forty-three years and seven months, a minister upwards of 12 years.

F I N I S.

www.ingramcontent.com/pod-product-compliance
Lightning Source LLC
Chambersburg PA
CBHW050324230426
43663CB00010B/1736